D1561525

WITHDRAWN
L. R. COLLEGE LIBRARY

CARL A. RUDISILL LIBRARY
LENOIR-RHYNE UNIVERSITY

IN GOD'S PATH

Ancient Warfare and Civilization

SERIES EDITORS

RICHARD ALSTON   ROBIN WATERFIELD

In this series, leading historians offer compelling new narratives of the armed conflicts that shaped and reshaped the classical world, from the wars of Archaic Greece to the fall of the Roman Empire and the Arab conquests.

Dividing the Spoils: The War for Alexander the Great's Empire

Robin Waterfield

By the Spear: Philip II, Alexander the Great, and the Rise and Fall of the Macedonian Empire

Ian Worthington

Taken at the Flood: The Roman Conquest of Greece

Robin Waterfield

In God's Path: The Arab Conquests and the Creation of an Islamic Empire

Robert G. Hoyland

IN GOD'S PATH

The Arab Conquests and the Creation of an Islamic Empire

Robert G. Hoyland

CARL A. RUDISILL LIBRARY
LENOIR-RHYNE UNIVERSITY

OXFORD
UNIVERSITY PRESS

DS
38.1
.H688
2015

OXFORD
UNIVERSITY PRESS

Oxford University Press is a department of the University of Oxford.
It furthers the University's objective of excellence in research, scholarship,
and education by publishing worldwide.

Oxford   New York

Auckland   Cape Town   Dar es Salaam   Hong Kong   Karachi
Kuala Lumpur   Madrid   Melbourne   Mexico City   Nairobi
New Delhi   Shanghai   Taipei   Toronto

With offices in

Argentina   Austria   Brazil   Chile   Czech Republic   France   Greece
Guatemala   Hungary   Italy   Japan   Poland   Portugal   Singapore
South Korea   Switzerland   Thailand   Turkey   Ukraine   Vietnam

Oxford is a registered trademark of Oxford University Press
in the UK and certain other countries.

Published in the United States of America by
Oxford University Press
198 Madison Avenue, New York, NY 10016

© Oxford University Press 2015

All rights reserved. No part of this publication may be reproduced, stored in a
retrieval system, or transmitted, in any form or by any means, without the prior
permission in writing of Oxford University Press, or as expressly permitted by law,
by license, or under terms agreed with the appropriate reproduction rights organization.
Inquiries concerning reproduction outside the scope of the above should be sent to the
Rights Department, Oxford University Press, at the address above.

You must not circulate this work in any other form
and you must impose this same condition on any acquirer.

Library of Congress Cataloging-in-Publication Data
Hoyland, Robert G., 1966-
In God's path : the Arab conquests and the creation of an Islamic empire / Robert Hoyland.
pages cm. — (Ancient warfare and civilization)
Includes bibliographical references.
ISBN 978–0–19–991636–8 — ISBN 978–0–19–991637–5 I. Islamic Empire—History—622–661.
2. Islamic Empire—History—661–750. I. Title.
DS38.1.H688 2014
909'.09767—dc23
2013043047e

CARL
LENOIR-RHYNE UNIVERSITY
LIBRARY

1 3 5 7 9 8 6 4 2
Printed in the United States of America
on acid-free paper

'To the great despair of historians men fail to change their vocabulary every time they change their customs'

—(Marc Bloch, *The Historian's Craft*, trans. Peter Putman, Manchester 1954, 28).

CONTENTS

C⋆

ACKNOWLEDGMENTS

C*

I am indebted to two particular sources for the writing of this book. The first is the many students to whom I have taught Islamic history and who have helped me think about the shortcomings of the traditional narrative. The Oxford graduate intake of 2010–11 were particularly influential, for I was then fully engaged in writing this book and we discussed some of its aspects in our seminars, so thank you Anna, Benedict, Charlie, Hasnain, Josh, and Ryan. The second is my undergraduate teacher and doctoral supervisor, Patricia Crone, who first introduced me to Islamic history and encouraged me to think critically about its origins and formation. In addition, there are the many colleagues with whom I have had interesting discussions that have helped shaped some of the ideas presented in this book. Although there are too many to name them all here, I would particularly like to thank Aziz al-Azmeh, Amikam Elad, James Howard-Johnston, Hugh Kennedy, Marie Legendre, Milka Levy-Rubin, Andrew Marsham, Fergus Millar, Harry Munt, Arietta Papaconstantinou, Richard Payne, Gabriel Reynolds, Christian Robin, Sarah Savant, Petra Sijpesteijn, Adam Silverstein, Jack Tannous, David Taylor, Luke Treadwell, and Kevin van Bladel. Of course, none are responsible for how I have used the wisdom that they imparted to me. My editor Stefan Vranka and reader Robin Wakefield put in a lot of work to improve this book's coherence and readability, and Michael Athanson gave freely of his time and expertise to help make the regional maps. Finally I am eternally grateful to Peter Waidler for his astute and thoughtful proofreading and to Sarah for her love and support.

Byron's Muse, October 10, 2013

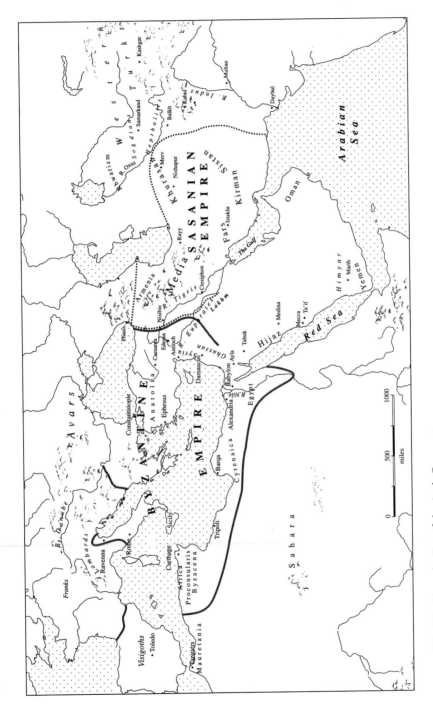

MAP 1 The World on the Eve of the Arab Conquests.

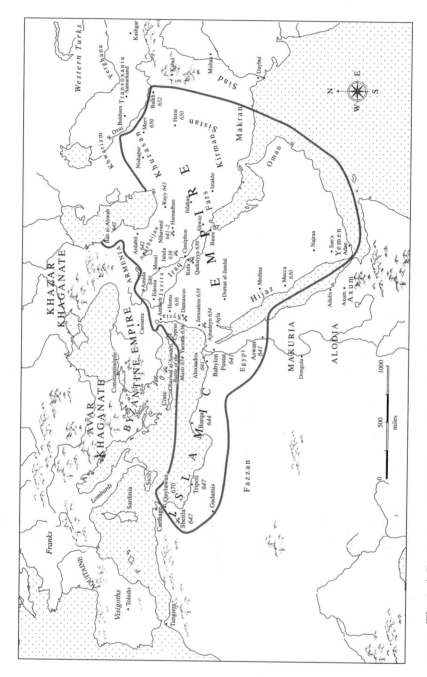

MAP 2 The Arab Empire in AD 685 (with approximate dates of major campaigns).

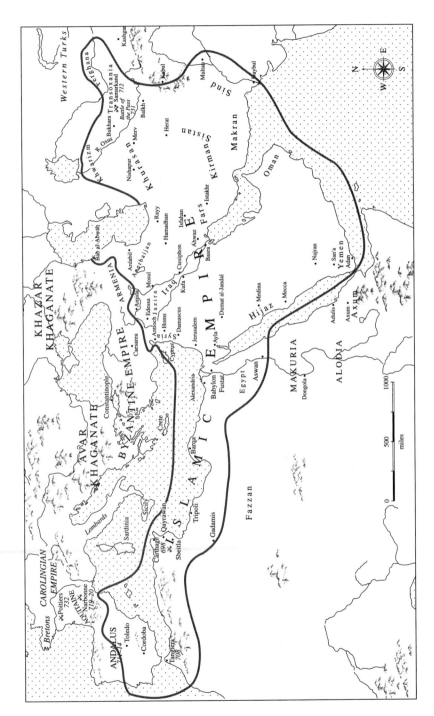

MAP 3 The Arab Empire in AD 750 (with approximate dates of major campaigns).

INTRODUCTION

There is an old Middle East legend that tells of a band of Christian youths fleeing the persecution of a pagan Roman emperor in the mid-third century AD. They leave their native city behind and seek refuge in a cave, where they soon fall asleep. When they go out on what they assume to be the following day they are astonished to hear church bells ringing out across the streets below and to see crosses on all the high buildings. Unbeknown to them, God had spared them from witnessing the cruel ravages of heathenism by putting them to sleep for two centuries, and so the youths passed overnight from a pagan world to a Christian one.[1] One experiences much the same feeling when one studies the seventh-century Middle East. Histories of the region up until AD 630 present an image of a largely Christian land, where Christ's word is fast gaining ground even in the deserts of Africa, the Persian Empire, and as far away as China. But when one turns to Muslim accounts to read about the post-630 world, then it appears that the prophet Muhammad's preaching was carried at breakneck speed from its birthplace in west Arabia across the whole Middle East by Arab soldiers, who then established unified rule over all the lands of the former Persian Empire and in all the southern and eastern provinces of the Byzantine Empire in only a few short years. The

Arabs are everywhere victorious; non-Arabs everywhere submit, convert, or are killed; and Islamic government is everywhere imposed—or at least this is the picture that ninth-century Muslim historians painted and it is one that has been widely accepted ever since.

The problem with this narrative is not so much that it is wrong, but that, like all histories told from the standpoint of the victors, it is idealizing and one-sided: the role of God and Islam is played up and the role of non-Muslims is mostly ignored. It is the aim of this book to try to give a more rounded account of this undeniably world-changing phenomenon. The main strategy for achieving this is a simple one: I will give precedence to seventh- and eighth-century texts and documents over later ones. Our earliest extant Muslim sources date from the ninth century, and even though their authors were using earlier materials, they inevitably shaped them in the light of their own world. This is of course always so, but the problem is magnified in this case because the political and religious landscape of the ninth-century Middle East was so dramatically different from that of the seventh century. It may seem very odd to an outsider to this field why this strategy of privileging earlier sources over later ones would not have been used before—is it not just standard practice for modern historians? The problem is that the early sources are overwhelmingly of Christian provenance and in languages other than Arabic, and so they fall outside the usual purview of Islamic historians—and it is also assumed that they will be either prejudiced or ill-informed. Christian authors inevitably had their own preconceptions and biases, but the Arab conquests did affect them concretely and directly, and so there is very good reason to refer to their works to write about this subject. Moreover, those living in the decades shortly after the conquests still understood the late antique world in which these events had occurred and so can help us to understand what these events meant in their own time as opposed to what they meant to the inhabitants of the ninth-century Islamic world. But I do not want simply to champion non-Muslim sources over Muslim sources; indeed, it is my argument that the division is a false one. Muslims and non-Muslims inhabited the same world, interacted with one another, and even read one another's writings. In this book, the distinction I make is simply between earlier and later sources, and I favor the former over the latter irrespective of the religious affiliation of their authors.

This strategy allows me to put back a number of elements missing from the traditional narrative. The first is process. The word most associated with the Arab conquests by Western scholars is "speed." "The speed of the Arab expansion is staggering," says one; another speaks of its "near-miraculous speed," like "a human tsunami speeding outwards." This reflects the assumption that the Arab conquests were over and done with in a few short years. For example, a famous modern medievalist sums up the situation with this sentence: "The Muslim Arab armies conquered half of one empire, that of east Rome, and all of another, Sasanian Persia, and most of this process was completed in six years, 636–42."[2] This massive compression of the duration of the conquests means that the process by which they were achieved is lost. The Arabs' victories were certainly stunning, and their progress was much faster than that of settled powers like the Romans, but it is comparable with armies comprising a high proportion of nomads (the Mongols actually covered a larger area in just seventy years). To help make clear the varied pace and extended duration of the conquests I have decided to proceed chronologically and to take the narrative up to the 740s, which is when the Arab conquest juggernaut finally runs out of steam. As in all human ventures, things did not always go to plan: the Arabs suffered some reverses and had to come to an accommodation with some peoples, but none of this diminishes the impressive scale of their overall achievement.

The second element that needs to be put back is the voices of the vanquished and of the non-Muslim conquerors. The ninth-century historians wanted to create a distinctively Arab Muslim history, which meant downplaying the role of non-Arabs and non-Muslims and placing God, Muhammad, and the Muslims center stage. President Barack Obama, when asked whether he thought the American people had a special mission, diplomatically replied that every people likes to think that it is special. And it is the specialness of their people that these ninth-century Muslim historians were trying to portray. Like the Christian historian Eusebius before them, they wanted to record the implementation of God's plan for His chosen people. Just as Eusebius of

Caesarea (d. 339) began his *Ecclesiastical History* with Christ, so Muslim historians made a strong distinction between profane time, when "barbarity" (*jahl*) prevailed, and sacred time, when Muhammad founded his community at Medina. This act is linked with the initiation of raiding by Muhammad and later full-scale conquest, which were approved by God, so these historians say, as a means of propagating Islamic rule across the world. "It is a sign of God's love for us and satisfaction with our faith," as one Muslim general explained to a Christian monk, "that he has given us dominion over all religions and all peoples."[3] But this is an idealized, simplified, and homogenized picture, whereas the reality was complex and variegated. Wars are messy affairs—the composition of the opposing sides and the reasons for which they are fighting are often diverse and shifting. However, those who wage the wars and those who document them have a strong interest in portraying the situation as black and white: believers against infidels, good against evil, justice and freedom against tyranny and oppression.

Third, I will emphasize the pre-history of the Arab conquests. Muslim sources give the impression that Muhammad and his companions invented the world anew; rather, they refashioned the world that they found. To understand this, however, one needs to be familiar with the culture of the Middle Eastern lands that the Arabs appropriated. Here non-Muslim sources are particularly useful, for they can inform us about the period before the Arab conquests (commonly now referred to as Late Antiquity in acknowledgment of the fact that some elements of the ancient world still endured). This means that we can work forward from this time and see how events unfolded and changes occurred from the sixth to the eighth century. If, however, we follow the usual practice of Islamic historians and work backward from the ninth-century sources, we hit a wall with the time of Muhammad and will end up concluding with medieval Muslim authors that Islamic civilization flows directly from pre-Islamic west Arabia.

Finally, I will try to broaden the horizons of the narrative rather than focus narrowly on Muhammad's movements in west Arabia and the activities of his successors. Arab tribesmen had been serving in the armies of Byzantium and Persia in large numbers in the fifth and the sixth centuries, and some powerful clans had managed to establish petty states on the margins of these empires. A new world power, a Turkic confederation, had seized control of vast swathes of the lands between Persia and China in the late sixth century and was launching attacks against the Persians. The 1,500-year-old civilization of Yemen had collapsed in the mid-sixth century and many of the ancient settlements of northwest and east Arabia were shrinking. And the two superpowers of the region, Byzantium and Persia, engaged in all-out war for more than two decades in the early seventh century. Yet even experts narrow their vision to concentrate wholly on Muhammad's west Arabia and consider it sufficient simply to say that the Arab conquests happened and succeeded because of the religious zeal of the Muslims without any reference at all to broader socio-economic factors. I do not want to belittle the role of religion but rather to expand its remit. Religion is integral to the conquests and the evolution of an Islamic Empire, but religion is not just piety and devotion, especially not in the seventh century; it is as much about power and identity as spiritual yearnings and righteous behavior.[4]

To reduce this later Islamicizing perspective I will speak of "Arab" conquests rather than "Islamic" conquests. Both terms are to some degree inaccurate, since the conquerors were neither all Arabs nor all Muslims, and the meaning of both terms was in any case evolving in the immediate aftermath of the conquests. Nevertheless, contemporary observers mostly referred to the conquerors in ethnic rather than religious terms, and even if some of the conquerors were not Arabs their descendants often came to think of themselves as such, and so it seems preferable to use the term "Arab," while bearing in mind that we are not talking about a nationalist endeavor nor an immutable racial category.[5] Islamicists would say that religion plays a greater role in the object of their study, but that is a dubious claim. When the Vandal king Geiseric was asked one day by his ship's captain whither he should sail, he replied: "Against those with whom God is angry of course,"[6] and this accords well with the spirit of the conquerors treated in this book. Furthermore, if we use the term "Islamic conquests" we cannot distinguish between the many different conquests achieved over the centuries by many Muslim groups (Iranians, Turks, Kurds, Berbers, etc.). This causes much confusion among students, and among quite a few experts too, for it tends to be assumed that the Arabs conquered most or all of the lands that are majority Muslim today, whereas a large proportion of them were actually conquered much later, by local Muslim dynasties, of non-Arab origin, or were Islamized slowly by traders, missionaries, and wandering ascetics.

In general, this book tries to emphasize complexity and ambiguity and to give voice to groups that are not normally heard. Historians writing at a considerable remove from the events they are describing tend to simplify, schematize, telescope, and idealize their narratives. Since our modern accounts of the Arab conquests have relied upon ninth-century writers for this seventh-century phenomenon, they have tended to perpetuate and intensify these tendencies, stressing the miraculous speed and success of the conquests and the religiosity of the conquerors. My aim is to reintegrate these conquests and their impact into the fabric of human history, against the prevailing trend to see them as utterly exceptional, and I hope thereby to make them more explicable according to the usual norms of human behavior. The achievements of the Arab conquerors were immense, but they can be properly appreciated only if we also take account of the difficulties and reverses that they had to overcome.

A Note on Methods and Conventions

Since my stated intention is to give voice to groups not normally heard, I include quite a few quotations from these groups. This will also allow readers to see for themselves what the sources say and the foundations on which my reconstruction rests, which is important in this highly contested subject, where even the existence of Muhammad and Mecca is disputed. These quotations are all referenced in the notes (sometimes bundled together for convenience), along with modern academic works that are particularly relevant to the point being made. For texts that inform the broader picture that I present, however, the reader should consult the Select Bibliography at the end of the book. References are given in full on their first occurrence in the notes or in abbreviated form where they are included in the Select Bibliography.

A Note on Arabic

Since this book is intended for a broad audience, Arabic names and words are given without diacritical marks according to the principle that if you are an expert you do not need them and if you are not they will not help you. I have, however, maintained the consonants *hamza* and *'ayn*. The *hamza*, indicated by an apostrophe, is effectively a glottal stop, that is, a closing of the throat, and exists in East London dialects, as in "bu'er" (for "butter"). The *'ayn*, indicated by a reverse apostrophe, is similar to the *hamza*, but rather than close the throat, one expels a little air, as though making a small cough. Names in Arabic are usually given in the form x ibn x (x son of x), sometimes followed by an epithet (*nisba*) that further specifies a person's identity, usually the person's tribe, profession, or place of origin.

Chapter One

THE SETTING

I n an oft-quoted passage, the Byzantine historian Theophylact Simocatta refers to the empires of Byzantium and Persia as "the two eyes of the world," the divinely ordained realms responsible for maintaining order and civilization amid a sea of inferior untrustworthy barbarians. Of "the Saracen tribe," for example, he writes that they were "most unreliable and fickle; their mind is not steadfast and their judgement is not grounded in prudence."[1] They needed to be kept in check so that justice and harmony could reign, but they were not a serious problem, for the two empires would always prevail. And yet this comfortable world order, which had endured so long, was suddenly turned upside down by the Arab conquerors not long after Theophylact had finished his work sometime in the 620s. In the end, he had no successor; the genre of secular history, going back more than a thousand years to Thucydides, came to an abrupt end, as though in sympathy with the way of life that it had so well described and now was no more.

This and a number of other seemingly dramatic changes, in particular the rise of the new religion of Islam, have led many scholars to see the Arab conquests as the last nail in the coffin of the classical world and as the herald of a medieval society. This was the view of the Belgian scholar Henri Pirenne, who let the western (Germanic) "barbarians" off the hook, arguing, against the English historian Edward Gibbon, that they were responsible for extending the life of the Roman Empire and not for destroying it. The fifth and sixth centuries could now be rehabilitated and rebranded as an age when classical values remained in vogue, reshaped by Christianity and the "barbarian" customs of the likes of the Franks, Goths, and Lombards, but certainly not effaced. Accordingly the somber epithet of Dark Ages could now be replaced by the cheery sobriquet of Late Antiquity. However, the eastern (Arab) "barbarians" became Pirenne's bête noire. The Arab capture of North Africa and the Levant made the Mediterranean into a barrier rather than a conduit, so Pirenne maintained, and thus southern Europe was cut off from the east, causing it to stagnate. On the plus side, however, the Arabs kept Byzantium busy and this allowed new forms of statehood to blossom in northern Europe, culminating in the Carolingian Empire.[2]

Islamic historians have also tended to see the Arab conquests as a turning point, though from their perspective it is the beginning of the new and not the end of the old. In this they are governed by medieval Muslim sources, which reset the clock and made the establishment of the prophet Muhammad's polity and the launch of the Arab conquests the starting point for Islamic history. These sources, mostly composed by writers living in Iraq in the ninth and tenth centuries, have no acquaintance or sympathy with the Late Antique world that the Arabs overran and pay little heed to it in their writings, thus reinforcing the sense that when one travels from the pre-conquest Middle East of Theophylact Simocatta and enters the post-conquest world of the first Muslim rulers, one is crossing a watershed, exchanging one society for a totally different one. This is of course merely an illusion of the sources, but unfortunately it is made concrete by the fact that two different sets of modern historians (Late Romanists and Early Islamicists) with very different agendas, linguistic skills, and suppositions work either side of the divide. It is the aim of this book to try to smooth out this artificial rupture, to focus on continuities as well as changes, on processes as well as events. This can only be achieved by first understanding what went before, and this is the subject of the rest of this chapter, for, as with all world-changing phenomena, there was a long buildup to the event, a lengthy period in which key transformations took place in the Middle East that made the conquests both possible and likely.

The Superpower Confrontation

To understand the Arab conquests we need to go back all the way to the second and third centuries AD, when the Roman Empire made a great push to the east. This began with Emperor Trajan's war of AD 106 against Persia and was followed up by numerous expeditions eastward by high-ranking military men and emperors. One by one they annexed the lands of the once-independent dynasties of Petra, Palmyra, and Edessa, which brought Rome into direct contact with the pastoralist tribes that these dynasts had formerly managed on her behalf. Under Emperor Septimius Severus (193–211) two extra legions were created for service in the east, meaning that eight legions were now stationed in the zone that stretched from the new province of Mesopotamia (in modern southeast Turkey and northwest Iraq) southward to Arabia. It looked as though Rome would gradually come to dominate the whole of the Middle East. However, the game changed in 224 when the energetic Sasanian dynasty took over the Persian Empire (which comprised Iraq and Greater Iran), for it pursued a more centralizing and expansionist policy than its predecessors.[3] The Sasanians launched a series of devastating attacks upon Rome's eastern flank in the mid-third century, achieving numerous victories and even managing to capture the Roman emperor himself. Only the intervention of the prefect of Palmyra, who rallied an army of townsmen and tribesmen, saved Rome from Persia's seemingly unstoppable onslaught. Thereafter the two empires came to a grudging acceptance of one another, eyeing each other warily across the Syrian desert, mostly respecting each other's sovereignty except for occasional skirmishes and forays to extract tribute and captives and to make a show of strength for audiences back home (Figure 1.1).

Though the western portion of the Roman Empire suffered instability and loss of territory during the fourth and fifth centuries, the eastern part continued to flourish, now based at a new capital, Constantinople, on the site of the ancient Greek city of Byzantium, which is the name that modern scholars use when referring explicitly to the Christian East Roman Empire (though its own citizens kept thinking of themselves as Romans). The geopolitical situation described earlier—the empires of Byzantium and Persia in a sort of cold

FIGURE 1.1 Emperor Justinian I at court: mosaic, San Vitale, Ravenna; Yazdgird III at hunt: silver plate, Bibliotheque Nationale, Paris. Note the very different styles of legitimation and projection of power practiced by these two empires.

war standoff—remained relatively stable through the fourth and fifth centuries, but the sixth century witnessed a sharp escalation in hostilities. Major clashes occurred in 530–32, 540–45, and 572–90. The last of these confrontations ended on a hopeful note. The youthful Persian emperor Khusrau II fled to Constantinople, seeking the Byzantines' help against rival challengers at home. Khusrau was granted troops and he went on to successfully recapture his throne; all looked set for a new era of peace and cooperation between these two superpowers. However, when Byzantium was rocked by a military coup in 602, Khusrau decided that the time was ripe to renew hostilities and he launched an all-out attack on his erstwhile ally. The onward march of his forces seemed impossible to check: Syria was captured by 610, Palestine by 614, Egypt by 619, and Anatolia as far as the walls of Constantinople itself by 626. Yet the Byzantine emperor Heraclius, who had wrested the imperial throne from its usurper in 610, made a dramatic comeback by marching through the Caucasus and attacking Persia from the north, supported by a large contingent of Turks.

This enabled him to strike at the heart of his enemy's empire, advancing on the capital, Seleucia-Ctesiphon, sacking royal residences as he went and putting the defeated and disgraced Khusrau to flight.

At one point it had looked as though the Persians were going to steal the whole show; thus in the very early seventh century the head of the Georgian church told his Armenian counterpart: "The king of kings (Khusrau II) is the lord of the Romans as much as of the land of the Aryans."[4] But now the tables were turned and Heraclius was able to dictate terms to a humbled Persia. Khusrau's son made peace with Heraclius in 628 and agreed to restore to the Byzantines all of the lands seized by the Persian troops. In 630 Heraclius celebrated the triumph of the Christian world by restoring the relics of the cross of Jesus to Jerusalem, entering the city in great pomp and ceremony, only sixteen years after its sack at the hands of the Persians. Again, all looked set for an irenic future, and the picture looked even rosier for the Byzantines, when the general Shahrbaraz, who "had presented himself to Heraclius as a slave" and whose son had become a Christian, acceded to the Persian throne in April 630 with the aid of "Persian and Byzantine troops."[5] It looked as though Persia would become a vassal of Byzantium and possibly even a Christian one at that. But yet again these hopes of a lasting peace between the two superpowers were shattered. Shahrbaraz was not of the royal house of Sasan and, despite the endorsement of Heraclius, was murdered by disgruntled Persian nobles. The Persian Empire descended into civil war, leaving its borders, already neglected during its quarter-century long conflict with Byzantium, woefully exposed.

The Spread of Universalizing Monotheism

In the course of this last great war of antiquity, Christianity had become more intimately linked to the fate of the Byzantine Empire. It was the Virgin Mary who was thought to have saved Constantinople in its hour of greatest need, when Persians were baying outside the very walls of the city. Heraclius's campaign against the Persians was a holy war; he was a new David and he led an army of crusaders who fought for God's cause. This worldview began to take form in the aftermath of the conversion of Constantine the Great to

Christianity in AD 312, which at once made it acceptable, even fashionable, to be a Christian. Importantly, this move allied the fledgling Christian church hierarchy with political power; patriarchs, bishops, and monks could now call on imperial backing to enforce their will. Churches and monasteries gradually replaced pagan temples and theaters, city councilors slowly ceded their power to Christian clergymen, non-Christians became ever more suspect and liable to persecution, grand councils determined orthodoxy and harried those who would not conform. In short, the Roman Empire became Christianized. The imperial office itself was remodeled, reflecting the unprecedented situation that its holder now shared the same faith as a rapidly increasing number of his subjects and so had an interest in determining and defending their common beliefs.

This link between religious and political power became ever stronger in the coming centuries, and the cold war scenario between Byzantium and Persia gave it additional impetus: being Christian gradually became equated with being pro-Byzantine, and non-Christians were viewed with ever greater suspicion as potential sympathizers with Persia, an accusation frequently leveled at the Jews. In this situation, political conflicts took on a religious coloring. Thus, when the dynasty of Himyar, which ruled Yemen at this time, converted to Judaism in the late fourth century, Byzantium began to suspect it of pro-Persian tendencies. In the early sixth century, the ambitious Christian rulers of Ethiopia sought to extend their sway over Yemen and justified this move by portraying it as a holy war against the Jewish Himyarite dynasty. Their success was celebrated across the Byzantine world as a victory for Christianity. And the efforts of one Himyarite king to suppress pro-Ethiopian elements in his realm in the 520s were written up as an attempt by a Jewish tyrant to persecute innocent Christians, who courageously suffered for their faith. Known as the *Martyrs of Najran*, this story circulated far and wide in many different languages and served as a powerful and emotive piece of propaganda.

Christianity is perhaps the most glaring example, but it is a feature of the Late Antique religions that they were inextricably linked with power, a fact that was hugely significant for the emergence of the Islamic empire. Zoroastrianism never managed to gain quite the same status in the Persian world, but its clergymen certainly sought imperial backing. One third-century Zoroastrian high priest boasted in an inscription that "the king of kings conferred on me the staff and belt and created for me a higher rank and dignity, and at court and in kingdom after kingdom, place after place, throughout the whole empire he gave me more authority and power in matters of the divine services, and created for me the title 'chief-priest of Ahura Mazda,' after the name of Ahura Mazda, the Deity."[6] Judaism managed to win over the ruling dynasty of Yemen in the fourth to fifth century, as mentioned, and the Khazar elite of the southern Russian steppe in the eighth to ninth century. Buddhism was also very successful at this time, enjoying the patronage of the Chinese emperors and of numerous minor polities in Central Asia, and later, in the seventh century, it was adopted by the ruling dynasty of the Tibetan Empire. The Persian prophet Mani (d. 274) and his successors made great efforts to win powerful backers for their religion, which we call Manichaeism; it was popular across Central Asia and China, and in 762 it became the creed of the ruling clan of the Uighur Turks.

It was nevertheless Christianity that clearly had the greatest reach at this time. It spread eastward in the fifth to seventh century, through Iran and into Central Asia, even reaching China. By the mid-seventh century there were twenty Christian dioceses east of the river Oxus, including Samarkand and Kashgar. One can observe a similar process in Arabia. As early as the mid-fourth century emissaries were being sent from Constantinople "to persuade the ruler of the people (of Himyar) to become Christian and to give up the deceits of heathenism,"[7] and this momentum was sustained via Byzantium's Christian ally in the region, Ethiopia. The church in the Persian realm was very dynamic and established offshoots in all the islands and coastlands of east Arabia in this period, and Christian missionaries were active in all the frontier zones of Mesopotamia, Syria, Palestine, and north Arabia. The tribal folk of these latter regions are portrayed as accepting the new faith as a result of the power of the Christian God, made manifest by the miraculous deeds of various holy men. By their transition from paganism to "true belief," the tribesmen were considered to have entered the civilized fold: "Those who were formerly called the wolves of Arabia became members of the spiritual flock of Christ."[8]

These tribes became acculturated to the wider Roman world primarily through the influence of Christianity, and they were often encouraged to settle, which further aided the integration process. For example, one celebrated fifth-century ascetic of the Judaean desert converted a great number of tribesmen and they begged to remain near him; he marked out the site of a church for them, with their tents around it, and he assigned them a priest and deacon. "In consequence they became extremely numerous and spread out to form various encampments."[9] By the early seventh century it is possible to speak of a fledgling Arab Christianity, based in the settlements of Rusafa (in northern Syria), Hira (southern Iraq), Najran (northern Yemen), and a number of places in the Roman province of Arabia stretching from Jabiya in the north, in modern southwest Syria, to Petra and Kilwa (Figure I.2) in the south, in modern south Jordan and northwest Saudi Arabia, respectively. Some of these Arab Christians rose to become members of the Byzantine and Persian elite, and we see them hosting ecclesiastical meetings and sponsoring church building. One of them, a certain Sharahil, son of Zalim, left us a fine testimony

FIGURE I.2 Arabic inscription from Kilwa, a Christian settlement in northwest Saudi Arabia, ca. late seventh century. © Christian Robin.

FIGURE 1.3 Lintel of a martyrium with foundation inscription in Arabic and Greek, dated 567 AD, from Harran in southern Syria. © Author.

to this phenomenon in the form of an inscription carved onto the lintel of a chapel for a martyr named John, which had been commissioned by Sharahil in the year 567 (Figure 1.3). He ordered that the text of the inscription be in two languages: Greek to show that he was an educated member of Byzantine Christian society, and Arabic to make clear his roots, his local identity, and his pride in his Arabophone culture.[10]

The Rise of Peripheral Peoples

We do not know anything about Sharahil outside of his inscription, but we do see a number of his Arabophone contemporaries playing a substantial role in the imperial armies. The superpower rivalry that began in the third century AD meant that both empires were overstretched and had desperate need to swell the ranks of their military. Men who showed that they and their followers were skilled at waging war were welcomed with open arms and could negotiate for high stipends and titles. Furthermore, whereas before, in the glory days of the

Roman Empire, "barbarians" had been separated and distributed across different units and served under an imperial commander, now they entered service as whole groups and under their own leaders. This imperial policy of seeking out strong leaders and giving them subsidies and titles led to the emergence of ever larger and more powerful groupings as chosen leaders competed with one another for power and status. There were, for example, some fifteen chiefs of the Goths when they first appeared in the west in the fourth century, but by the sixth century there were just the two major kingdoms of the Visigoths and Ostrogoths, and they wielded enough military muscle to be able to dictate their demands to the Byzantine emperor.

The rise of such kingdoms in the peripheral regions of the Byzantine and Persian Empires in the fourth to sixth century is characterized by sociologists as secondary state formation. Groups that enjoyed frequent, sustained, and intensive contact with empires begin to establish rudimentary state structures of their own. Thus in all the border regions around the Byzantine Empire we see hybrid polities emerging: Romano-Germanic kingdoms in western Europe, Romano-Moorish kingdoms in north Africa, and Romano-Arab kingdoms on the periphery of the Levant. They retained their own distinctiveness—using their own language among themselves, preserving their own styles of dress, burial rites, and other customs—but they were proud of their ties with the empire. King Masuna of Altava, in modern west Algeria, proclaimed himself "king of the peoples of the Moors and the Romans,"[11] and the chiefs of the Arab tribe of Ghassan enthusiastically commissioned Arabic poetry and at the same time vaunted their imperial titles in their inscriptions and their patronage of Christianity.

In the old Chinese classification, these were "cooked" barbarians in that they had been moderated by close and prolonged interaction with the empires and adopted many of their ways. Beyond them lay barbarians who were less cooked and some who were downright raw. They, too, coveted the material riches that empires possessed, but being more distant from centers of settlement, they had less easy access to them. However, if they spotted a weakness in the imperial defenses they would seek to enrich themselves by extortion, demanding tribute and taxing trade routes. The late sixth and early seventh centuries presented just such an opportunity, and a number of peoples on the margins of empires seized their chance to raid the two empires. The situation was in many ways the same as had bedeviled the western half of the Roman Empire in the fifth and sixth centuries, when various "barbarian" groups carved out principalities for themselves and over time created independent kingdoms. The east had seemed immune from such depredation, since its more complex and diverse economy allowed it to pay for better defense and support a bigger army. But Byzantium and Persia's dangerous infatuation with defeating each other in the late sixth and early seventh centuries depleted their resources and left them exposed to attack.

The most powerful of these new peoples were the Turks. They had been one faction among many within a loose tribal coalition on China's northern frontier, but their khagan (chief) Bumin, with his brother Ishtemi, made a bid for power in 552 and established themselves as the new masters of this region, probably aided by the fact that China was particularly weak and disunited at this time. Subsequently they expanded westward, vanquishing in the 560s the Hephthalite (White Hun) confederation that had dominated Central Asia for the previous century. These Turks are unusual among steppe powers in that they have left us a number of inscriptions, in Sogdian and Old Turkish, which recount their exploits and ideas, including this reminiscence of an eighth-century ruler concerning the founding of his realm (Figure I.4):

> When the blue sky above and the dark earth below were fashioned, human beings were created between the two. My ancestors, the khagans Bumin and Ishtemi, rose above the sons of men. Having become the masters of the Turk people, they established and ruled its empire and fixed the law of the country. Many were their enemies in the four corners of the world, but, leading campaigns against them, they subjugated and pacified them, making them bow their heads and bend their knees. They pushed eastward to the forest of Qardirkhan and westward to the Iron Gate; thus far did the realm of the Turks reach. They were wise khagans, they were valiant khagans; all their officers were wise and valiant; all their nobles as well as common people were

FIGURE I.4 Statue from Zhao Su (Mongolkure) in northwest China, depicting the khagan Nili (d. ca. 600) with a crown on his head and holding a vessel and short sword in his hands. © Sören Stark.

just. This was why they were able to rule an empire so great, and why, governing the empire, they could uphold the law.[12]

By 583 the empire had split into eastern and western portions. The former, in Mongolia, primarily contended with China, engaging it in major confrontations in the late sixth and early seventh centuries. The western Turks, occupying the area from the Black Sea to Lake Issykul (in modern Kyrgyzstan), sought to challenge Persia, but two of the latter's commanders of the eastern marches defeated them in a series of battles in the late 580s and mid-610s. Instead, the Turks sent out feelers to Byzantium, whose emperors were happy to receive such powerful aid against their archenemy and to buy the silk and other luxury goods from China that they were trading. Byzantine courtiers perhaps smiled when envoys from the khagan referred to him as "great lord of the seven races, master of the seven climes,"[13] and yet it was only with the aid of the Turks that Heraclius was able to defeat the Persians in 627.

In the mid-sixth century another "barbarian" group, the Avars, began their rise to prominence. They seem to have been traveling westward from Central Asia, pushed along by the advance of the newly created Turk polity. They reached northern Caucasia in the winter of 557 and sent envoys to Constantinople, whose inhabitants marveled at their long plaited hair. The Byzantine emperor agreed to pay them a subsidy and directed them to attack various unruly elements in the Balkans. Gradually the Avars subjugated all the peoples of that region, including the Bulgars and Slavs, and raided as far afield as the river Elbe, coming into confrontation with the Franks. But this military might was soon turned against Byzantium and in 582 they conquered the strategic town of Sirmium (modern Sremska Mitrovica in Serbia). Clashes continued for many years, with the Avars most often having the upper hand, and they culminated in full-scale attacks on Constantinople itself in 619 and 626. The latter assault was particularly terrifying for the capital's residents, since it coincided with a simultaneous attack on the city by the Persians. The Byzantine navy was, however, able to stop all communication between the two enemy forces across the Bosphorus and harried the small ships of the Slav contingent. Lack of supplies and the immensity of Constantinople's encompassing walls gave rise to discontents and the siege was called off. The Avars never quite recovered their prestige, and the Slavs and Bulgars soon broke away to found their own polities.

The Avars were also constrained to the east by yet another emerging political player, the Khazars, who established themselves in the lower Volga region sometime between the 630s and 650s. They seem to have begun as a group within the Turk confederation, which was at that time coming under severe pressure from the recently established Tang dynasty in China. The Khazars' territory stretched from modern Ukraine to western Kazakhstan, and their rule lasted some three centuries (ca. 650–969), making them a particularly long-lived example of a steppe empire. The reason for their longevity was their evolution into a highly successful trans-Eurasian trade hub, connecting the northern forest zones with the Byzantine and Islamic empires. Moreover, the regime reinforced its own distinctiveness and independence by converting to Judaism in the eighth to ninth century. The Khazars were, in short, a formidable power and presented the Arabs with a serious challenge on their northern flank, especially in the period 708–37, when the two sides came together as equals and battled each other for supremacy of Caucasia.

In some ways, the rise of these peripheral peoples is a success story. By close and constant interaction with the empires they had learned to organize themselves in a more sophisticated way so that they were now capable of orchestrating major coordinated military action. They were not homogeneous entities but coalitions of numerous groups of different origins and ethnicities atop of which often sat a presiding dynasty. However, the resources that they obtained by extortion and pillage allowed them to buy loyalty, to unite fragmentary and diverse groups into more cohesive wholes, to articulate a sense of identity, and to promote their own culture. For the empires, there was a danger in this development in that some of these peoples became powerful enough to challenge them. The Persian emperor Peroz (457–84) made use of the Hephthalites of Central Asia to fight his younger brother, who had usurped the throne, but he was later to die at their hands when the relationship turned sour. A century later the Persians allied with the newly ascendant power in Central Asia, the Turks, to destroy the Hephthalite kingdom, but later the Turks struck a deal with Byzantium and reinforced the emperor Heraclius with enough troops to defeat Khusrau II. The Avars only appeared on the scene in the mid-sixth century, but they were soon able to cause the Byzantines a major headache, and their surprise attacks on Constantinople almost brought about the demise of the empire. Yet these peoples, the Arabs included, did not attack an empire in order to destroy it, despite what imperial citizens claimed; rather, they sought to appropriate some of its wealth for themselves, or even to make themselves its new masters.

Arabia and the Arabs

The most successful of the peripheral peoples were the Arabs, whose conquests are the subject of this book. They are very difficult to write about because

the term "Arab" has, as one would expect, meant different things to different people at different times since it was first introduced into the historical
record almost three millennia ago. A recent academic study into the nature of
pre-Islamic Arabs concluded that they were nomadic, camel-rearing, religiously
fanatical desert warriors, essentially lumping together all the stereotypes about
them held by settled peoples, on whose writings the author had relied for his
data.[14] These stereotypes have endured into our age, reinforced by films such
as *Lawrence of Arabia*, and so it is immensely difficult to persuade even educated
people that Arabs were not all nomadic desert-dwellers, and indeed that some
were sedentary and even members of the imperial elite. The idea of Arabia as a
harsh unchanging desert world populated only by heroic, martial Bedouin has
a romantic fascination for Western culture—and for many Middle Eastern
societies too, which have regarded the Arabian deserts and their denizens as
the source from whence they all hailed. In reality, Arabia has harbored a number of very different peoples, some of which did not define themselves as Arabs,
and some of which possessed advanced and complex cultures. It was also not as
remote as is generally assumed, but was heavily exposed to the influences and
machinations of empires and enjoyed mercantile contacts with other polities,
such as Ethiopia and India.

To the Assyrians and the Israelites, the Arabs were the inhabitants of the
Syrian desert, which lay between Iraq and Palestine, and of the vast empty
lands to the south (i.e., the Arabian Peninsula). These arid regions therefore became known as "the land of the Arabs" or, more popularly, "Arabia."
Subsequently, by an understandable piece of circular reasoning, all who lived
in the area known as Arabia were frequently referred to by outsiders as Arabs
(and sometimes Arabians—Greek-speakers used both *Arabes* and *Arabioi*). For a
long time the label was probably of only loose significance to those to whom it
was applied, who used more specific words to identify themselves, such as the
name of their tribe or region, but two developments gave it greater substance.
The first was the rise of the Nabataeans, who were identified as Arabs, spoke
an Arabic dialect, and established a kingdom in the second century BC that
encompassed "the whole territory from the Euphrates to the Red Sea." The
second was the annexation by the Romans of this realm in AD 105. Elements

of the old kingdom blended with imperial traditions to create a distinctive culture in this new province of "Arabia," many of whose inhabitants now began to
call themselves Arabs and were referred to as such by outsiders.[15]

The geographical extent of this province pretty much overlapped with the
former Nabataean kingdom, equating to modern southern Syria, all of Jordan,
southern Palestine/Israel, and northwest Saudi Arabia. It had no fixed southern
and eastern borders; the land there was dry and barren bar scattered oases, and
so was of little interest to the Romans. Yet some of the inhabitants of these
desert territories were proud to consider themselves part of the empire. A military unit from the tribe of Thamud, for example, erected a temple in honor of
Marcus Aurelius (161–80) in their hometown, not so far north of Muhammad's
Medina.[16] Over the centuries, the province came to generate a strong sense of
identity among its inhabitants, even though they were quite diverse in other
respects. A bird-augurer named Rufinus, temporarily resident on the island of
Thasos in the third century AD, calls himself an Arab because, as he emphasizes
in an epitaph for his son, he was a native of Qanawat in the north of Roman
Arabia. A funerary inscription concerning two soldiers, which dates to 522 and
was found in the Jordan Valley, stresses that they hailed "from the lands of the
people of the Arabs." And a couple of sixth-century monks from a monastery
near Jericho are described as Arabs on their tombstones.[17] Some may have been
linked by a common language, Arabic, but this was a polyglot land, and in the
end it was principally an attachment to their province that bound them.

These Arabs were settled folk, citizens of the Roman/Byzantine Empire,
but there were also Arabs who lived as nomadic pastoralists, refusing to be
subject to taxes and the dictates of bureaucrats. Settled people would always
draw a clear distinction between themselves and these nomadic Arabs,
regarding the latter as devoid of civilized values. Yet despite their apparent
marginality, it is the nomadic Arabs who feature more prominently in Late
Antique sources, and this is for two main reasons. In the first place, they
were converting to Christianity. In this they were influenced by the early
Christian ascetic movement, which saw the arid lands on the periphery of
the Byzantine and Persian Empires populated by hermits and monastic
communities. A whole new genre of literature arose that celebrated the more

heroic representatives of this movement and their devout exploits. In texts of this genre the indigenous inhabitants of the desert lands loom large, usually designated as Saracens or Tayyaye, the terms used by Byzantine and Persian citizens for the nomadic Arabs. Sometimes they are portrayed as predatory creatures whose attacks are foiled by the anchorite's appeal to God, and at other times they are characterized as impure beings whose lives are then enlightened by the piety of a holy man: "numerous were their superstitions and they were the most ignorant of all the peoples of the earth until the moment when the light of Christ came to them." A good example of such a desert missionary is Ahudemmeh, who, according to his acolyte, assiduously visited all the camps of the nomads in northern Mesopotamia, instructing them in the faith and preaching to them the word of God. He inaugurated churches, which he cleverly named after tribal chiefs, who would therefore feel encouraged to maintain them, "and thus he inclined the hearts of the Arabs to the love of God."[18]

In the second place, the nomadic Arabs were serving in the armies of Byzantium and Persia in increasing numbers. The term "nomad unit" and the names of commanders of such units appear in inscriptions at this time, and a document from around the year 400 lists "Saracen" cavalry regiments at locations in Egypt, Phoenicia, and Palestine.[19] Given the benefits that association with the empires could bring, especially titles and stipends, many chiefs actively sought to win the recognition of the authorities. An early example of such a figure is Imru' al-Qays ibn 'Amr, whose exploits are celebrated in an epitaph inscribed on the lintel of his tomb, which lies in the basalt desert southeast of Damascus and is dated to AD 328. It records how he asserted his authority, on behalf of Rome, over various tribes as far south as Najran, on the northern edges of Yemen. And over the following three centuries there were many who strove to emulate him, flexing their muscles and making ever grander demands. Much feared was Queen Mawiya (fl. 370s), who ravaged the eastern provinces when she did not receive her usual payments, but who showed herself to be fully at home within the Byzantine Empire, renewing the alliance once her requests were granted, and even giving her daughter in marriage to a high-ranking member of the imperial army. Then there was

Abikarib (fl. 530s), who was appointed by the emperor Justinian the Great to maintain order among the pastoralist tribes in Palestine and to halt the incursions of tribes from outside the province. He achieved great success in this position, "for both to the barbarians over whom he ruled and no less to the enemy Abikarib always seemed a man to be feared and an exceptionally energetic fellow."[20] He also features in a contemporary Syriac manuscript from the Palmyra region, where he is addressed as "king" by the copyist, and in a Greek papyrus from Petra, where he acts as an arbiter in a property dispute between two residents of the city. It would seem, then, that these Arab leaders were becoming increasingly involved in the life of the province to which they were assigned by the imperial authorities, acting as local powerbrokers in the lives of the settled communities on the margins of the empires.

By the time of Abikarib we can speak of Romano-Arab and Perso-Arab polities. A number of the dynasties lasted three, four, or more generations, suggesting that they possessed sufficient political power to ensure succession from one generation to another and to instill allegiance. They had bases of varying degrees of permanence where they could store wealth, receive embassies, conduct a rudimentary administration, and hold court. All had organizational structures for relaying commands and all could muster substantial military manpower, their key attraction to their imperial masters. In addition, all had at least modest revenues, deriving from imperial payments, booty, and extraction of tribute from weaker tribes; this they used to win loyalty and to extend patronage, which is manifested to us in building inscriptions and collections of poetry. The latter, composed in Arabic, praised patrons and scorned enemies, and in general presented an idealized picture of Bedouin life: meals shared with guests around the fire, amorous liaisons with the women of neighboring camps, fast camel rides across the desert, battles won and lost, honor defended, and always the heroic struggle against fate, time, and the elements. The homogeneity of the themes presented and the norms espoused clearly reflected and reinforced a body of shared values and experiences. This poetry contributed to the formation of a broad Arab identity, and the hybrid Arab polities that sponsored it paved the way for the coming Arab Empire by assimilating customs and practices of both the settled and the nomadic worlds.

The rise to prominence of these dynasties was very much a consequence of the stepping up of hostilities between Byzantium and Persia, which made both of them court those who could provide military assistance. As the conflict between these two empires intensified, greater power was granted to their favored tribal allies. This was undertaken first by the Persian emperor Kawad (488–531), who appointed the fearless Mundhir ibn Nu'man (504–54), a chief of the tribe of Lakhm based in the southwest Iraqi settlement of Hira, as sole overlord of the tribes in his lands. To counter this man, who for half a century "forced the Roman state to bend its knee," the various clans loyal to the Byzantines were brought together under Harith ibn Jabala (529–69), a chief of the tribe of Ghassan, now granted the title of "king" by the emperor himself—"a thing which had never been done by the Byzantines before." The military power at the disposal of Harith was demonstrated later in this century when his son was exiled by the emperor Maurice (582–602). This impelled his men to go on a rampage in Syria and Arabia, which so terrified the inhabitants of the countryside, claimed one contemporary, perhaps with some exaggeration, that they "fled for refuge to the cities and did not dare appear outside."[21]

Byzantine and Persian citizens employed the terms "Saracen" and "Tayyaye" to designate the nomads of Arabia and the imperial borderlands, whereas they used the term "Arab" to refer to the settled inhabitants of the provinces of Arabia. It is important to bear in mind, however, that the various tribes on the edges of the empires did not call themselves "Saracens" or "Tayyaye." Indeed, we know that they felt some degree of affinity with the settled Arabs. For example, the aforementioned Imru' al-Qays, whom the Romans called a Saracen, styled himself "king of all the Arabs" (al-'arab), seemingly referring to the provinces of Roman and Persian Arabia and their inhabitants. And a poet who was born in the lifetime of Muhammad sang: "You call us nomads but our name is the Arabs."[22] Language was almost certainly a crucial ingredient in this shared identity. Sharahil ibn Zalim and the prophet Muhammad were contemporaries and to both of them it was evidently important to compose in their native tongue. Sharahil made a point of having the dedication of the martyrium that he had paid for written in Arabic as well as Greek, and he is the first person we know of who did this. Muhammad stressed that the revelation he brought from God was in "the Arab tongue" (*lisan 'arabi*), and that he was the first prophet to employ it.[23] The revelation, he emphasized, could have been conveyed in a foreign (*'ajami*) tongue, one more conventionally used for such discourse, such as Greek or Aramaic. However, as God is made to say in the Qur'an: "We made it an Arabic Qur'an so that you can understand" (43:3; cf. 12:2) and "We have imparted to you (Muhammad) an Arabic recitation so that you can warn the mother of towns and those who live around it" (42:7; cf. 6:92). Clearly the inhabitants of Muhammad's west Arabia were primarily Arabic speakers and participated to some extent in this newly burgeoning Arab identity. For centuries they had interacted with their northern neighbors in Byzantine Arabia, but very much in a subordinate position. In the seventh century they would come to play the dominant role and would win the support of many of the inhabitants of Byzantine and Persian Arabia by playing up their shared Arab identity and Arab tongue.

The Mid-Sixth-Century Crisis and the Unraveling of Empire

The rise of these peripheral peoples is likely to be connected, at least in part, with a decline in the fortunes of the empires of Byzantium, Persia, and China in the fifth and sixth centuries, which came to a head in the second half of the sixth century. This means that we should probably consider the Arab conquests as an outcome of this decline rather than its cause.[24] A feeling that matters were going downhill is certainly noted by contemporaries. "There was a time," narrates an eyewitness of the Avar raids around Constantinople in 619, "when things were going well for us and there was no warfare to terrify us; but the summit of prosperity, as they say, was changed through our carelessness and tripped us up, for we were not able to maintain our good fortune untarnished." Little more than a decade later, a Jewish merchant, native of Palestine but on business in Carthage, was to confirm this view: "The territory of the Romans used to extend until our times from the ocean, that is from Scotia, Britain, Spain, France, Italy, Greece and Thrace, as far as Antioch, Syria, Persia and all the East, Egypt, Africa and the interior of Africa . . . but now we see Rome humbled."[25]

Although politically correct scholars hate to use such value-laden terms as "decline," this perception of shrinkage and diminution given by contemporaries does seem borne out by the evidence. A number of minor polities, like Georgia and Ethiopia, which had still been thriving in the early sixth century, seem to splutter and lapse into torpor toward the end of that century. The kingdom of Yemen, ancient Sheba, is so enfeebled that, despite a continuous history going back a millennium and a half, it becomes a puppet state first of Ethiopia, then of Persia. The rest of Arabia is similarly hard hit: the commerce in the Arabian port cities of the Persian Gulf that had boomed in the Hellenistic and Roman period slows to a trickle in the fifth and sixth centuries. In the oases and pilgrimage sites of northwest Arabia not a single inscription in any language or script is to be found that is dated to the sixth century despite a rich epigraphic tradition that stretched back more than a thousand years. Even the rich olive oil producing lands of northern Syria show a sharp retrenchment in building inscriptions and economic activity in the late sixth century.[26]

As far as contemporaries were concerned there were two key factors responsible for this downturn: recurring bouts of bubonic plague, commencing in 542, by which "nearly the whole human race was annihilated," and the increasing frequency and intensity of confrontation between Byzantium and Persia. As a historian writing in 580 put it: "Nations have been wiped out, cities enslaved, populations uprooted and displaced, so that all mankind has been involved in the upheaval." Both phenomena had a major depressing effect upon the population, in turn affecting the economy, which in pre-modern times was very sensitive to demographic fluctuations. It has also been postulated that environmental catastrophe played a part in this mid-sixth-century recession. Chroniclers from Ireland to China mention crop failures, abnormal cold, and prolonged reduction of sunlight in the year 536–37, and this is attributed to ash clouds resulting from volcanic eruptions or meteorites crashing to earth. A substantial and sustained reduction in harvests would certainly trigger major social unrest further down the road, and one could see this as the ultimate cause of the change and upheaval of the late sixth and early seventh centuries, provoking empires and steppe peoples alike to fight over diminishing resources. Many modern historians are, however, wary of such ideas, in part because they do not understand the science, and in part because they focus principally on human actions rather than environmental factors. Of course, even if disaster hits, humans can still influence their fate by the way they respond to it; one thing for sure, though, is that the choice of the Middle Eastern superpowers to engage in large-scale warfare was the wrong response.[27]

Whatever the reason, it is clear that the empires of Byzantium and Persia failed to keep in check the steppe peoples within and beyond their borders in the late sixth and early seventh centuries. The Turks, Avars, and Arabs are all able to make significant encroachments over the course of this period. The same can be said for China where the Wei dynasty collapsed in 534 and decades of infighting ensued, which was reduced somewhat by the Sui dynasty (589–618) but only properly brought under control with the establishment of the Tang dynasty by Emperor Gaozu (618–26). The Persian Empire suffered the most, since its capital, Seleucia-Ctesiphon, was dangerously close to the steppe lands, and the deserts and mountains within its realm favored regional autonomy and limited centralization. Ignominious defeat at the hands of Emperor Heraclius and an ensuing civil war fatally weakened the regime's ability to respond when the Arabs overran their lands. The capitals of the Byzantine and Chinese empires, on the other hand, were far from the steppe and extremely well defended, and the empires themselves, organized around large bodies of water (the Mediterranean Sea and the Yellow and Yangtze Rivers, respectively), were reasonably well integrated. This meant that though they also suffered many defeats at the hands of steppe raiders, they were able to weather the storm. The Avars and Turks clearly had ambitions to penetrate further into the lands of Byzantium and Persia, but they were coming from the difficult northern and eastern sides of the two empires, where they faced substantial man-made and natural obstacles, whereas the Arabs were directly adjacent to the soft southern underbellies of these empires, and so it was they who ultimately triumphed in this seventh-century great game.

Chapter Two

THE FIRST BATTLES (630–640)

B y the summer of 628 the bitter war between the empires of
Byzantium and Persia was finally over. It had begun a full quarter of a century earlier and in the course of these years tens of
thousands of lives had been lost, the livelihoods of many ruined, and a number of cities sacked. Inevitably, both imperial armies had endured enormous
losses, and raiding by various groups, including Arab tribes, was now endemic
in marginal areas. Yet contemporary observers assumed, understandably, that
such ancient and powerful states had the resources and organizational capacity
to reassert themselves. As the victors, the Byzantines could at least feel encouraged that they enjoyed God's support and with the advent of peace would be
able to repair their defenses and reestablish security. Persia, on the other hand,
had suffered a crippling defeat at the hands of Heraclius and the Turks, and
many of its local nobles were openly hostile to the ruling family for bringing
such shame and ruin upon them and their nation. They murdered Khusrau II,
who had initiated the ultimately unsuccessful campaign against Byzantium,
which ushered in a period of bloodletting and strife. Various candidates fought
for control of the state, including a daughter of Khusrau II, but most ruled
for a very short time and held sway over a limited portion of the realm. Only
around 632–33 was the succession crisis resolved, when a grandson of Khusrau

named Yazdgird took charge. In the meantime, the Persian lands had been left critically exposed to potential invaders.

Some Arab tribes of northeast Arabia had already begun to test the will of the Persians to defend their southern borders by launching exploratory raids, but a much more potent threat came from Caucasia. A khagan of the Turks had spotted an opportunity and in 629 he led out a huge army and "spread terror and dread over the face of the earth." He began by ravaging the east Caucasian kingdom of Albania and then moved westward to Armenia, where he learned that one of Khusrau's leading generals was marching against him. This turned out to be the celebrated Shahrbaraz, who had achieved so many victories against the Byzantines in the previous two decades. He picked the head of an Arab cavalry unit and sent him with 10,000 men to "trample the Turks beneath the hooves and chests of the horses, and scatter them like dust in the wind." But the Turks had prepared an ambush and while one party of them appeared to flee, causing the Persian contingent to pursue them, another party fell upon the Persians from the rear and sides and massacred them. The Turks now looked set to add Persia to their dazzling list of acquisitions. It was not to be, however, for "the cauldron of the North had turned his face against his own sons." A deadly power struggle had broken out at the top; the khagan himself was killed and the Turk confederation imploded. They had squandered their opportunity and the way was now left open to armies from Arabia.[1]

The Arabian Peninsula (Map 2.1)

The land of Arabia might at first seem an unlikely home for world conquerors, since huge distances and vast desert expanses had kept it divided into petty kingdoms, ephemeral chiefdoms, and isolated oasis communities for centuries, but this began to change around the year AD 300. The kingdom of Himyar, based in southwest Yemen, managed to subjugate the various principalities around it to become the dominant force in South Arabia. Its leaders made two rather dramatic policy decisions. First, they broke with the past by rejecting the old pagan gods and converting to monotheism: no pagan inscriptions have been discovered that postdate 380, bringing to an abrupt

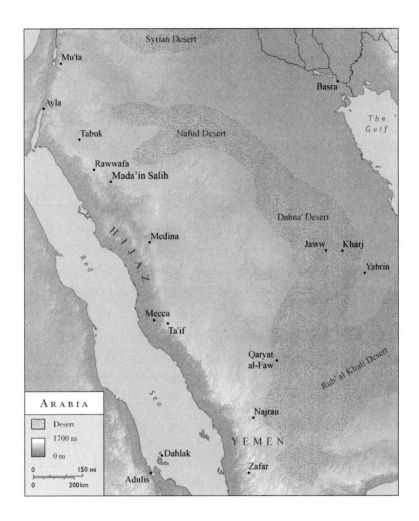

MAP 2.1 The Arabian Peninsula.

end a 1,300-year-old tradition of polytheism, among the ruling elite at least. Judaism seems to have been the preferred variety of monotheism, though some favored Christianity, especially those with close links to Christian Ethiopia on the other side of the Red Sea. Second, they used the combined resources of their realm to expand northward and succeeded in bringing under their sway many of the Arab tribes of central and north Arabia. Some they chastened by conquest, as is reported in triumphal terms in a number of royal inscriptions, but many they wooed with subsidies and titles. A fifth-century chief of the tribe of Kinda won just such an accolade for the loyal military support that he gave to Himyar and he proudly celebrated this honor by having his name etched on a rock, in the south Arabian alphabet, together with the title "King of Kinda." He and his descendants became so powerful that they attracted the attention of Byzantium and Persia, who vied with each other to draw them over to their side.[2]

The ascendancy of the Himyarite monarchy was, however, challenged by the Christian Ethiopian kingdom, which invaded Yemen on the pretext of defending the Christians of that land against the oppression of the ruling clan of the Himyarites, who were mostly Jews. It achieved a resounding victory in this venture and this ushered in nearly half a century of Ethiopian tutelage over Arabia (ca. 525–72). Much of this period was dominated by one particular Ethiopian general, named Abraha (ca. 535–65), who strove to present himself in the manner of a Himyarite king (Figure 2.1), adopting all the old royal titulature and writing official statements in the local prestige language. He also maintained, and even extended, south Arabian domination over the lands to the north, as is recorded in a number of inscriptions that boast at length about his victories. In the latest text, from the 550s, he tells us that he now controlled towns right across Arabia, including Medina (ancient Yathrib), and had driven the prince of the tribe of Lakhm back to his camp at Hira in southwest Iraq. The most famous text, which commemorates the repair of the dam of Marib (Figure 2.2) and the consecration of a church in the same city in 548, suggests that he had genuine political clout, for it records how envoys from Ethiopia, Byzantium, Persia, and three Arab vassal states had arrived to pay their respects.

Abraha's kingdom of Arabia did not endure long, however. The sons were not able to sustain their father's triumphs and ruled no more than a few short years. A local Himyarite prince came to power with Persian support, but when he was killed by disgruntled Ethiopians, the Persians decided to impose direct rule. This occurred sometime in the early 570s and heralded the end of the south Arabian civilization that had flourished for more than a millennium and a half. Presumably the half century of Ethiopian domination followed by

FIGURE 2.1 Stone relief from Zafar, capital of Himyar in Yemen, depicting a Himyarite king with crown and staff; ca. fifth–sixth century AD. © Paul Yule.

another half century of Persian rule had a deleterious effect on the ancient culture, for, though Yemen was a major supplier of troops to the Arab armies, very little of its long tradition of literature and history became a part of the Islamic worldview beyond the haziest of recollections.[3] Not long after the Persians took charge of south Arabia, in 582, the Byzantine emperor Maurice cast off the tribe of Ghassan as an imperial ally and exiled its chief. For a couple of decades this left the field open to the tribe of Lakhm, based in southern Iraq. Its chief endeavored to exert his authority as far afield as west Arabia and he evidently achieved some success, for east Christian sources describe him as "king of all the Arabs in the Persian and Byzantine empires."[4] However, his conversion from paganism to Christianity in 594 made him suspect to his Persian masters, especially when the emperor Khusrau sought to launch an all-out war against Byzantium, and so he had the Lakhmid chief poisoned and appointed a Persian official to keep the Arabs in check. The Persian Empire

FIGURE 2.2 Dam of Marib, capital of Saba/Sheba in Yemen, northern sluice system.
© American Foundation for the Study of Man.

now claimed the whole of Arabia, but it is unlikely that they were in full control of anything more than the southwestern tip and the eastern coast, and even this might have been fairly tenuous, given how much of Persia's military resources were tied up with its war against Byzantium.

Unfortunately, our contemporary sources offer almost no information at all on Arabia in these crucial decades. Later Muslim writers suggest that in the absence of any political direction from neighboring states a number of local leaders stepped in to fill the vacuum. Since the usual structures of political authority had broken down, these leaders were not from the ranks of the traditional holders of power; rather they claimed authority on religious grounds, arguing that they had been called by God to govern their people. None invoked pagan deities but presented themselves as monotheist leader-prophets,[5] presumably influenced in different ways by the various versions of Christianity and Judaism that were by this time fairly well established in Arabia. Not surprisingly, it is one particular leader-prophet that we hear most about in later Muslim sources, namely, Muhammad, who was based in the central west Arabian settlement of Mecca. He was of little consequence to the outside world until after his death, and so we have no contemporary external sources to elucidate his life; if we are to escape the sacralizing tendencies of later Muslim writers, we are therefore obliged to rely on what we can infer from his religious teachings enshrined in the Qur'an. These tell us that Muhammad sought to persuade his countrymen to adhere to the pure monotheism that had been established by Abraham, who was, he claimed, their ancestor. He initially attempted to spread his message solely by preaching, but he received a hostile reception from most of his fellow Meccans and had to make a journey in search of refuge (a *hijra*), ending up in the nearby oasis town of Medina. The time of peaceful preaching was over now, he decided, and it was time to use force to carry out what he perceived to be God's will. He drew up an agreement with a number of groups in Medina to create a single community (*umma*) dedicated to "fighting in God's path" (*jihad fi sabil Allah*), that is, in His cause, against His pagan enemies. All who promised to be faithful to the agreement were obligated to contribute to the war effort and to support the other members of the *umma* above anyone else.

After founding this polity at Medina in 622, Muhammad launched a number of raids against neighboring tribes and settlements with the aim of recruiting them to his mission. He also kept trying to win over the Meccans and he finally realized this objective by a mixture of warfare and diplomacy in 628. He sealed the deal by marrying the daughter of Abu Sufyan ibn Harb, who was one of the most powerful men of Muhammad's tribe, namely Quraysh. After cementing the alliance between the Meccans and Medinans, Muhammad went on to bring a third town into their coalition: the fertile oasis of Ta'if, which was dominated by the tribe of Thaqif. This was achieved in 630 and together the three towns and their allied tribes made a formidable fighting force. It is difficult to be sure what Muhammad's intentions were at this point. Later Muslim authors and, following them, modern historians assume that he was bent on world domination from the beginning, but it is inherently unlikely that he expected to spread his message so far from the outset. Certainly the Qur'an suggests that he had more local objectives: God wanted him to "warn the mother of towns [assumed to be Mecca] and those who live around it" (42:7; cf. 6:92), and He gave him "an Arabic Qur'an" (12:2 and 43:3) in accordance with the general principle that He "has only ever sent a messenger with a message in the language of his own people so that he makes it clear for them" (14:4). Muhammad's target audience, then, was, initially at least, the Arabic speakers of his own region. He was aware, though, of the wider world: his followers originally prayed facing Jerusalem and he knew that this was the world's first monotheist sanctuary, and it may be that, having attracted many fighters to his cause, he now aimed to capture this cherished prize.[6] Whether true or not, Muhammad's west Arabian coalition did direct their efforts northward. They had already subjugated the nearby oases of Fadak and Khaybar in 628, but now they went much farther to the north, challenging the Byzantine Empire directly.

While Muhammad led this expedition to the north in 630, delegations were sent to other parts of Arabia inviting them to join forces with Muhammad. Medieval Muslim authors, in part wishing to play up the achievements of their prophet and in part striving to systematize their source material, claimed that these delegations succeeded, whether by diplomatic or military means, in winning all of the Arabian Peninsula to Muhammad's rule by the time of his death in June 632, but that subsequently many of its tribes apostatized and seceded and had to be coerced to return to the fold by Muhammad's successor, Abu Bakr. This rebellion of the Arabian tribes (Arabic: *ridda*), required at least a year (632–33) to quash, they say, and only then could the Arab conquests (Arabic: *futuh*) commence, in the twelfth year of Muhammad's community (633–34). One could imagine that the tribes of southwest Arabia had begun to join the new movement already in Muhammad's lifetime, especially when they saw how successful it was. But east Arabia is separated from the west by vast inhospitable deserts, including the aptly named Empty Quarter, and in any case, as we shall see further on, its tribes were already launching their own raids against Persia. It is more likely, then, that not that much of Arabia outside the western flank had been brought under the control of Muhammad's forces by the time of his death. Abu Bakr's task, therefore, was not to reconquer

Arabia, but simply to conquer it, or at least to win it over to the movement's cause. Possibly he did not fully accomplish even this, for, according to a contemporary Armenian chronicle, only *after* the Arabs had invaded Syria and Iraq did "they then penetrate with royal armies into the *original* borders of the territory of Ishmael."[7]

Byzantine Arabia, Palestine, and Syria (Map 2.2)

Muhammad's campaign northward, into the Byzantine province of Arabia, in 630 was apparently planned in response to intelligence about military preparations against his coalition by some neighboring pro-Byzantine Arab tribes.[8] Khalid ibn al-Walid, a tough no-nonsense soldier, led a detachment northwest to Dumat al-Jandal, an important stop on a desert trade route from southern Syria to northern Arabia, while Muhammad himself commanded the main body of men and marched directly northward. He passed by Mada'in Salih, the southern capital of the ancient Nabataean Kingdom, and reached Tabuk, an oasis in the far northwest of modern Saudi Arabia. There is no natural border between the Arabian Peninsula and the lands to the north of it; crossing from modern Saudi Arabia to Jordan, one observes no change in the scenery— the same imposing sandstone mountains, volcanic outcrops, and bleak sandy desert continue for a while as one heads northward (Figure 2.3). It was quite natural then that Muhammad, encountering no resistance at Tabuk, should continue on another 125 miles to Ayla, modern Aqaba, the northernmost port of the Red Sea, and on another 65 miles to Udhruh, very near Petra, the main capital of the Nabataean Kingdom. This was in any case the route that traders between west Arabia and southern Syria had been used to taking for many centuries now. The terms of the peace agreements Muhammad concluded with these and neighboring settlements differ considerably, suggesting that there was no collective negotiation by an agent of the Byzantine government, but rather the towns had been left to fend for themselves and the head persons of each place had to bargain as best they could.

Presumably, the Persians who had nominally occupied this region during the years 614–28 had been too busy establishing their hold over cities and

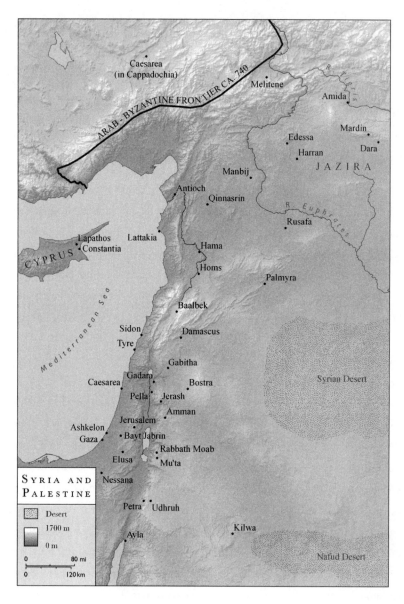

MAP 2.2 Syria, Palestine and Jazira.

FIGURE 2.3 View of scenery around Mada'in Salih, northwest Saudi Arabia. ©
Laïla Nehmé.

extending their conquests of Byzantine lands to worry about the security of
outlying areas. In such a situation it is not surprising, as contemporary evidence makes clear, that Muhammad's followers had precursors. One chronicle
records that in 610 "a band of Arabs came out of Arabia into the regions of
Syria; they pillaged and laid waste many lands, committed many massacres of
men and burned without compassion or pity." A monk of Mar Saba monastery
in the Judaean desert tells us that two months after the sack of Jerusalem by
the Persians in 614 the monks were still unwilling to return to their monasteries in the desert "for fear of the Saracens," and a monk from a monastery
near Jericho describes the depredations of bands of "Hebrews and Saracens."
The situation was not immediately improved when the Byzantines took back
control of this region, for, as one paymaster told a group of Arabs who came
to claim their subsidies for keeping the desert roads safe: "The emperor can
barely pay his soldiers their wages, much less you dogs!"[9]

Before we get into the accounts of the battles themselves, it is worth making clear that we have no good descriptions of the tactics or weaponry employed by any of the parties involved. As we said in the last chapter, the genre of Greco-Roman classicizing history, which had treated politics and warfare and was written by those who had experience in these matters, had passed away. The men who subsequently chronicled military affairs were mostly clergymen on the Christian side and storytellers and religious scholars of different sorts on the Muslim side. Their purpose in writing was to show the workings of God, not the machinations of man. Storytellers, or we might say preachers, had served in Arab armies from an early stage, encouraging the troops by recalling past glories and heroic exploits, so adding a human dimension to the bare facts. They give us an impression, for example, of the characters of the early warriors (Abu 'Ubayda as prudent, Khalid ibn al-Walid as impetuous, 'Amr ibn al-'As as wily), and of the self-image of the conquerors: "soldiers by day and monks by night," emphasizing their passion for jihad and *zuhd* (simple living).[10] We almost never receive from any writer, however, reliable details about troop strength and movements, specific planning, weapons deployed, layout of the site, and so on. In particular, the numbers given by our sources are very erratic, and the reader must just bear in mind that provisioning large numbers of soldiers was very difficult in the time before mechanized agriculture and transport. An army of 5,000–10,000 men is already very substantial, and 30,000–40,000 near the limit of what it is possible to sustain, especially in less fertile areas.

The first sure contemporary information that we get about the movements of the west Arabian armies comes from a chronicle that would seem, from the precision of its report, to depend on a local source. It tells us that in the year 945 of the Greeks (AD 634), "on Friday 4 February, at the ninth hour" a Byzantine force engaged "the Arabs of Muhammad" in Palestine, twelve miles east of Gaza. Nothing is said about the course of the confrontation, but it is simply noted that "the Byzantines fled, leaving behind their patrician," whom the Arabs killed, and that "some 4000 poor villagers of Palestine were killed there, Christians, Jews and Samaritans, and the Arabs ravaged the whole region." This would appear to correspond to an equally brief notice in Muslim sources about a battle in the spring of 634 at Dathin, described as one of the villages of Gaza, in which a general was killed.[11]

As the banditry continued, the governor of Palestine, based in the regional capital of Caesarea, felt that he should take action, for the Arabs were now entering the agricultural areas and nearing major settlements. He marched south toward Bayt Jabrin, which bore the grand name of Eleutheropolis, that is, "Freedom City." However, the Arabs had prepared an ambush for him and at an opportune moment leaped out of their hiding places, screaming and shouting, and fell upon a unit of Samaritans, who unfortunately for them were at the front and faced the full brunt of the Arab onslaught; they buckled under the force of the attack and "every one of them perished by the sword." Seeing this, the commander retreated, precipitating the hasty and disorderly flight of his men. The chronicler of this rout, though he had no Byzantine victory to boast of, managed to give a positive twist to his account by lauding the bravery of the governor, who, having fallen off his horse in the path of the pursuing Arabs, waves away his attendants, bidding them to save themselves "lest you and I shall drink the cup of death together."[12] This confrontation is probably to be equated with what Muslim sources call the Battle of Ajnadayn, which took place in July 634, since it too involved the death of a high-ranking Byzantine official.

Another encounter occurred in the vicinity of Rabbath Moab, to the east of the southern stretch of the Dead Sea. Here the austere and barren mountain range that accompanies the traveler from Arabia gives way to the more gentle and fertile highland region of the northern Jordan valley. Rabbath, renamed Areopolis by the Romans, is situated at the point of this transition and lies on the ancient road known as the Kings' Highway, linking the cities of Ayla and Amman. The remains of a pagan temple are still visible today, but in Muhammad's time Rabbath was a major Christian center, important enough to have its own bishop attend the council of Ephesus in AD 449. Here, then, the Arabs might have expected stiff resistance, but again they caught their opponents unawares. A contemporary source says that a Byzantine force was encamped in the vicinity and that the Arabs, "falling on them unexpectedly, put them to the sword and put to flight Theodore, brother of the emperor

Heraclius." One might wonder that such a senior figure in the Byzantine establishment would be involved—perhaps there is confusion with an assistant of
the provincial governor (*vicarius*) of the same name (i.e., Theodore), who was
also fighting the Arabs in this region.[13] However, numerous sources, Muslim
ones included, do agree that Heraclius's brother was involved in an early confrontation with the Arabs and that, chastened by his defeat, he hurried back
to Constantinople.

The Arabs pressed on and, taking the desert route in order to avoid major
centers of settlement, they arrived at Bostra by the autumn of 634, in the
south of modern Syria, just across the border from Jordan. It was a rich and
prosperous city, the capital of the Byzantine province of Arabia; situated in
a large fertile plain it served as an important market for pastoralists coming
to sell their animal products and to buy grain, oil, wine, and manufactured
goods. To the northeast rose the volcanic hills of the Hawran, in which all
sorts of fruits were grown, including the grapes that provided the wine extolled
in pre-Islamic Arabic poems. Christian and Muslim chroniclers are agreed
that the capture of Bostra was a brief affair, for the city simply surrendered
to the Arabs on the agreement that its residents' lives and property would be
safeguarded in return for payment of tribute. In the sixth century there would
have been a military commander based at Bostra, responsible for the troops
stationed in the province of Arabia and for the overall security of that province. But it is possible that after the Persian occupation military resources were
concentrated in Damascus, only sixty or so miles to the north, or at least that
a new commander for Bostra was not yet in place, which would explain why
the city appears not to have put up any resistance.

Contemporary chroniclers record very few clashes between Arab and
Byzantine armies in this region, but other types of sources suggest that acts of
despoliation and looting were common. On the other side of the river Jordan,
in Jerusalem, the newly elected patriarch, Sophronius, a former monk with a
passion for Greek learning and rhetoric, had strong feelings about the invaders.
In the letter he wrote to mark his elevation to the headship of the Palestinian
church in 634 he rails against "the Saracens who, on account of our sins, have
now risen up against us unexpectedly and ravage all with cruel and feral design,

with impious and godless audacity." Later in the year the security situation was so bad that he could not travel to Bethlehem and was obliged to give his Nativity sermon in Jerusalem. As happened to the Israelites at the hands of the Philistines, he laments, "so now the army of the godless Saracens has captured the divine Bethlehem and bars our passage there, threatening slaughter and destruction." The patriarch's last and most detailed description of the Arab attacks appears in his sermon on the Holy Baptism, which he delivered on the feast of the Epiphany, December 6 of either 635 or 636. He urges his congregation to eschew sin, for this is the reason "why the vengeful and God-hating Saracens, the abomination of desolation clearly foretold to us by the prophets, overrun the places which are not allowed to them, plunder cities, devastate fields, burn down villages, set on fire the holy churches, overturn the sacred monasteries and oppose the Byzantine armies arrayed against them." Of course, one cannot take such accusations at face value, since Sophronius is indulging in high rhetoric to ram home his message of repentance and abstinence from wrongdoing, but the threat was evidently real enough to make his sermon convincing.[14]

Chroniclers now focus on an encounter that, in retrospect, was viewed as turning the tide against Byzantium and in favor of the Arabs: the Battle of Yarmuk. The name refers to the river that flows westward along the modern border between Jordan and Syria, and empties into the river Jordan, just south of the Sea of Galilee. The Arabs were led by two of their most famous generals: the aforementioned Khalid ibn al-Walid and Abu 'Ubayda ibn al-Jarrah, who comes across as a tough but fair and pragmatic man. Both were from the prophet's tribe of Quraysh, but whereas the former was from a clan that long opposed Muhammad, Abu 'Ubayda had been a close companion of the prophet from the very start of his mission. The emperor Heraclius had traveled to northern Syria to obtain better intelligence about events and realized that matters were serious, and so he appointed his top general in the east, the Armenian Vahan, to take charge of the operation. Heraclius was particularly worried that the key city of Damascus was under threat, and so he dispatched messengers to instruct legions with spare capacity to release some troops for the defense of the Syrian capital. Vahan marched from Antioch with the main army, apparently routing a small Arab exploratory force on the way, in the vicinity of Homs. In the early summer of 636 "an enormous multitude of Saracens set out from Arabia and headed for the region of Damascus";[15] presumably the success of the initial Arab raids had encouraged many others to join the venture. Worried by this, Vahan wrote to Theodore, a patrician of Edessa and a senior financial administrator, to bring reinforcements, and he arrived with a further 10,000 men. Once all were assembled, they encamped together, right by the bank of the river Yarmuk.

The Byzantine force looked very strong, but fortune was not on their side. An initial encounter in July 636 resulted in a defeat for the contingent of Theodore. This led to an argument between the latter and the Armenians, who subsequently proclaimed their own general emperor while abjuring Heraclius. Theodore's men withdrew and the Arabs seized the moment to attack; some had been hidden in ambush around the Byzantine camp and they now jumped out and fell upon the enemy. The Byzantines attempted to flee, but the dense mud of the flood plain bogged them down and the heat of the sun overwhelmed them. Many thousands were either cut down by the sword or slipped down the steep sides of the river valley and were either crushed or drowned. The exact details of the battle are difficult to recover, but the loss of Byzantine life was evidently considerable, for it sent shock waves around the empire, even as far away as Gaul, where one Frankish chronicler spread news of the calamity. The latter and another Latin source blame at least some of the loss of Byzantine life on an outbreak of the plague, which was raging in Syria at that time. Heraclius realized that it would be a while before more troops could be mustered and so he issued orders to all the provinces to the effect that no one should try to engage the Arabs in open combat, but everyone should instead try to maintain their positions as best they could. He himself returned to Constantinople and is prematurely portrayed by later Christian and Muslim authors as bidding Syria a sorrowful farewell, "saying *sosou Syria*, which means, 'rest in peace, Syria', as if he despaired of ever seeing her again."[16]

This victory allowed the Arabs, as one writer put it, to "take firm possession of the provinces which they had not long since invaded, and locate their rule at Damascus, the most splendid city of Syria." From this firm base the

Arabs were able to extend their conquests to the rest of the Levant. Christian sources speak most about three key cities: Homs, ancient Emesa and the resting place of the head of St. John the Baptist; Jerusalem, the seat of a patriarch and numerous churches and monasteries; and Caesarea, the capital of Palestine and an important port. The capture of Homs gives us an insight into why many cities seem to fall with such apparent ease to the Arabs. It had tried to hold out against a siege during the winter of 636–37 hoping that the cold would make the Arabs give up and that Heraclius would be able to raise an army to relieve them. But as the winter wore on, disputes broke out, some arguing that it would be better to surrender now when they could negotiate reasonable terms, others countering: "How can we do that when the emperor is still in authority and power?" Finally, as it became clear that help was not forthcoming, the inhabitants sued for peace and they received, like Damascus, a written covenant guaranteeing them "security for their lives, possessions, churches and laws" in return for payment of 110,000 gold coins as the tribute of the city.[17] The relative fairness of the conditions of surrender encouraged many cities to submit rather than face a grueling blockade and possible slaughter, especially as they had already endured the hardship of the Persian invasion and occupation just a few years beforehand. Moreover, those cities adjacent to the Syrian desert—and that included all the settlements that submitted early on, like Bostra, Damascus, Homs, Amman, and Hama—were accustomed to dealing with Arab tribes and had relations with them on a number of different levels. They were also home to a moderate population of well-to-do and well-educated Christian Arabs, such as the Mansur family, who served as financial administrators for Heraclius in Damascus and continued to do so for the Arabs well into the eighth century.

As for Jerusalem the accounts of its capture are, as one might expect of this holiest of cities, charged with religious overtones, but they are annoyingly bereft of concrete detail. A late Christian source makes a brief reference to a two-year siege, but gives no details or clarification. Our only contemporary source reports that "the Lord's Cross and all the vessels of the churches of God" were taken away by sea to Constantinople for safekeeping, but of military matters simply says that having requested an oath from the Arabs that they would respect life and property, the people of Jerusalem submitted to the Arabs. Otherwise Christian writers focus on two particular events. First, there is the building of a mosque on the site of the former Jewish temple, which is related by a number of contemporary and near-contemporary authors and so there is no reason to doubt it. We even have a description of it from a Gallic pilgrim, who subsequently traveled to Iona in Scotland and recounted his travels to its abbot in the 670s. He tells him that he recalls seeing in the place where Herod's Temple once stood, near the eastern wall, a rectangular "house of prayer," which the Arabs had constructed "over some ruined remains." It was evidently a sizable building, for it could accommodate, he says, "at least 3000 people."[18]

Second, there is the visit of the caliph 'Umar I (634–44) to the holy city. This event is not reported by any early source and appears first only in a mid-eighth century chronicle, which concentrates on the meeting between 'Umar and the patriarch Sophronius. 'Umar was allegedly dressed in filthy garments of camel hair, and the patriarch, seeing this, offered him a clean loin cloth and over-garment, but 'Umar refused, only accepting in the end, after Sophronius's insistence, to wear the clean clothes for a short time until his own had been washed. There are a number of occasions in the Bible when clothes are washed or exchanged as part of a ritual of purification or investiture—such as when the high priest Joshua arrived before the angel of the Lord in dirty attire and is given new (priestly) robes in their stead (Zachariah 3:1–5)—but the exact message of the chronicler is unclear. In Muslim accounts of 'Umar's trip to Jerusalem, he is also wearing rough dress, but that is part of his image as a humble and simple man, who is wary of the trappings of civilization. Here it is Muslims urging 'Umar to put on smart clothes so that he will not appear lowly to the non-Muslims and 'Umar's refusal to do so is intended as a criticism of Muslims who covet fine attire after the fashion of the Byzantines and Persians and are seduced by earthly concerns.[19]

Caesarea, like all the Mediterranean coastal settlements, was much less acquainted with the Arabs than were the inland cities that bordered the Syrian desert. Its residents were more likely to be of the same doctrinal persuasion as Constantinople and the emperor, namely Chalcedonian (accepting the creed agreed upon at the council of Chalcedon in AD 451), and more likely to speak the same language, Greek, rather than Aramaic or Arabic. Moreover, as the provincial capital it had more to prove, had more to protect, and had a legion based in the city, and so would of course be expected to put up a fight. The new commander of the Arab forces in Syria, Mu'awiya ibn Abi Sufyan, recognized this challenge and so brought seventy-two siege engines, which hurled stones day and night. This went on from December 640 to May 641 until finally the massive encircling walls of the city were breached. Since the troops had obdurately refused to surrender, Mu'awiya decided to make an example of them, and all the 7,000 stationed there were killed save those who had managed to escape by boat to Asia Minor. The city was not razed, but its strongly pro-imperial ethos and the ease with which it could be supplied by sea from Constantinople meant that it was not deemed suitable by the Arabs as an administrative base. They preferred the inland cities with their closer access to the desert and their greater familiarity with Arabic and Arab tribes. Consequently, whereas many of the coastal cities declined after the Arab conquests (early Islamic Caesarea is only one tenth the size of Late Antique Caesarea), the inland cities—Damascus, Bostra, Jerash, Pella, Jerusalem, and so on—all enjoyed a considerable measure of growth.[20]

Iraq (Map 2.3)

After Khusrau II's murder of the chief of the tribe of Lakhm and its loss of imperial support, "all the Arabs of the Byzantine and Persian realms revolted and dispersed, each group acting according to his own will," observed one chronicler, "and they became powerful and caused much trouble in the provinces." For example, at Dhu Qar near Kufa, around the year 610, tribal groups loyal to the Lakhmids confronted and defeated other tribes that were allies of the Persians. It was probably a very minor encounter and only involved Arab factions, but it was later celebrated as the first victory of the Arabs over the Persians. Matters worsened when civil war broke out after the death of Khusrau II in 628 and reached a nadir in June 630 when the empress Boran came to the throne. Among the neighboring Arabs the word went around that

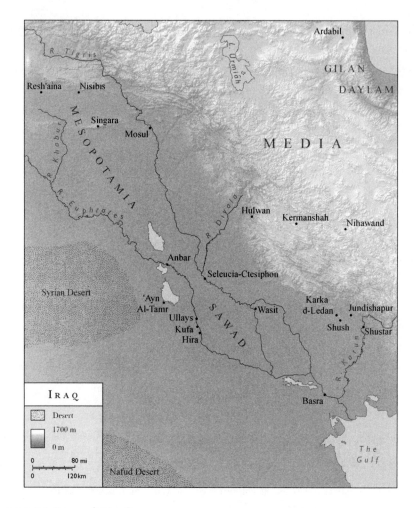

MAP 2.3 Iraq and West Iran.

"the Persians no longer have a king, they have sought refuge in a woman" and many took to pillaging the frontier lands of the empire.[21] Some men from northeast Arabian tribes went and joined those who were massing on the borders of Persia and started raiding the local nobles, seizing whatever they could. Later Muslim historians maintain that Abu Bakr participated in the planning of these attacks, but this is clearly a retrospective attempt to bring all fighting against the empires under the banner of Muhammad's community. They also wanted to provide a neat chronological schema: the mutiny of the tribes of

Arabia in year eleven of the community (632–33) had first to be suppressed before the conquests could be initiated in year twelve (633–34). However, since these historians also mention that Persian rulers of the period 628–32 were on the throne at the time of these raids, it is evident that, as was the case with the Levant, the various tribes living on the imperial frontiers had already begun to take advantage of the empire's weakness to plunder the outlying areas long before Muhammad's west Arabian coalition became involved.

The early clashes were principally between Arab tribes of different affiliations, and only local Persian officials were involved. At the oasis town of 'Ayn al-Tamr in southwest Iraq, for instance, a Persian garrison backed up by a division of Arab recruits levied from the tribes of Namir, Taghlib, and Iyad opposed the general dispatched by Abu Bakr, namely, Khalid ibn al-Walid. However, as the raids snowballed, the matter came to the notice of the regime's leaders and of contemporary chroniclers. We are lucky that an Armenian historian writing shortly after 660, referred to by modern scholars as Sebeos, took an interest and gave an account which, supplemented by a couple of other writers, allows us to get a reasonable picture of the march of events.[22] As happened in Syria, the success of minor skirmishes in the late 620s and early 630s paved the way for a large-scale invasion in 636, involving considerable numbers of tribesmen from the Arabian Peninsula. The invaders marched from central Arabia through the endless flat stony wastes of northeast Arabia until eventually reaching the beginning of the fertile alluvial lands of lower Iraq. Meeting little resistance, they pushed on in the direction of the Persian capital, Seleucia-Ctesiphon. This was a huge sprawling settlement established on both sides of the river Tigris, some twenty miles south of modern Baghdad, and comprising numerous palaces built in the course of the many centuries of the city's life. The Arabs laid siege to it through the winter of 636–37, but in the meantime Rustam, the prince of Media (northwest Iran), had assembled a huge army, including contingents from Armenia, Albania (modern north Azerbaijan), and Siunik (modern south Armenia). Such was the size and might of the army that Rustam, so it was said, "haughtily expected to trample all the southerners underfoot." The emperor Yazdgird participated too, rallying the troops with encouraging words and distributing stipends.

In the autumn of 637 the Persian army got under way. They crossed the river Tigris and slowly and inexorably drove the Arabs back, defeating them in the odd pitched battle (one is recorded in Muslim sources under the name of the Battle of the Bridge), until eventually they forced them right back to "their own borders," to the west bank of the Euphrates. Both sides then encamped there, by the village of Qadash (Arabic: Qadisiyya), a short distance to the south of Hira. In an initial encounter the Arabs were worsted, but a few days later they received reinforcements from Arabia of "a multitude of cavalry and 20,000 infantry" and thus heartened "they sped forward, covered with shields, eager to fight against the Persian troops." This seemed to throw the Persian army into confusion and many fled. A general rout ensued and many of the nobles were killed, including the princes of Armenia, Siunik, and Media. Some, such as Juansher, king of Albania, only escaped by hurling themselves headlong into the river Euphrates and swimming for their lives to the opposite bank. The engagement, referred to as the Battle of Qadisiyya in Muslim sources, took place on January 6, 638, and, like the battle of Yarmuk in the Levant, was retrospectively perceived as a turning point in the Arab conquest of the Persian Empire. It brought great fame to the key Arab general, Saʻd ibn Abi Waqqas, of the tribe of Quraysh, and it also brought immortality to Rustam, who is celebrated in the Persian national epic as a valiant but tragic hero, the last great noble knight of the Persian Empire, sorrowfully predicting that after him "lineage and honour will count for naught."

Having gained the upper hand, the Arabs now went back on the offensive. In the course of 638 they established control over lower Iraq and, so one chronicler informs us, "they began to collect the taxes."[23] This allowed them to keep their men fully fed and equipped, and, after subduing the area around Seleucia-Ctesiphon, they renewed their siege of the capital itself, maintaining their position for at least six months. Seeing that the situation in the capital was hopeless, Emperor Yazdgird arranged for the new general of the army of Media, Khurrazad, who was the brother of Rustam, to effect an evacuation operation. The plan was to get the emperor out of Seleucia-Ctesiphon to the comparative safety of a royal estate some seventy miles to the northeast. With much haste the contents of the treasury were packed up and the inhabitants of the capital assembled, and Khurrazad and his men led out the procession in the direction of their new home. On the way, however, they were unexpectedly attacked by a contingent of Arabs that had managed to make it across the river Tigris. A short battle ensued (probably that known as the Battle of Jalula' in the Muslim sources), but the Persian troops, jittery after their dismal defeat at Qadash, quickly gave up the fight and fled, obliging Yazdgird to take to his heels along with them. The Arabs appropriated the forsaken wealth and returned with it to the newly captured Seleucia-Ctesiphon. Yazdgird and his retinue hurried on to seek refuge in the Zagros mountain range (Figure 2.4), which protected Iran from any army marching from the plains of Babylonia and Mesopotamia, and stopped off on the way at the ancient city of Hulwan. In the course of the year 640 he was continually on the move, seeking a place where he could obtain a breathing space and the time to rally an army. He descended from the mountains, traveling southeast to Isfahan and then southward to Istakhr, the capital of Fars, which was the heartland and homeland of the Sasanian dynasty, where he knew he could count on the support of the local army.

FIGURE 2.4 View of Zagros Mountains from the plains of Iraq. © Hugh Kennedy.

The Jazira (Northern Mesopotamia; Map 2.2)

The clashes narrated so far all happened in the southern parts of the Levant and Iraq and quite close to the Syrian desert. By contrast contemporary observers report no battles occurring in the northern parts of these regions. This is possibly because settlements there all submitted to the Arabs without a fight. They had already suffered badly in the earlier Byzantine-Persian war of 603–28 and so would have been discouraged from making a stand, especially when news came in of the recent Arab successes in the south. The only other theater of war that we hear of is the Jazira. This term means "island" in Arabic and it refers to the territory that is virtually encircled by the northern arms of the mighty Euphrates and Tigris Rivers, comprising parts of modern northwest Iraq, northeast Syria, and southeast Turkey. It was the heartland of Aramaic Christianity, as indeed it still is today, though there are dramatically fewer Christians there now. "The whole land of the Jazira," wrote one local resident, "was rich in vineyards, fields and much cattle; there was not one single poor and miserable man in any village who did not possess a plough, donkey and goats."[24] There were also large areas of steppe well suited to grazing and these were the preserve of a number of powerful Arab pastoralist tribes. The territory's wealth meant that it was attractive to great powers and indeed was fought over by Byzantium and Persia for many centuries before becoming a border zone between the Byzantine and Arab states.

The Arab commander in Syria, Abu 'Ubayda, entrusted his kinsman 'Iyad ibn Ghanm, a man famed for his generosity, to oversee the subjugation of the cities of northern Syria. In 638, while 'Iyad was at the encampment of Qinnasrin, near the great Hellenistic city of Chalcis and just south of modern Aleppo, the governor of Byzantine Mesopotamia, John Kataias, came to meet him. His mission was to save his province from Arab occupation, but he did not have sufficient troops to achieve this aim by military means. Instead he promised to pay 'Iyad every year 100,000 gold coins "on condition that he would not cross the Euphrates either peacefully or by force of arms as long as that amount of gold was paid to him."[25] 'Iyad agreed and John, true to his word, returned to Mesopotamia to collect the annual tribute and then dispatched it directly to 'Iyad. However, the emperor Heraclius, on hearing about this deal, was furious that it had been arranged without his knowledge; he dismissed John and exiled him to Africa and replaced him with a military man, a general named Ptolemy.

When the next year's tribute payment was due, Ptolemy refused to authorize it and so 'Iyad crossed the Euphrates with an army and in the course of the year 639–40 he visited each city in turn to demand its submission. He began with Edessa in the west of the region and gradually made his way over to Nisibis in the east. The former opened its gates to him and was rewarded with a favorable treaty, which respected its inhabitants' lives and property and even allowed Ptolemy, who was based there, to leave for Byzantine territory together with his soldiers. The same conciliatory approach was taken by most of the nearby cities and they too were given generous terms. Tella and Dara, however, decided to resist. The former prepared for a siege, but 'Iyad launched a determined assault and after capturing it killed its guard of 300 soldiers. Dara lay right by the former Byzantine-Persian border and had endured Persian attacks many times before and so perhaps felt able to withstand an Arab advance (Figure 2.5), but it too was fairly quickly reduced and its resident soldiery was wiped out. 'Iyad then returned to Qinnasrin and for the next few decades the Jazira was governed from this distant base. This remoteness meant that Arab involvement in the province's affairs was minimal. We hear of no substantial Arab settlement, as occurred in Iraq and Syria, and being now isolated from the Byzantine realm it was no longer a focus of imperial patronage or persecution. Existing patterns of local government and tax-collection were left mostly intact: in the former Persian part of the region the same local aristocratic families were in charge as before the conquest, and Greek-educated Christians managed the ex-Byzantine lands. "The Christians were still the scribes, leaders and governors," observes one chronicler,[26] and this seems to have remained the case at least until the end of the seventh century.

FIGURE 2.5 The walls of Dara in southeast Turkey (as seen in 1978). © Jim Crow.

Who Were the Conquerors?

The impression one gets from the contemporary sources that we have looked at is that in the 620s and early 630s Muhammad's west Arabian coalition was only one among many Arabian groups trying to take advantage of the lax security situation created by the pre-occupation of Byzantium and Persia with warring against each other. On the margins of these empires raiding had become endemic already by the 620s. Even once the Arab conquests were under way in the late 630s, it is likely that some opportunists took the chance to enrich themselves under the cover of the chaotic political situation. A chief with the un-Arab and un-Islamic name of Qanan, for example, took some captives in southern Anatolia and he and his followers killed a Byzantine general who attempted to challenge them.[27] These other actors are, however, airbrushed out of history by later Muslim writers, or if mentioned at all they are recast as false prophets or claimed as loyal Muslims. Christian chroniclers inform us about some of these raiding parties who were not part of Muhammad's coalition, but they are not interested in the details of their identities and usually just refer to them using generic terms such as Saracens and Tayyaye. It is therefore all but impossible for us to probe beneath the surface of the storyline presented by later Muslim historians that the conquest venture was fully managed and directed solely by Muhammad and his successors from Medina. There are enough small cracks in this storyline for us to see that the Arab conquests were not initiated by Muhammad alone, but had begun before him and were being conducted by other leaders in other locations; yet we cannot easily recover their aims or identities.

On the positive side we do have contemporary information on the coalition of Muhammad in the form of his preaching (the Qur'an) and of the agreement that he drew up on arriving in Medina. What is most striking is the very simple but powerful program of action outlined by Muhammad: form a righteous community (umma), go to a safe place (hijra), and from there embark on jihad against the unrighteous (mushrikun). The latter are defined in the Qur'an as those who denied or diluted God's oneness, though we do not get to hear much about their side of the story. The foundation agreement that Muhammad made in Medina to combat them was effectively a mutual defense pact (all signatories were obliged to come to the aid of one another if attacked) and a war manifesto (all signatories had to join in the war effort against the common enemy). The term for a signatory was mu'min, meaning "faithful." As with the English word "faithful," mu'min could mean both loyal and believing. In the Qur'an it is mostly used in a very general way, but in the foundation agreement it seems to have a specific sociolegal sense, designating all those who pledged allegiance to the new community and its manifesto and who accepted that the one God and Muhammad were the supreme arbiters of the community.[28] The majority were Muslim, whether emigrants (muhajirun) from Mecca or converts from Medina, and Jews, along with possibly a few Christians and monotheists of other hues. The agreement explicitly states that "the Muslims have their religion and the Jews theirs," but for the purposes of the war effort all were "a single community."

Muhammad's coalition at this stage was, then, pluralist by nature, with everyone committed to waging jihad against the pagans whatever their own particular monotheist persuasion.[29] This remained the case for some time after Muhammad's death, though, once the Arab armies had entered Syria and Iraq, Jews became much less important and Christians much more so. Later Muslim historians play down this pluralist dimension, seeking to portray the conquests as a wholly Arab Muslim venture. The famous religious lawyer Ahmad ibn Hanbal (d. 856), when asked about the Jews and Christians of the community of Muhammad, went so far as to say that "this is a despicable question and one must not discuss it."[30] Fortunately, the eclectic and comprehensive method of data collection of many of these authors meant that they also transmitted material that did not conform to their overall message, allowing us sometimes to glimpse a different picture of the ninth-century consensus. For example, Muslim lawyers debated Muhammad's rulings about what share of the spoils of war should go to Jews and Christians who fought alongside Muslims.

A diverse soldiery is of course only what one would expect, for all major conquering forces in history have made use of groups external to their core supporters. Extra manpower from local sources is always welcome when an army is operating in regions where it is a small minority, and successful armies will therefore seek to woo possible defectors and recruit willing natives. Almost 80 percent of the troops in the British army in India, for example, were non-British. Very early on, Muhammad's west Arabian coalition encountered the Arab Christian tribes of the Syrian steppe and desert, a number of whom were allied to the Byzantine and Persian empires. They are often presented as having divided loyalties: some fought on the side of the empires and some on the side of the conquerors. Of the latter group some converted to Islam, but some evidently did not. In an early battle in southern Iraq, for instance, the chiefs of Namir and Taghlib came to the support of a Muslim general with men from their respective tribes "who were Christian"; they fought hard, though the battle was severe and prolonged, and the Muslim general encouraged the two men, saying to them: "You are an Arab even though you do not follow our religion."[31]

The conquerors were socially diverse too. The leadership came from the tribes of the oasis towns of west Arabia, in particular Mecca, Medina, and Ta'if, or else from the fertile highlands of Yemen, where the tribes were

mostly sedentary agriculturalists, as they still are today. A substantial proportion of the rank and file, however, were from nomadic pastoralist tribes;
the Qur'an regarded them with some suspicion, deeming them unreliable
and fickle, yet their military capability and ease of recruitment were crucial
to the success of the Arab conquests, as it was to the conquest plans of
Arabian townsmen after them right up until Ibn Sa'ud in the early twentieth
century. Nomads were mobile, accustomed to fighting to defend their honor
and kin and to supplement their income, and the percentage of men that
can be drafted in a nomad society is more than twice what is possible in a
settled society. Fickle or not, then, they were a crucial asset and evidence of
the drive to win them over to the west Arabian coalition is found in such
sayings as that ascribed to the caliph 'Umar I: "Be good to the nomads
(a'rab) for they are the root of the Arabs and a support for Islam" and in
general urgings for them not to leave the garrisons and return to Bedouin
life (al-ta'arrub).[32]

As the conquests progressed and more victories were achieved, many
groups who were neither Arab nor Muslim sought to join the conquerors. This
is of course a standard feature of imperial armies: the initial conquerors will be
relatively few, but once they have proved successful they quickly attract other
peoples to their cause, especially those who, for whatever reason, were not fully
assimilated or did not enjoy equal status within the original polity. Examples
are the Daylam from the southwest coastlands of the Caspian Sea, and the
Zutt, Sayabija, and Andaghar, who were said to hail originally from India, but
who had served in the Persian armies before Islam. Some were on bad terms
with their former masters and so jumped at the opportunity to better their
lot. In this category are the Luwata Berbers, who had suffered in the course of
the Byzantine recapture of North Africa in the 540s and had to some extent
been excluded from Byzantine society, and so not surprisingly they were quick
to join the invading Arabs in the 640s. Others simply did not want to be on
the losing side. For instance, units of the Persian elite cavalry (asawira) offered
their skills in the aftermath of the disastrous Persian defeat in southern Iraq
in 638 on the condition that they were given the top rate of stipends, and a

contingent of Slavs defected from the Byzantines when promised resettlement in Syria, wives, and payments in money and kind.[33]

Muslim historians tend to assume that these non-Arab non-Muslim collaborators converted once they had changed sides. Thus of one such group in southern Iraq it is reported that "they settled among the tribe of Tamim in Basra in the days of 'Umar I, converted, fought with the Muslims and distinguished themselves; so people said: 'although you are not Arabs, you are our brothers and our people.'" However, we do occasionally learn that conversion was not necessary or immediate. The north Mesopotamian monk John of Fenek, writing in the 680s, informs us that among the Muslim armies were "not a few Christians, some belonging to the heretics and some from us." One Muslim source speaks explicitly of the troops of the Daylam who had fought alongside the Muslims "without having embraced Islam."[34] And though the Persian cavalry are said to have converted very soon after their defection in 638, they sport very un-Islamic names like Mah Afridhun and Mahawayh until the late seventh century. It is true, though, that in this age when so much of the fabric of life was expressed in religious terms, collaboration and conversion were often perceived as pretty much the same thing.[35]

In short, then, the composition of the conquerors was quite mixed and changed over time, though the core was made up of tribesmen from Arabia and the frontier lands of the Byzantine and Persian empires. Medieval and modern historians alike apply the label Arab to this core, but it is difficult to know for sure how far and how deep this Arab identity extended in the early years. The term is extremely rare in pre-Islamic Arabic poetry, but that may be just because the poets tend mostly to be focusing on their own tribe or allied/ rival tribes. In the early Islamic period some Arabian tribes were accused of not being Arabs; thus one member of the tribe of 'Abd al-Qays mocked the Azd tribe of Oman by saying that "in their old age they had themselves circumcised and claimed in their delusion to be Arabs, though they are Persians (*ajam*)."[36] In this genre of satirical poetry, however, it is common to cast doubt on the pedigree of opponents. What one can say with some degree of confidence is that the conquests brought about a deepening and broadening of Arab identity, for garrison life has a homogenizing effect on soldiers, and the

Arab Muslim leaders set the tone. Moreover, such a successful and momentous event inevitably imparted a degree of solidarity, pride, and common feeling to those who participated in it, and it brought them into contact with numerous other peoples, which gave them a greater sense of their own distinctiveness. In general, it is when humans leave their homeland and dwell in a foreign country that they think of the bigger grouping to which they belong, whereas at home among their countrymen they will adopt more local terms. Similarly, the conquerors dealt with one another by reference to clan and tribe, but when confronted with Persians, Byzantines, Berbers, Sogdians, Turks, and so on, they placed more weight on their broader affiliation, their Arabness. And this was reinforced by the fact that they were conquerors, which gave them a sense of superiority to these other peoples.[37]

Fighting for Gain, Fighting for God

We should not, then, view the conquests as a sort of nationalist enterprise, as was sometimes proposed by late nineteenth-century European scholars inspired by the emergence of the German and Italian nations. Though Arab identity certainly existed before Islam, it was the conquests that entrenched it and spread it and the early Muslim rulers who commissioned writers and poets to give it substance and shape. So what was it that motivated the conquerors to venture forth? It could be argued that there is no need to postulate a particular reason. Tribes living on the margins of states will frequently turn upon those states to supplement their incomes, whether by pillage, ransoming prisoners, or extorting subsidies. Usually they are quickly chased away or bought off by the agents of state security, but if not they will return in bigger numbers, and soon the affair, if not checked, will snowball into far-reaching conquest. This is what is termed an autocatalytic process: a small initial event triggers and drives a chain reaction that evolves on an ever faster and bigger scale. This is sometimes adduced to explain the explosion of Viking raids that occurred after the highly profitable attack on the English island of Lindisfarne in 793, and also the European rush to embark upon maritime exploration after Columbus's "discovery" of the New World in 1492. One might object that this would have only led to disorder and not a state, but if large territories were won, adept leaders would step forward to manage the situation, as happened with the Vikings and much later with the Mongols. This certainly fits with what we learn from contemporary descriptions of the early stages of the Arab conquests where random minor raids yielded success and soon prompted the participation of much larger numbers of Arabian tribesmen. In this view, Muhammad's coalition would have been just one of many groups profiting from the disorder caused by the Byzantine-Persian conflict, though their superior organization and ideological commitment helped them to become the dominant group.

The accidental view of history (i.e., history as fallible human responses to random acts and events) is not, however, a commonly held one, and usually an array of push and pull factors has been proposed. The most popular factors cited are easy availability of plunder due to the weakness of the Byzantine and Persian empires (on the pull side) and economic/environmental impoverishment in Arabia (on the push side). The case for imperial exhaustion has been frequently advanced, though never actually documented, and Heraclius's defeat of the Persians and subsequent failure to prop up their government at their hour of greatest weakness has recently been described as "Heraclius's gift to Islam." The idea that there was a worsening economic and/or environmental situation in Arabia was in vogue in the first half of the twentieth century, but fell out of favor thereafter. However, recent archaeological surveys of east and west Arabia reveal a substantial drop in settlement activity in the fifth and sixth centuries, and the collapse of ancient Yemen after a tradition of 1,500 years is startling and must have had a negative impact on neighboring communities. Presumably, Arabia suffered the same sort of fall in economic activity in the fifth and sixth centuries as Europe did in the fourth and fifth centuries, and, as happened in Europe, a number of Arabia's residents turned to raiding their imperial masters in order to make good the shortfall in their income. Given that political instability and economic retraction were afflicting numerous areas from the Balkans to China, it is possible that this deterioration in material conditions was much more widespread. Plausibly there were climatic and/or environmental stresses affecting large parts of Eurasia that were putting empires under strain and leaving them more exposed to the predations of steppe and desert peoples around them, but this needs further investigation.[38]

In recent years, and especially since the rise of radical Muslim groups like al-Qa'ida, the most often cited pull factor is Islam, which is assumed to have unified the diverse Arabian tribesmen under one banner and filled them with the zeal to do God's work in fighting all non-believers and to bring God's rule to the whole world. This is the message that ninth-century Muslim historians propagated, and modern Western scholars have recently embraced it. "Faith was the driving force behind the Muslim conquests," as one has succinctly put it.[39] Some of these scholars, however, have felt a little uneasy that a religion that "embodied an intense concern for attaining personal salvation through righteous behavior" should also have impelled its followers to take up arms. They have, therefore, striven to play down the role of violence in the conquests, though we cannot view them, concedes the doyen of this view, "as entirely a pacific operation, devoid of violence against, or coercion of, the conquered populations."[40]

Such opinions reflect an attempt to present Islam more positively in a world in which Islamophobia has been growing. But such apologetic aims, though noble, are out of place in works of history. All empires have relied on violence and coercion for their existence, and yet, since the imperial elite is always small in relation to the numbers of their subjects, all empires make use of a range of non-violent strategies to maintain their rule: co-opting the willing, rewarding collaboration, promising protection in return for submission, playing divide and rule, and so on. The Arab empire was no exception to this, and so needs no special treatment. Moreover, by the time the Arabs arrived on the scene, the use of violence for religious ends had long been regarded as acceptable, if not commendable, in the Middle East, at least in certain situations. When in 388 a band of Christians attacked a Jewish synagogue in northern Syria, the emperor thought to apply Roman law and punish the culprits, but Ambrose, the bishop of Milan, dissuaded him, pointing out that the pious should not have to defer to the impious. And when in the 620s the emperor Heraclius wished to rally his troops to fight the Persians, he emphasized that "death in battle opens the way to eternal life" and so urged them to sacrifice themselves to God for the sake of their compatriots and "to seize the martyrs' crown."[41] These exhortations accord well with similarly encouraging remarks in the Qur'an: "Let those who would trade this life for the hereafter fight in God's path; and We will recompense well whomsoever does fight in God's path, whether he dies or achieves victory" (4:74).

The Qur'an is equally explicit about the rewards that those who fight for Him can expect in this life: "God has promised that you will take much booty and He has expedited this for you" (48:20), so "consume the booty that you have captured as a lawful benefit" (8:69). And it is made abundantly clear that "God favors those who go out to fight with their own wealth and lives over those who stay behind" (4:95). Since God was sanctioning the fighting and the acquisition of booty, there is no need to debate whether Muhammad's west Arabian soldiers fought more for gain or for God—the two were inseparable. They were also mutually reinforcing: the gains won by fighting for God made His warriors more desirous to serve Him in war and worship. One should not think, however, that this idea goes hand in hand with trying to convert the conquered peoples. In many ways it runs contrary to it, for the gains will be diluted if they have to be shared with everyone. This point is made very strongly by a number of Arab Muslim generals seeking to motivate their troops on the eve of war: "This land is your inheritance, which God has promised you," says Sa'd ibn Abi Waqqas to his soldiers before the battle of Qadisiyya, "and you have been tasting it and eating from it, and killing its people, collecting taxes from them and taking them prisoner until today," and so it is crucial that you fight now to maintain this situation.[42] It is, in effect, a literal understanding of "the righteous shall inherit the earth," as the Qur'an itself notes (21:105), explicitly quoting the Psalms of the Bible (37:29).

There is a downside, however, in assuming faith to be the prime instigator of the Arab conquests. Besides the difficulty of assessing whether one group is more zealous than another (why should we think that the Byzantines and Sasanians had less zeal for their faith than the Arabs?), this explanation focuses very narrowly on one time and place, early seventh-century west Arabia, and one man, Muhammad, and ignores broader currents of world history. To take a modern example, Mohamed Bouazizi, the Tunisian fruit-vendor who set himself on fire in December 2010, may well have been the spark that kindled the Arab spring, but a proper reckoning of this phenomenon would have to take into account high youth unemployment, rising food prices, restricted access to positions of power, and so on. Of course, the prophet Muhammad played a much more crucial role in the uprising that followed his death, and his politico-religious message and organization were key to the future direction of the conquests. However, the fact that other peoples, such as the Turks and Avars, were also striving to conquer Byzantium and Persia at this time, and the fact that there were many prophetic figures active in Arabia in the early seventh century, suggests that we need to think more broadly about the ultimate causes of the Arab conquests.

Chapter Three

EASTWARD AND WESTWARD
(640–652)

fter losing a substantial number of troops at Yarmuk in 636 the emperor Heraclius had sent word to his generals and governors not to engage the Arabs in battle in order to conserve precious manpower and to buy time to raise a new army and devise a fresh strategy. He may also have hoped that God would restrain the Arabs as He had done a few years before with the Persians. But as city after city capitulated, panic began to set in. This was intensified by the death of the emperor in February 641, which triggered a succession crisis: some backed Heraclius's son by his second wife, his niece Martina, who favored accommodation with the Arabs, and others took the side of a grandson of Heraclius, the ten-year-old Constans, represented by a senior general named Valentine, who advocated a more hawkish policy toward the Arabs. Amid scenes of rioting, Valentine entered Constantinople in September 641; Martina and her son were deposed, and the young Constans was crowned. Using the latter's tender age as a pretext, Valentine sought to usurp the de facto military and political powers of the imperial office for himself, but this offended popular opinion and he was arrested and brought before Constans. The young emperor magnanimously accepted his plea that he had only acted out of a desire to save the empire from the Arabs and appointed him head of the imperial guard. Only two years later, however, Valentine's failure to achieve any significant military successes weakened him and he was hanged by an angry mob. Constans was now secure on the throne, but this meant that an adolescent was in charge of the Byzantine Empire at a moment when it faced an existential threat from the Arabs.[1]

In the Persian realm, the proverbial situation had come true: the head had been severed and consequently the body floundered. With Yazdgird on the run and the economic powerhouse of southern Iraq in Arab hands, the Persian Empire ceased to function as an integral entity. The local chiefs and nobles of Iran, wearied by three decades of warfare and civil strife and unnerved by the Arab successes, began to negotiate separate agreements with the conquerors that would preserve as much of their authority and wealth as possible. Families were often pitted against one another, sometimes victims of an Arab policy of divide and rule and sometimes using the Arabs to settle old scores. For example, in return for being left in power in Media (northwest Iran), Khurrazad offered to help the Arabs capture Rayy, now a suburb of modern Tehran, but once a proud and ancient city that served as the seat of the noble family of Mihran. The incumbent head of this family had connived in the murder of Khurrazad's father. There was, therefore, bad blood between the two families, and Khurrazad got his revenge by showing Arab forces a secret way into Rayy, which allowed them to surprise the city's defenders. They looted and ransacked the houses of the Mihranids, who were afforded no mercy, but gave safe passage to the family of Khurrazad, who was allowed a free hand to establish himself and his offspring in the city. For the Arabs, as for many conquerors before and after them, such pragmatic deals made good sense in lands difficult to access, the subjugation of which would demand substantial resources and manpower. In the mountainous regions around the Caspian Sea, for instance, numerous local arrangements were made. To the south the lord of Damavand signed a pact of non-aggression in return for the right to maintain his rule and ancestral title. And the prince of Gurgan and a Persian-appointed potentate in Darband, on the east and west side of the Caspian, respectively, were exempted from tax in exchange for providing military assistance against any potential enemies of the Arabs.[2]

Of the Arab command structure in this period we hear very little in our contemporary sources. The Armenian chronicler Sebeos does confirm to us the existence of some sort of overall ruler, for he distinguishes between the general or prince (ishkhan), who was based in Damascus, and the king (ark'ay or t'agawor), who resided in Arabia. The latter did not get involved in the fighting—when the Arabs marched out from the desert, "their king did not go with them"—but he does seem to have had responsibility for major decision making. Thus it was the king, says Sebeos, who ordered that ships be assembled and equipped to carry out naval raids against the southeast shores of Iran.[3] These rulers in Medina are portrayed by later Muslim sources as the successors (caliphs) to Muhammad and as being in overall control of all worldly and religious matters. Responsibility for practical day-to-day planning was, however, borne by the commander-in-chief in Damascus, which for the period 640–60 was Mu'awiya, the son of Abu Sufyan ibn Harb, whose daughter the prophet Muhammad had married and whose cousin 'Uthman became the third caliph (644–56). Evidently, the clan of Abu Sufyan, the Umayyads, had managed to take firm hold of the reins of the conquest enterprise from a very early date, and Mu'awiya's very long term in office, twenty years as commander in Syria and twenty years as caliph (661–80), served to entrench their position.

Egypt (Map 3.1)

It was a member of a related clan, 'Amr ibn al-'As, who launched the most lucrative campaign of this period: into Egypt. This land was a jewel in the Byzantine crown because of the size and constancy of its tax remittances and its harvests, both a consequence of the fertility of the Nile valley. Every year it would dispatch some 300 million bushels of grain to Constantinople, keeping its citizens and the empire's soldiers supplied with bread. Yet despite its wealth, the country's enemies were few, principally the Nuba to the south and the nomadic Blemmyes in the eastern desert regions. The latter are singled out for censure in numerous writings for their lack of regard for the lives of

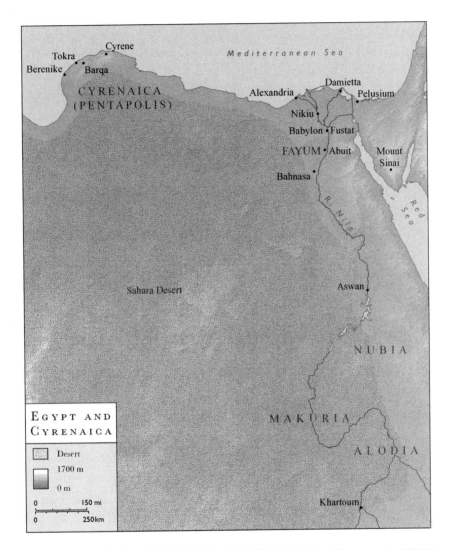

MAP 3.1 Egypt and adjoining countries.

monks and the property of monasteries, but their raids were only minor irri-
tants and, after the brief incursion in AD 269 of Zenobia, "queen" of Palmyra,
Egypt faced no further external aggression until the seventh century. Perhaps
because of this the armies of Egypt were ill prepared when they were obliged
to face the onslaught first of the Persians, in 617–19, and subsequently of the
Arabs, in 640–42. In the summer of 633 Heraclius ordered his governor of

Numidia (modern west Tunisia/east Algeria) to defend Egypt against Arab attacks, and a couple of years later he sent a certain John of Barqa (modern northeast Libya) to accomplish the same task. Presumably, then, there was some buildup to the main Arab invasion in 640, but since the Muslim sources mention nothing about this we cannot be sure of the identity or objectives of these earlier raiders.[4]

For the period 640–43 we are lucky to have at our disposal the chronicle of someone who lived through the Arab conquest of Egypt, one John, bishop of Nikiu, though our good fortune is tempered slightly by the fact that we have this text only in the form of a late Ethiopic translation of the Arabic version of the original Coptic account.[5] The chronicle covers events from Creation to 643, but frustratingly there is a lacuna from 610 to 639, which means that we only have the word of Muslim sources that ʿAmr ibn al-ʿAs set out in the winter of 639–40 with a contingent from Palestine. They say that he traveled westward along the coastal road until he reached Pelusium, at the eastern edge of the Nile Delta, and captured it after a month or so of sporadic fighting. Although this is not verified by any contemporary source, it would certainly make sense for an army invading from the east to subdue Pelusium in order to secure their supply lines as they marched westward. ʿAmr then turned southwest in the direction of Babylon, now a suburb of modern Cairo. At this point John of Nikiu picks up the story, and he makes it clear that there were in fact two Arab armies. In addition to that of ʿAmr, which is the only one mentioned by the Muslim sources, a second Arab army had been marching from the south, perhaps first sailing across the Red Sea from Arabia and then traveling overland to reach the Nile. After passing to the west side of the river, it proceeded northward until reaching Bahnasa, ancient Oxyrhynchus, which lay about 100 miles south of Babylon, near the southern entrance to the fertile Fayum oasis, presumably intending to join up with their comrades to the north.

ʿAmr ibn al-ʿAs, "paying no attention to the fortified cities," had by now reached a place called Tendunias, plausibly the Umm Dunayn of the Muslim sources, which now finds itself on the edge of modern Cairo, on the east bank of the Nile. His objective was to gain control of the Byzantine stronghold of

Babylon, a little to the south, but he was distressed to learn that the Arab division coming from the south was now on the west side of the Nile. Rather than attempt a siege of Babylon while the Arab forces were separated, he sought to entice the Byzantines out into the open. He divided his own army into three units and placed them at the three points on the triangle formed by Babylon (to the south), Tendunias (to the north), and Heliopolis (to the northeast) (Map 3.2). The plan was that while 'Amr's unit, situated in front of Heliopolis, engaged the Byzantines head-on, the Arab unit placed just north of Babylon would march out and attack them from the rear. The tactic worked and in the early summer of 640 the Arabs achieved their first major victory on Egyptian soil.

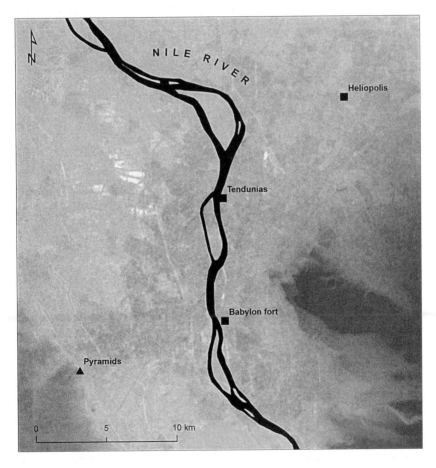

MAP 3.2 The Battle of Heliopolis.

The Arab success had a number of significant consequences. The most
immediate one was that the Arabs took control of Tendunias, for its garrison
had been destroyed in the course of the battle of Heliopolis, any surviving
soldiers having quickly taken to their heels and fled. A second consequence
was that it brought home to the population that this was no mere ephemeral
raid; the threat was real and a plan was urgently needed for how to contain
it. Many voted with their feet. As John of Nikiu says, presumably with some
exaggeration: "a panic fell on all the cities of Egypt, and all their inhabitants
took to flight and made their way to Alexandria, abandoning all their possessions, wealth and cattle." Even senior military figures quailed; for example,
the general charged with defending the Fayum fled to the Delta city of Nikiu,
whereupon the southern Arab force marched upon the capital of this rich
agricultural oasis and captured it after a bloody battle. Others decided that
their interests were best served by collaboration, and John tells us of officials
who "began to help the Muslims"[6] by arranging transportation and the construction of bridges. Concerning two senior administrators, who were charged
with organizing the swift provision of rations to the Arabs, John says that they
"loved the heathen and hated the Christians"—we know from the survival of
their correspondence that they had remained Christians, but presumably collaboration with the Arabs was deeply unpopular.[7] Some went more fully over
to the other side, which is recorded by John in laconic terms: "they apostatized
from the Christian faith and embraced the faith of the beast."

Despite their substantial victory at Heliopolis, the Arabs still found it difficult making further headway in their conquest of Egypt. Many of the major
cities in the Nile Delta were protected by water, which served as a blockade,
impeding the entry of horses. Others, such as Nikiu and Damietta, shut their
gates and steadfastly refused to surrender. John goes so far as to say that 'Amr
spent twelve months in warring against the Christians of northern Egypt, but
"failed nevertheless in reducing their region" (ca. March 640–41). This was
a slightly hollow boast, but it is true that the Arabs had not yet managed to
take out the most crucial targets. In particular, the great fortress of Babylon
remained in Byzantine hands. It occupied an area of some five hectares; the
walls were more than fifteen meters high and three meters thick while the

circular towers rose higher still and were at least thirty meters in diameter. Moreover, the Nile came right up to the western walls where a small port allowed the Byzantines to get in and out by boat.

The Arabs began to besiege it after the Nile floodwaters had receded, in September 640. They lacked the machinery to break down the walls and so concentrated on sapping the morale of those within the fortress. They constructed a large, low bridge over the river near Babylon to prevent the passage of ships to Nikiu and Alexandria and to facilitate the movement of their own horses and supplies across the river. They arrested officials and confined them in iron and wooden fetters, they pillaged property, burned crops, and "put to the sword all the Byzantine soldiers whom they encountered." But perhaps most damaging to the morale of the besieged was the news of the death of the emperor Heraclius, who had ruled for over thirty years and had earlier freed Egypt from the yoke of Persian domination, and also the ensuing struggle for the succession, which made it unlikely that help would come from Constantinople any time soon. So when 'Amr promised that the lives of the troops garrisoning the fortress would be spared, they decided to surrender and evacuated their positions on the second day after the festival of the Resurrection, in April 641, after a siege of some seven months. Now 'Amr began the slow but inexorable march on Alexandria, pushing the remaining Byzantine troops northward, their numbers swollen by the garrisons of towns like Nikiu and Kariun, who abandoned their posts at the sight of the approaching Arab soldiers. The latter attempted an early attack on the metropolis itself, but the defenders on the walls rained down stones on them and they were obliged to retreat. There, in the early summer of 641, they pitched camp and hunkered down in preparation for a lengthy blockade of Alexandria.

Modern scholars often argue, on the basis of later witnesses, that the Egyptians who were anti-Chalcedonian (that is, they rejected the creed agreed upon at the council of Chalcedon in AD 451) welcomed the Arabs and only the Chalcedonian Egyptians opposed them.[8] However, John of Nikiu never once intimates that he or his fellow anti-Chalcedonians were in any way well disposed toward the conquerors. He also makes clear that the Arabs themselves were indiscriminate in their slaughter and that the disunity among the Egyptians lay not in sectarian differences but in how to face this challenge: whether it was better to submit and make peace or to stand and fight. "A great strife had broken out between the inhabitants of Lower Egypt, and these were divided into two parties." Of these, one sided with Theodore, the commander-in-chief of the army in Egypt, who was determined to resist, whereas the other side felt that their interests were best served by negotiation and accommodation with the invaders. And this indecision seemed to grip the very highest echelons of government. The elder son of Heraclius promised to send Theodore a large force in the autumn of 641 with which to repel the enemy. However, upon his premature death, his younger brother chose not to respect this promise, and furthermore he reappointed Cyrus, who had been Chalcedonian patriarch of Alexandria during the 630s, but who had been sacked for his conciliatory stance toward the Arabs. Indeed, it was known that Cyrus not only favored paying tribute to the invaders in exchange for peace but had recommended offering one of the emperor's daughters in marriage to 'Amr, "with a view to his being consequently baptised in the holy bath and becoming a Christian, for 'Amr and his army had great confidence in Cyrus and regarded him with great affection."[9] This proposal had angered Heraclius's elder son, but his successor gave Cyrus power and authority to make peace with the Arabs, to check any further resistance against them, and to establish a system of administration appropriate for the new circumstances.

Cyrus arrived in Alexandria in early September 641. He went to the great Caesarion church in the city to celebrate the feast of the holy cross on September 17, and the people covered the whole route and chanted hymns in his honor. Presumably many supported the dovish policy of Cyrus and thought that some sort of deal with the Arabs was the best way forward for Egypt. Once he had consulted with the elite of Alexandria, Cyrus went to Babylon, seeking by the offer of tribute to procure peace and put a stop to the war in Egypt. 'Amr welcomed his arrival and said to him: "You have done well to come to us." And Cyrus answered, saying to him: "God has delivered this land into your hands; let there be no enmity henceforth between you and Rome." They fixed the amount of tribute to be paid and agreed that the Arabs would keep to themselves for eleven months, not intervening in

Egyptian affairs, while the Byzantine troops in Alexandria would be allowed to remove all their possessions and equipment and proceed home by sea. No other Byzantine garrisons could replace them and they were to cease all fighting against the Arabs, while the latter for their part were to desist from seizing any churches and meddling in Christian concerns. Furthermore, Jews were to be permitted to remain in Alexandria. As a guarantee, the Arabs would take as hostage 150 soldiers and 50 civilians.

Cyrus returned with a heavy heart to Alexandria and reported the terms of the agreement to Theodore, the commander-in-chief, so that he might inform the emperor and persuade him of the merits of the treaty. He also acquainted the populace with the results of the deliberations and the conditions of the agreement. Many were at first incensed by what they perceived as an excessively favorable settlement for the enemy and they rose up against the patriarch and sought to stone him. But he said to them: "I have made this treaty in order to save you and your children," and though overwhelmed by tears and grief he entreated them to be reasonable. Grudgingly the Alexandrians complied and raised the sum of gold that had to be handed over to the Arabs. Those Egyptians who had fled and taken refuge in Alexandria begged to be able to return to their homes and Cyrus negotiated this on their behalf. And so the Arabs "took possession of all the land of Egypt." Cyrus died not long afterward, the following Easter, and so he did not live to see the handover of Alexandria, which happened in accordance with the treaty at the end of September in the year 642. Theodore left the city with his troops and officers and 'Amr made his entry without any obstruction. Looking back, the event seems momentous, marking the end of a millennium of Greco-Roman dominion over Egypt and the beginning of an even longer period of Muslim rule, but what perhaps struck contemporaries more was that they had lost God's favor. "None could recount the mourning and lamentation which took place in that city. . . . They had none to help them and God had destroyed their hopes and delivered the Christians into the hands of their enemies." Yet this was not then seen as final, for "the strong beneficence of God will put to shame those who grieve us, and He will make His love for man to triumph over our sins and bring to naught the evil purposes of those who afflict us."

Our chronicler, John of Nikiu, halts his narrative here, but other sources report that there was one Byzantine attempt to recapture Egypt. The emperor Constans dispatched an Armenian general named Manuel with instructions to oust the Arabs. According to a mid-eighth-century account he meets with 'Amr ibn al-'As and approaches him in a disdainful manner, saying: "I am not Cyrus the bishop who gave you money out of fear of you, for he was a pious monk, whereas I am a man of arms, war and valour," and he warns him to leave at once "or I will destroy you." However, in battle he is quickly worsted by 'Amr. Muslim sources are also familiar with the Armenian Manuel. In their version Constans resolves to recapture Egypt when its inhabitants send him a letter informing him that the number of the Muslims in Alexandria was small and the condition of the Byzantines there was pitiful. Accordingly, Manuel set sail from the imperial capital with 300 ships packed with warriors. Initially they were successful: they expelled the Arabs garrisoned in Alexandria and launched guerrilla raids against those stationed in the villages around the city. News of this reached 'Amr and he set out toward them with an army of 15,000 men. He engaged the enemy and a struggle ensued that was so heated that it made it into Muslim apocalypses as one of the precursors to the final battle of Armageddon. The Arabs were in the end victorious and this time they used various machines of war to breach the walls of Alexandria. A proportion of the inhabitants decided to leave for lands still under Byzantine control and thenceforth Alexandria remained in Muslim hands.[10]

Southward from Egypt: Nubia and Ethiopia

To the south of Egypt, between modern Aswan and Khartoum, a number of kingdoms flourished, the most well-known of which were Nubia (Nobadia), Makuria, and 'Alwa (Alodia), heirs to the ancient civilization of Meroe. Christianity gradually percolated into the region in the course of the fourth and fifth centuries, and various Greek and Latin sources inform us about the activities of both Chalcedonian and anti-Chalcedonian missionaries in the sixth century. Arab forces were dispatched from Aswan around 650 to test the defenses of this land. Possibly it was meant as no more than an exploratory raid, but they received something of a bloody nose. Fighting was unexpectedly fierce and what particularly shocked the Arabs was the awesome velocity and accuracy that the Nubian archers were able to achieve, obliging the would-be invaders to retreat "with many wounds and blinded eyes."[11] The Arabs immediately requested a truce and the governor of Egypt at that time signed an agreement whereby the Nubians would provide one slave a day in return for various foodstuffs. In addition, merchants and messengers were to be allowed to go about their business without hindrance from either side and fugitives were to be returned.

Although the Arabs were repelled, their attack may have prompted the different kingdoms of this region to ally, for the next time we hear from this part of the world there is a "great king," under whom are thirteen kinglets. He had been prevailed upon to come to the aid of the Coptic patriarch, who had been imprisoned by the governor of Egypt, and to make a show of strength to the Arabs of Egypt who were in the habit of kidnapping the Nubians and selling them as slaves. In 747 he marched out from Nubia with a huge army, accompanied by an equal number of horses, which, so an eyewitness tells us, were trained to fight with their forefeet and hindfeet in battle. They used them to good effect, killing and capturing a good few Arabs and taking much plunder; hearing of this, the governor of Egypt, not having any means of resisting, prudently decided to release the patriarch before the Nubians reached the capital. An Arabic papyrus of 758, issued by another governor of Egypt, was addressed to "the lord of Makuria and Nubia," suggesting that these two kingdoms had fully merged.[12] In both cases we get the impression that this distant realm wielded considerable influence and this is reinforced by the account of the grandeur of the visit of George, son of King Zachariah of Nubia, to the court of the caliph at Baghdad in 836, which caused much excitement among the local Iraqi Christian community. In the tenth and eleventh centuries, certain Nubian rulers even managed to extend their authority over Upper Egypt. And Nubian civilization continued to flourish well into the late Middle Ages, as is evidenced by the wide dissemination of Nubian-style pottery and documents in the old Nubian language, which is closely related to certain Nubian dialects still spoken in Sudan today.

The resilience of Nubia meant that the Arabs did not attempt to push farther southward to Ethiopia via an overland route. There was of course the option of attacking by sea, and one might have expected this to happen, for Ethiopia had been an important trade destination for west Arabians and it had invaded Yemen and ruled it for a time in the middle decades of the sixth century. Now there was a chance for the Yemenis to get their own back. Yet no major naval campaigns seem to have been launched from Arabia. In fact, the only incident we hear of is the attempt by a small Ethiopian fleet to raid the coast of west Arabia, which was repelled by a force hurriedly dispatched by Muhammad in 630 or, more likely, by the caliph 'Umar I in 641. It is tempting to connect this with the prophecy in a late seventh-century Christian apocalypse that the Byzantines would attack the Arabs "from the sea of the Kushites (Ethiopians) and inflict desolation and destruction on the wilderness of Yathrib (Medina),"[13] but we have no way of verifying this. We are, however, informed by numerous Muslim sources that later Umayyad rulers used to exile those who incurred their wrath to the island of Dahlak, which was only a short hop from Adulis, the port city of ancient Ethiopia, in modern Eritrea. Presumably, then, an Arab raiding party had made it this far in the course of the seventh or early eighth century. We do not know why it did not establish a foothold on the mainland, but possibly because, as in Nubia, it faced strong resistance from the natives or else because the rewards were deemed insufficient, since the kingdom of Axum was by this time long past its prime.

Westward from Egypt: Cyrenaica and Tripolitania (Libya)

The lands to the west of Egypt proved to be a much easier prospect for the Arabs, and John of Nikiu tells us that as soon as 'Amr ibn al-'As had concluded a treaty with the patriarch Cyrus and accepted the submission of Alexandria, he dispatched a raiding party to the Pentapolis. This refers to the region of modern northeast Libya, also called Cyrenaica, which comprises five prosperous Roman cities, including Berenike (modern Benghazi), Barqa (modern al-Marj), and Cyrene, the capital. It is at least a 600-mile march away from

Alexandria, via a very flat coastal road hemmed in to the south by desert. The Pentapolis itself is dominated by the mountain range known as the Jabal Akhdar, which attracts enough rainfall to provide a fertile hinterland for the settlements in its shadow. The governor of the province, together with his troops and the richer residents, withdrew into the ancient city of Tokra, which had been equipped with strong walls a century before, and so offered those sheltering within the hope that they might be able to ride out the passing Arab storm. And sure enough, John informs us, once the raiders had seized a good amount of plunder and captives they retired to whence they came. Muslim sources have 'Amr attacking a number of other places in the area, even entering and pillaging Tripoli, but again the impression conveyed is of raiding expeditions rather than the establishment of a permanent presence. As one early ninth-century Muslim scholar affirmed: "No tax collector entered Barqa (probably meaning all Pentapolis) at that time; rather they would send the tribute when it was due."[14]

Muslim sources also attribute to 'Amr the first Arab encounter with the Berbers, in this case with the Luwata tribe, which inhabited the pre-desert lands to the south of the coast of Cyrenaica. They are presumably to be identified with the Laguatan of the Byzantine sources, who were famed for never having been conquered and for possessing countless thousands of men. They played a major part in the great Berber revolt against the Byzantines in the 540s, and, though they were suppressed, it would seem that Byzantine rule was never really reestablished in this interior region, and so the Luwata enjoyed a high degree of autonomy in the century before the Arab conquest. 'Amr continued this arrangement; he did not attempt to fight the Luwata, but concluded an agreement with them that, according to the earliest Muslim historians, stipulated that they pay a sum of money in tribute which would be raised by "selling whichever of their children that they wished." No clarification is given, but probably this is an allusion to the vibrant slave trade of Africa. St. Augustine, for example, lamented the ubiquity of slave merchants in Africa, who "empty a large part of the land of its human population, exporting those whom they buy—almost all free men—to provinces overseas."[15]

John of Nikiu ends his narrative at this date (ca. 643) and from this point on we are deprived of any detailed seventh-century account of the Arab conquest of North Africa. No contemporary resident felt impelled to record Byzantium's gradual loss of these lands, or if they did it has not come down to us. Two mid-eighth-century chronicles, both produced in Spain but incorporating material from Syria, give us the barest outlines of the next Arab offensive. It was led by ʿAbdallah ibn Saʿd, a foster brother of the caliph ʿUthman, who had installed him as governor of Egypt in 645 instead of ʿAmr ibn al-ʿAs. After reaching Tripoli, the chroniclers say, ʿAbdallah "advanced in war upon Cidamo and Lebida." The former refers to the oasis town of Gadamis, southwest of Tripoli, where the Arabs perhaps went to parley with local Berber tribes. The latter is Leptis Magna, to the east of Tripoli, one of the most magnificent and today one of the best preserved Roman cities in the world (Figure 3.1), though when the Arabs arrived there it was but a shadow of its former self, since it had suffered badly when the Byzantines recaptured it from the Vandals in 533. After carrying out many depredations, ʿAbdallah "received in loyalty the conquered and devastated provinces, and he soon reached Africa still thirsty for blood." It would seem, then, that after passing Tripoli ʿAbdallah proceeded westward along the coast and entered what the Romans called Africa (Arabic: Ifriqiya), which corresponded to modern Tunisia and eastern Algeria. This would have taken him into the interior of the province of Byzacena, described by Isidore of Seville (d. 636) as "rich in oil and so fertile in its soil that seeds that are sown there return a crop nearly a hundredfold."[16] Apparently ʿAbdallah's goal was to challenge the patrician Gregory, who had been appointed governor of Africa by the emperor Heraclius, but who had raised a rebellion against Constans "together with the Africans." He began minting his own coins and allegedly "controlled everything between Tripoli and Tangiers." He perhaps saw himself as acting to save the Byzantine Empire, which seemed to be disintegrating before his eyes: Africa had produced Heraclius, who had freed Byzantium from the clutches of the Persians, so maybe it could now help relieve the Arab threat.[17]

Gregory was based at this time, in the summer of 647, in Sbeitla, ancient Sufetula, which can still boast a fine forum and capitolium and the remains of

FIGURE 3.1 The theater of Leptis Magna in Libya.

a number of temples and churches. It was not in itself of great commercial or cultural significance, and did not even possess a fortress or strong city walls, but it was situated near the Kasserine pass through the Tebessa mountain range and so stood in the way of any invaders' march westward. This, plus the relative fertility of the region, which facilitated the provisioning of troops, perhaps explains why Gregory took up position here. Hearing that 'Abdallah was proceeding from the coast toward him Gregory went out with his men to head off the aggressor. No details of the battle are given except for the laconic notice that "the battle line of the Moors turned in flight and all the nobility of Africa, along with Count Gregory, was extinguished." Having achieved this great victory, 'Abdallah returned to Egypt laden with booty. No indication is given that the Arabs had any base in Africa at this point and Muslim sources expressly state that when the Byzantines saw the extent of the Arabs' plundering after the battle of Sbeitla they asked 'Abdallah ibn Sa'd to take from them money on the condition that he leave their country. He accepted their request and returned to Egypt "without appointing anyone over them or establishing any garrison there."[18]

Iran (Maps 2.3 and 3.3)

At the same time 'Amr was pushing into Egypt, other Arab armies were seeking to consolidate their hold on Iraq and to prepare the ground for extending their conquests into Iran. To realize these aims they needed a headquarters. They could have used the Persian capital, Seleucia-Ctesiphon, but it was such an enormous sprawling site that it was likely deemed unsuitable for a military base, and perhaps also it smacked too strongly of the ancient régime. Instead

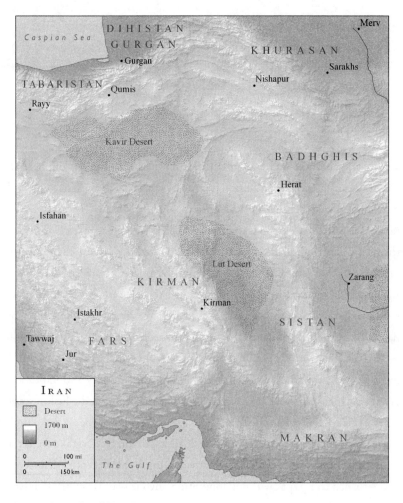

MAP 3.3 Central and East Iran.

they established two large garrisons, Basra and Kufa. The former, notes a contemporary chronicler, was founded by Abu Musa al-Ash'ari, a native Yemeni and early companion of Muhammad, "at the point where the Tigris flows into the great sea, situated between cultivated land and the desert." The latter, Kufa, was commissioned by another early companion of Muhammad and a veteran of campaigns in Persia, Sa'd ibn Abi Waqqas; it was located farther to the north, at a bend on the Euphrates opposite the old Arab Christian settlement of Hira.[19] Though they were initially only intended for the quartering of Arab troops, who would then be sent off to participate in further conquests to the north and to the east, the garrisons soon became flooded with large numbers of prisoners-of-war brought from all over the Middle East and Central Asia and with men hoping to get rich by offering services to the newly wealthy Arabs, making them into booming cosmopolitan cities.

In the early 640s the Arabs launched incursions into Iran from three different directions. One line of advance took them into Khuzistan, a province in the far southwest of modern Iran. At its heart was the mighty Karun River, which begins in the Zagros Mountains and then flows west and south, emptying into the Persian Gulf right next to the river Tigris. The Sasanian dynasty had invested much money and labor in the region, restoring and building canals in the north to increase agricultural yields, in particular of cereals, sugarcane, and rice, and so it was a rich prize for whoever could control it (Figure 3.2). The cities of Jundishapur and Karka d-Ledan submitted, but Hormizdan, a senior Persian general, managed to muster some troops and hold the other two key cities of the province, Shush and Shustar. He initially struck a deal with Abu Musa, promising to pay tribute, but after two years, having reinforced his position, he broke the peace and killed the men who served as ambassadors between them. Abu Musa dispatched troops, against which Hormizdan sent a number of squadrons, but all were defeated. The Arabs began with Shush, ancient Susa, the favorite residence of Darius the Great, and within a few days they had taken it. "They slew all the distinguished citizens and seized a building called the house of Daniel, appropriating the treasure that was stored there," including a silver chest containing a mummified corpse, said to be either that of the prophet Daniel or of King Darius himself. Next

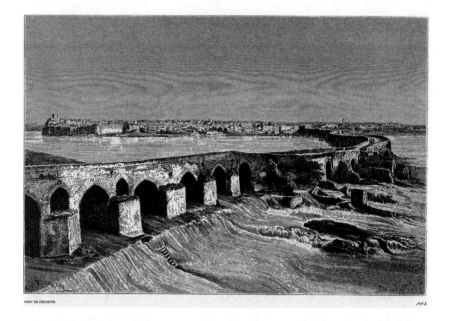

FIGURE 3.2 Bridge over the river Karun at Shustar in southwest Iran. Drawing from ca. 1880 by Jeanne Dieulafoy.

the Arabs moved on to another ancient city, Shustar, which lay on an island in the river Karun and was well protected on all sides. For two years they besieged it without making any progress. But then a native of Qatar who lived there conspired with a friend who had a house on the walls to let them in on the proviso that they receive a third of the spoils. The Arabs on the outside agreed to this and the two men gave them access by tunneling under the walls. "Thus the Arabs took Shustar, spilling blood as though it was water."

The second and principal line of the Arab march into Iran was via the same ancient route through the Zagros Mountains that Alexander the Great had taken long before and that the Mongols would take long after. Crossing from Iraq, they passed Kermanshah and proceeded to Nihawand, which commands entry into the rich agricultural lands of the Iranian plateau. It was crucial for the Persians, after losing the fertile plains of southern Iraq, to halt the Arab advance here before they lost yet another major center of food production. The contemporary chronicler Sebeos evidently considered the encounter important, for he paid careful attention to its dating: "It happened in the first year of Constans, king of the Byzantines, and in the tenth year of Yazdgird, king of the Persians," namely 641–42. The Arabs fielded "40,000 men equipped with swords," he says, against which the Persians mustered "a force of 60,000 fully armed men." For three days the two sides confronted each other, with heavy losses diminishing the infantry of both parties. Suddenly a rumor circulated among the Persians that their enemy had received reinforcements. In their nervous state the Persian troops did not wait to confirm this information, but during the night abandoned their camp. The Arabs made an attack against the Persian position the following morning, but found no one there, and so instead they raided the surrounding area. "Spreading forays across the whole land they put man and beast to the sword; capturing twenty-two fortresses they slaughtered all the living beings in them."

Third, the Arabs conducted attacks all along the southern coastal flank of Iran from the mouth of the Tigris to the ports of northwest India. Again it is Sebeos who is our main informant, and he tells us that his source is "men who had been taken as captives." The Arab king, he says, dispatched ships from east Arabia to raid all along the southern coast of Iran as far as the borders of India. In the early stages, they would return to their bases in east Arabia, but after a time they sought to establish a garrison in southwest Iran so that they could follow up the naval attacks with maneuvers on land. The man responsible for organizing this was 'Uthman ibn Abi al-'As, of the tribe of Thaqif, who had served as governor of Bahrain and Oman from 636 to 650 and commanded operations against the coastal region of Fars from 640 to 650. He captured the town of Tawwaj, southwest of Shiraz, in 640 and stationed troops there. Their numbers were presumably limited, however, for they were unable to capture the mountain strongholds of Istakhr and Jur. This was only achieved once there was a new governor of Basra installed in 649, namely 'Abdallah ibn 'Amir, who was of the prophet's tribe of Quraysh and seems to have been an energetic and competent leader. He mobilized the extensive manpower based at Basra to launch a major assault on the heartlands of the Sasanian royal family at Fars. According to Muslim sources, Jur and Istakhr put up a fierce fight, but both eventually fell sometime in the early 650s. The latter allegedly suffered the massacre of 40,000 of its inhabitants, including many of the Sasanian elite who had sought sanctuary there in the homeland of their kings.[20]

The Arabs wished to ensure that there would be no Sasanian-led comeback, and this is why they visited such harsh treatment on southwest Iran, eliminating the members, supporters, and strongholds of this royal house. With this done, they had one obvious task left: to remove the last Sasanian ruler. An Arab army marched from southwest Iran all the way to the northeast, "the land of the Parthians," to catch up with Yazdgird, who was now holed up in Merv, in modern Turkmenistan, having been "spurned by the grand nobles" of Iran. Khurrazad, the prince of Media (northwest Iran) after the death of his brother Rustam, had also headed eastward, intending to join up with the other Persian troops fighting the Arabs, but, Sebeos tells us, unfortunately without clarification, he rebelled and "fortified himself in some place." Muslim sources maintain that he disagreed strongly with Yazdgird over their next course of action. Whereas the latter wanted to go to the Turks or the Chinese to plead for support against the Arabs, since they were the only peoples with sufficient surplus manpower, Khurrazad was adamant that he should not abandon his own people and that it would be a dangerous move to enter foreign lands when in such a position of weakness. His own preference was to make some sort of deal with the Arabs to buy themselves time.

Whatever the reason, Khurrazad decided that he personally would throw in his lot with the Arabs. This was a disaster for the emperor; the powerful army of Media was crucial to his aim of defeating the fast approaching Arab forces and their defection unsettled those left behind. He turned eastward, but the Arabs caught up with him and quickly routed his troops. Yazdgird survived this encounter but was murdered only a short while later in obscure circumstances. Contemporary authors give few details, but stories and speculation inevitably ran rife about his demise. The most popular version relates that he hid in a mill on a river by the gate of the city of Merv, the owner of which discovered him, killed him, and brought his head to the governor. There are, however, numerous different theories about the identity of the killer (the miller, a Turk, a coalition of east Iranian lords angry at the straits that the family of Sasan had brought them to), the manner of death (a blow to the head or drowning), and whether it was an accident (perhaps the miller did not realize who the intruder was) or a conspiracy (a deal between Mahawayh, governor of Merv, and the Buddhist prince Nizak, the latter offended because Yazdgird had spurned his request to marry his daughter).[21]

The slaying of Yazdgird at the hands of a steppe people was certainly a momentous and shocking event, but it had happened before: the emperor Peroz I and his army had been cut down by the Hephthalites in Gurgan in AD 484, and yet the Persian Empire had lived on. There was, then, the chance of a comeback this time too, and certainly Yazdgird's sons still struggled to recapture their birthright. Peroz III, the elder son, begged and cajoled the Turks and Chinese to give him troops and during the first Arab civil war (656–60) he made some progress in east Iran, even striking his own coins. At this time the emperor Gaozong (650–83)—or perhaps rather the real power in China, the indomitable empress Wu (655–705)—established a protectorate in the far east of Iran named the "Persian area command" and recognized Peroz as its chief. However, in 663 the Arabs resumed their eastward advance, forcing the young prince to retreat and to seek refuge in the Chinese capital, Chang'an (modern Xi'an), where he set up a Persian court in exile. He, or perhaps his son Narseh, made another attempt in 677, but the Chinese force would accompany him only part of the way; the enterprise came to nought—marching from so far east to attack the Arab garrison cities that lay so far west, in Iraq, was just too difficult. Peroz died in his makeshift court in Chang'an around 680 and is commemorated by a statue inscribed with the legend: "Peroz, king of Persia, grand general of the right courageous guard and commander-in-chief of Persia." The name of his brother Bahram also lived on, not so much for what he did, but for what nostalgic Persians hoped that he might do, and these hopes they poured into poetry anticipating the return to past glory that would accompany "the coming of the miraculous Bahram."[22]

Caucasia (Map 3.4)

Eastward and westward the Arabs made substantial gains over the course of the 640s, but northward, beyond the Jazira and northern Iraq, the mountainous

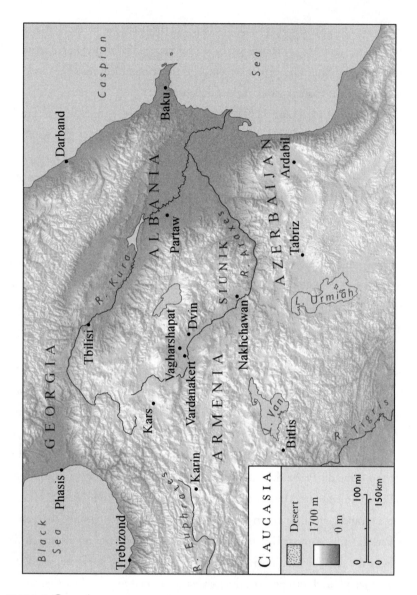

MAP 3.4 Caucasia.

nature of the terrain presents a more serious challenge to would-be invaders. Up until AD 428 much of these lands had belonged to the kingdom of Armenia, equating to modern eastern Turkey, Armenia, and the northwest tip of Iran. Increasingly, however, the superpowers of Byzantium and Iran became involved in the affairs of this region and after 428 it became divided up between the two of them, though the ruggedness of the country meant that the various noble families of Armenia maintained a fair degree of autonomy and their celebrated martial prowess made them valued as allies by both sides. Nevertheless, Mu'awiya, the new Arab commander-in-chief in the west, was determined to cut his teeth on this proud land. For this task he selected Habib ibn Maslama, a formidable warrior with a stern temperament, who was described by one Christian chronicler as "a wicked Syrian man." Habib took the easiest pass across the mountains to the northeast of the Jazira, and then marched along the northern shore of Lake Van. Continuing northeast he would have passed quite near the towering Mount Ararat, which attains a height of more than 5,000 meters. It was now the beginning of October and there was already snow on the ground. Not to be put off, the Arabs came up with the plan of bringing bulls and making them go on ahead of them to tread down the path. Thus they were able to forge ahead and enter the district of Ayrarat, the administrative center of Armenia, and to raid the capital, Dvin, some twenty miles south of modern Erevan. The Armenians had not been expecting an attack now that the winter had set in, and so they were caught unawares. The Arabs were able to plunder successfully across a wide area, and by means of smoke, dense volleys of arrows, and ladders they were able to enter the city of Dvin itself, in October 640, putting many of its residents to the sword and carrying off many captives and riches.[23]

Three years later, in the summer of 643, the Arabs launched another campaign against Armenia. This was part of a much wider assault on the whole region, perhaps intending to test the defenses of the northwest limits of the Persian Empire, which, it should be remembered, still endured at this time. The Arab army initially marched to the region of Azerbaijan, to the northeast of Lake Urmiah. There they split into three divisions of some 3,000 men apiece. One went northwards up the valley of the great Araxes River, past Dvin, and raided all around a great arc of territory to the north of the city, as far as the shores of the Black and Caspian Seas. A second division headed northwest into the southern Armenian highlands, in the area around the modern border between Turkey and Iran. The third division besieged the strategic city of Nakhchawan, which commanded the Araxes valley south of Dvin. The second division had the most difficult task, for the local inhabitants could retreat into high mountain redoubts. It attacked two fortresses but suffered many losses and so withdrew. It captured a third fortress, but the next day Theodore Rshtuni, the Byzantine-approved commander in Armenia, fell upon them in a surprise attack. Out of 3,000 men, "the elite of all the Arab troops," none survived save a few who escaped on foot and found safety in the lowland fens. To make known his victory Theodore selected 100 of the best Arab horses and sent them off to the Byzantine emperor as a gift. Hearing of this defeat, the third Arab division called off its siege of Nakhchawan and all the Arabs beat a hasty retreat, with only the booty taken by the first division to console them for this otherwise disastrous campaign.

Armenia, therefore, remained a free ally of the Byzantines for a while longer. However, in the year 652–53, Theodore Rshtuni, perhaps influenced by the news of the death of the Sasanian emperor Yazdgird, resolved to switch sides. The Armenians did not submit as conquered subjects, but agreed to act as vassals, which probably suited the Arabs, since their failed venture of a decade before was still fresh in their memory and they were in no hurry to return to fight this rugged country and its hardy inhabitants. The arrangement was quite a good one for the Armenians, since they were exempted from tribute for three years and then only had to pay whatever amount they deemed fair. They had to maintain 15,000 cavalry ready to give aid to the Arabs if they requested it, but in return they kept their autonomy. The document drafted by Mu'awiya stated: "I shall not send emirs to your fortresses, nor an Arab army—neither many, nor down to a single cavalryman." Moreover, if anyone were to attack Armenia, the Arabs would send troops in support, as many as required. This move was not, however, universally popular in Armenia. Sebeos, probably echoing the sentiment of many of the clergy, laments that Theodore "made a pact with death and contracted an alliance with hell, abandoning the divine covenant."

Cyprus and Arwad

The ease with which a Byzantine army was able to sail into the harbor of Alexandria in 646 and retake the city made Mu'awiya realize that the Arabs needed a navy to safeguard their gains. Moreover, if they were ever to capture Constantinople, an assault by sea would be a crucial accompaniment to a land attack. At once, then, he press-ganged workers at the shipyards of Egypt and the Levant to set about constructing a fleet. Three years later they were ready and Mu'awiya decided to test out his new force with an attack on Cyprus. An emotive account by a contemporary is preserved in a mid-eighth-century chronicle and gives us a vivid narrative of this first Arab naval raid.[24] In the spring of 649, Mu'awiya issued the command and the fleets came together off the coast of Syria, some 1,700 boats in all, their masts resembling a huge floating forest. Those watching from the shore were awestruck at the size of the armada, under which the waves of the sea were all but invisible. The sailors stood on the top decks in the full finery of their fighting gear, boasting that they were going to destroy the luxurious capital of the Cypriots, which had never before been subjected to the predations of any invader.

When they drew near to the island, Mu'awiya ordered the crew to lower the sails and to maintain the ships just short of dry land. He wanted to use clemency toward the islanders and so he gave them a chance to submit in exchange for guarantees of safety. He positioned his own ship at the head of the whole fleet and said to his companions: "Let us stay here and see whether the Cypriots will come out to us to make a peace agreement so that they and their country will be spared from ruin." Time passed, but no one came to sue for peace. At last Mu'awiya yielded to the recriminations of the Egyptian contingent, which was becoming impatient, and gave the go-ahead for a ground assault. When the Cypriots saw the large number of ships, they assumed that they were Byzantine vessels, and so when the Arabs reached land, they were able to drop anchor, arm themselves, and come ashore without encountering any opposition. Mu'awiya, together with his chiefs and loyal retinue, made straight for the capital, Constantia, and, after subduing it, he established his camp in the bishop's residence. The Arab soldiers, who had scattered across the island, collected a huge amount of gold, slaves, and expensive clothing and brought it to Mu'awiya, who was delighted at the quantity of the accumulated loot and the captives, male and female of every age. The gold and silver along with everything else was divided into two portions, for which the two armies, that from Egypt and that from Syria, cast lots. After a few days they loaded their human booty onto the ships, some destined for Alexandria, others for Syria.

Mu'awiya took this opportunity to launch a naval attack in the direction of Constantinople, but was repelled and driven off in flight. Still undaunted, Mu'awiya turned his attention instead to Arwad, which is a small island just off the coast of Syria. He made every effort to capture it, using siege engines and the like, but its inhabitants stood firm, protected by the large fortress that lay within the island's capital. He then sent a bishop to persuade them to vacate the island and go to Byzantium, but the islanders imprisoned him and paid no attention to his message. Since winter was now setting in, Mu'awiya went back to Damascus, but when spring arrived he returned to Arwad with many more troops and settled in for a long siege. When the islanders saw the mighty forces that were arrayed against them, they decided to accept guarantees of security for their lives and an offer to relocate wherever they wished, some of them going to Byzantine territory and others leaving for Syria. When the inhabitants of the island had departed, Mu'awiya ordered its fortifications to be destroyed and the city to be set on fire and razed to the ground. They did this to the city, it was said, "so that it would never again be rebuilt or resettled," and, one would assume, so that it could not be used as a base by the Byzantines from which to launch attacks against the Syrian coast.

In that same year, AD 650, the Arabs returned once more to Cyprus, under a commander called Abu l-A'war, who was fiercely loyal to the Umayyads and had turned out to be a competent admiral. The reason for this second assault was the news that a large force of Byzantines had been quartered on the island, presumably sent from Constantinople to hold it for the empire. The Byzantine troops encouraged the populace to stand firm and not to panic, but when the troops and natives actually sighted the Arab ships on the horizon and saw their number, their courage deserted them and they took flight. The rich citizens and the soldiers escaped by ship to Byzantine territory; others attempted to avoid death or slavery by shutting themselves up in the city of Lapathos. The Arabs roamed freely across the mountains and the plains hunting for plunder and slaves; "they winkled the natives out of the cracks in the ground like eggs abandoned in the nest." Then they settled their sights on Lapathos. For several days they tried the effect of promises of peace, but finding the Cypriots unreceptive they began to bombard the city with catapults from all sides. When the inhabitants saw that it was hopeless and that no help was on its way, they petitioned Abu l-A'war to give them a pledge that their lives would be spared. He showed clemency readily and sent them the following instructions: "The gold and silver and other assets which are in the city are mine. To you I give a peace agreement and a solemn pact that those of you who so wish may go to Byzantine territory, and that those who prefer to stay will neither be killed nor enslaved." Thus the city was taken, its treasures were loaded onto the ships with the rest of the booty, including slaves, and the Arabs sailed back to Syria in victory. A contemporary inscription records this mass enslavement, estimating the number taken away to have been 120,000 in 649 and 50,000 in 650; this is probably an exaggeration, or at least a generous estimation, but must surely reflect the fact that the numbers affected were very substantial.[25]

The Success of the Arab Conquests

All the victories achieved by the Arabs in the 630s took place within a relatively short distance of the Syrian desert: Palestine and Syria on the west side, Iraq to the east, and the Jazira to the north. In the 640s, however, they extended significantly the radius of their attacks, proceeding westward to Egypt, eastward into Iran, and northward into the Caucasus. The latter proved hard going for the Arabs, since they were not accustomed to such mountainous terrain, but in Egypt and Iran they were able to subdue the key cities and assume overall control of all of their territories. This was a stunning achievement and it inevitably raises the question of why the Arab conquests were so successful. For contemporary observers the answer was simple: God had decreed it, whether as a way of punishing people for their sins (as many Christian leaders said) or as a way of rewarding the Arabs for their adherence to the true faith (as the conquerors said). But how should we explain it?

The weakness of the Byzantine and Persian empires certainly played a part in their swift defeat. The continual outbreaks of war between these two powers since 502, and in particular the almighty clash of 603–28, was a huge drain on their finances and manpower. Recruitment of troops was also adversely affected by the recurrent bouts of plague that troubled the whole region from ca. 550. Plague spreads fast in areas of high population density, where contagion works its deadly spell, but in open areas, where human occupation is sparse, it quickly loses its power. Thus the core regions of Byzantium and Persia—the coastal cities of the Mediterranean and the agricultural settlements of southern Iraq—were hit hard, whereas the inland areas closest to the Syrian steppe and the vast grazing lands of Central Asia were much less troubled by it. A clear illustration of the limited manpower available to Byzantium is given by Heraclius's famous expedition from Caucasia to Iraq to strike at the heart of the Persian Empire. His force was only 5,000 strong, whereas the khagan of the Turks who had come to his aid was able to field 40,000 men. So when Chinese sources casually observed that in 627 the Turks defeated the Persians, not mentioning the Byzantines at all, they were in effect right.[26] It was now the steppe world that called the tune. As the loser in this titanic struggle, Persia suffered a crisis of confidence and its noble families suspected that the ruling Sasanian dynasty had forfeited the favor of the gods. For the first time in 400 years the Sasanian's royal prerogative was being challenged and a catastrophic civil war was unfolding at the very moment that the regime was at its weakest.

Yet it was not only the enfeebled state of their opponents that facilitated the Arabs' advance. The image of the Arab conquerors as "a horde of nomads with no military experience" and as outsiders to the civilized world,[27] which is sometimes peddled even in scholarly literature, is wrong on both counts. Over the previous three centuries or so, numerous Arab tribesmen had provided military service to the empires of Byzantium and Persia. Some served in regiments who fought as part of the imperial army while others acted as independent vassals allied to the empire and fighting alongside them when called upon. A good example is the sixth-century Arab chief Atfar whom a contemporary observer describes as "an experienced man of war, well-trained in the technology of the Byzantine military."[28] These Arab allies of the empires, though they continued to fight for their imperial masters for a while, soon began to switch to the west

Arabian coalition of Muhammad and his successors. In part, this was because they saw that the latter were winning victories and gaining plunder, but it was also because the province of Arabia had, over the five centuries of its existence, nurtured various ties—commercial, personal, and so on—between the tribes of the marginal lands of Syria, Jordan, and west Arabia, and this made it easier for members of the west Arabian coalition to appeal to their brethren to the north. For example, 'Amr ibn al-'As, the general who led Arab troops into Palestine in 634, was related by blood, via his maternal grandmother, to the tribe of Bali, which was one of the first of the Arab tribes allied to Byzantium to change allegiance and fight with the west Arabians. One chronicler of the first Arab-Byzantine encounters notes that "the Byzantine soldiers of [the province of] Arabia fought the Arabs of [the province of] Arabia."[29] And Muslim sources state that the Christian Arab tribes who fought on the side of the west Arabian coalition at the Battle of Yarmuk were "in their homeland." The same goes for the Persian realm, where the tribes "whose homeland was Iraq" fought against the agents of Persian imperial rule.[30] From this perspective the Arab conquests began as an Arab insurrection, that is, the early conquerors were not invaders coming from outside the empire but insiders trying to seize a share of the power and wealth of the Byzantine state. This helps explain why the Arab conquests were not particularly destructive: the leadership already had close acquaintance with the empires and they wanted to rule it themselves, not destroy it.

The loss of their Arab allies was a severe blow to the empires of Byzantium and Persia. After the defeat at the Battle of Yarmuk in 636, a substantial number of Christian Arabs went over to the side of the victors, with the result that Heraclius "was unable to raise any more troops to oppose them." Conversely, the west Arabians could draw on substantial numbers of nomads, for, as we noted in the last chapter, the percentage of men that can be drafted in a nomad society is much higher than in a settled society. A census of the garrisons of Kufa and Basra conducted during the reign of Mu'awiya by the superintendent of the military register revealed that they contained 60,000 and 80,000 fighting men, respectively.[31] If we assume that nearly as many again were to be found in garrisons across the rest of the conquered lands, this would then yield a figure of at least 250,000, which is a very impressive military force by any standards, and especially as measured against the enfeebled armies of Byzantium and Persia. This advantage of manpower would not have helped the west Arabians if they had not also had good organization, and this is where Islam comes in. Modern scholars tend to emphasize the zeal that it imparted, but more important was the clear motivation and plan of action that it gave: emigrate to a garrison and fight in God's path (*hijra* and jihad) against His enemies. It was a clear and simple message, and one that could bring together people of different backgrounds for a common cause.[32] The basis on which all signed up to join Muhammad's community was acceptance of him and God as the sole arbiters of government. After Muhammad's death this responsibility went to his successors, the caliphs, who similarly acted, in theory at least, as the ultimate authority for the conquest society in both religious and worldly matters. This meant that, even though the succession was often contested, there was a transparent command structure in place to give at least some overall direction to the conquests.

But the Arabs did not only employ military means to further their aims. They also made heavy use of agreements to respect life, property, and customs in return for submission and tribute. Such agreements were part of an ancient Middle Eastern tradition of rules for military engagement, examples of which exist from as far back as the third millennium BC. The dominant model at the time of the Arab conquests was the Roman/Byzantine *deditio in fidem*, whereby a community offered its surrender (*deditio*) in anticipation of a promise from the victors to act in good faith (*fides*), usually safeguarding the lives, possessions, and laws of the community in return for the fulfillment of certain conditions, all of which was set out in a treaty (*pactum*) accompanied by binding oaths. Although the fate of the conquered was now in the hands of the conquerors, there was an expectation of justice and mercy: "Not only must we show consideration to those whom we have defeated by force," acknowledges the Roman statesman Cicero, "but we must also receive those who, having laid down their arms, have made recourse to the good faith (*fides*) of our generals, even though their battering rams have struck against our walls."[33] The same basic principle applied in the Persian sphere too—Emperor Khusrau II urged his generals to "put to the sword all those who offer resistance," but he also instructed them to "receive in a friendly way those who will submit and keep them in peace and prosperity."[34]

Arab commanders recognized that such deals spared them from prolonged sieges, which tied up valuable military manpower, and won over to their side potentially troublesome enemies. Ninth-century Muslim historians, wishing to systematize the conquest accounts, often maintained that everyone the conquerors met was offered the same three choices of conversion, surrender and payment of a poll tax, or death in battle, but enough non-standard reports have survived to allow us to glimpse a more variegated picture. For example, the Samaritans of Palestine agreed to act as guides and spies in return for exemption from land tax, and the Jarajima, longtime residents of the Black Mountain region around Antioch, served as frontier guards on the condition that they paid no tax and kept any booty they took when they fought alongside the Arabs. The Persian governor of Darband and his troops were spared payment of tribute in return for rendering military service, and indeed "it became accepted practice that those non-Muslims who went into combat against the enemy (on behalf of the Arabs), and also those whose only contribution was to maintain readiness to fight, should be relieved of tribute."[35]

In short, a conciliatory attitude and the widespread use of co-option via tax exemption were instrumental in the success of the Arab conquests. The old idea, still commonly encountered in modern scholarly literature, that the native population welcomed the conquerors, is wrong. It is only with hindsight and with the intention of ingratiating themselves with the Muslim authorities that later Christian authors would offer positive assessments of the Arab invasions. It is true, though, that anti-Chalcedonian Christians had faced persecution at the hands of the Chalcedonian authorities in the late sixth and early seventh centuries, and this is likely to have alienated elements of the anti-Chalcedonian communities of Syria and Egypt and made them more amenable to accommodation with Arab rule once the initial period of fighting and looting had ended and it had become clear that the Arabs were going to leave people to practice their own faith in peace as long as they paid tribute.

The Beginnings of Arab Government

Although we can discern traces of a command structure in the execution of the early conquests, we have almost no contemporary information about the caliphs in Medina (632–60). This is possibly because some 650 miles of mountain, steppe, and desert separate Medina from cities like Damascus and Basra, or because the turbulence of these years disrupted the usual channels of communication. Whatever the reason, writers who lived at the same time as the first four caliphs—Abu Bakr (632–34), 'Umar (634–44), 'Uthman (644–56) and 'Ali (656–60)—recorded next to nothing about them, and their names do not appear on coins, inscriptions, or documents. It is only with the fifth caliph, Mu'awiya (661–80), that we have evidence of a functioning Arab government, since his name appears on all official state media. Having been stationed in Damascus as governor of Syria for twenty years (640–60), he had worked with the local provincial administrators and so was much better placed than his predecessors, based in faraway Medina, to begin the job of establishing a centralized state, which was crucial if the conquests were going to result in a lasting legacy. This made him unpopular, though, for many resented ceding any of their booty and autonomy to a central agency. Many felt that things had been better before Mu'awiya began his state-building activities and they attributed their ideas of how government should work to the caliphs before him, especially to 'Umar, who gradually acquired the status of model statesman and an arbiter on all matters to do with statecraft. For example, he was said to have insisted that the state should circulate wealth to its members rather than hoard it from them. When the question was put to him: "O commander of the faithful, would it not be a good idea to store up this wealth for emergencies that might arise," he replied: "This is an idea that Satan has put into your head. It would not affect me adversely, but it would be a temptation for those who come after me."[36]

How then were the conquered territories governed in the time of the Medinan caliphs? The answer is that to a substantial degree the existing systems that were already in place kept on ticking over. For example, until at least the 650s considerable quantities of regular Byzantine coins, mostly struck in

Constantinople, continued to arrive and circulate in Syria, and Sasanian silver dirhams remained the principal currency in Persia until the 690s. A Syrian author of Damascus, writing around 660, still speaks of "our empire" and "our emperor"; he is aware that "others" hold Jerusalem, but confidently asserts that "as long as the head and the empire remain firm, all the body will renew itself with ease." A contemporary of his, the monk John of Fenek, explains the squabbles between the Arabs in terms of ancient disagreements between the Byzantines and Persians, as though their empires still structured the fabric of his world. Old thinking died hard, but also it was not at once appreciated that the Arab conquests would lead to a permanent occupation, let alone to a new civilization. In Damascus, as our Syrian writer notes, Christians still predominated, their churches had not been harmed, and the city walls remained intact. Moreover, Arabic-speaking tribesmen had long constituted a substantial proportion of the region's population and so would not have seemed so alien as we now tend to think.[37]

The day-to-day running of the machinery of state was initially left, then, to continue in much the same way as it had before the conquests, conducted by much the same staff. In Egypt, for example, the system of *pagarchs* (in charge of cities and their agricultural hinterland) and dukes (in charge of the regional divisions of the country) and the offices that went with them initially remained in place.[38] Two major policy innovations were made in the Medinan period, however, both of which had very long-term repercussions. First, it was decided to pay all soldiers a stipend (*'ata'*), the rate varying according to length of service, and this was to be funded out of direct taxation. Second, a poll tax was introduced, which comprised varying annual rates according to the wealth of the payer and exemptions for women, minors, and the poor. This type of tax may have been employed for convenience, since it is easy and transparent to calculate and enforce (one person, one payment), and so was often imposed at a time of upheaval or invasion (the Mongols prescribed it for their subjects, for instance). Muslim sources suggest, however, that it was modeled on the Persian poll tax, which was also graded according to ability to pay and included exemptions for the elite (corresponding to the conquerors in the Arab case).[39] The stipend system is also sometimes attributed to a Persian precedent, though it

may have suggested itself simply because the Arabs formerly in the employ of
the empires had become accustomed to receiving stipends in return for military service. In order to facilitate payments to the Arab troops, they were, in
Iraq and Egypt at least, kept together in a small number of garrisons, which
were positioned at a slight distance from existing population centers: Fustat
(near Babylon of Egypt), Kufa (near Hira), and Basra (near Ubulla). Whether
intentional or not, this had the effect of allowing the soldiers to bond with one
another while at the same time isolating them somewhat from the local people.
This promoted a sense of group solidarity and reduced the chance of soldiers
going native in the early decades, as may well have happened if they had been
paid via land grants and dispersed across the countryside, which was common
practice among the invaders of the West Roman Empire.[40]

We would know very little about these measures if it were not for Egypt's
gift to scholars: the vast quantities of documents on papyri that have been preserved by the country's dry unforgiving climate. Among them we find numerous texts related to the local Arab administration in the country from as early
as 642. The new armies had not only to be paid, but also to be fed, housed,
and equipped, which led to a flurry of documentation as demand notes were
dispatched and receipts were issued for a wide variety of goods, such as grain,
oil, fodder, blankets, saddles, and horses. To meet the heavy demands of maintaining the army, Arab governors paid close attention to fiscal matters and
movements of people, as is clear from the floods of letters issued by governors
cajoling and ordering lower officials to chase up overdue taxes and to round up
errant taxpayers. One of the earliest texts to survive is number 558 in the collection amassed by Archduke Rainer in Vienna; it describes itself as a "Receipt
for the sheep given to the *magaritai* and others who arrived, as a down-payment
for the taxes of the first fiscal year" (Figure 3.3). It sounds prosaic, and the
papyrus looks very scrappy, but it can tell us much about the world of the new
conquerors. First, it is dated very exactly by two different dating systems—the
Egyptian Christian era of the martyrs and the Islamic calendar—to April 25,
643. The Muslims counted from the year of Muhammad's *hijra*, when he left
Mecca to go and found his new community in Medina, in 622. Already by
643 it is being used in documents, and not long thereafter we find it used in

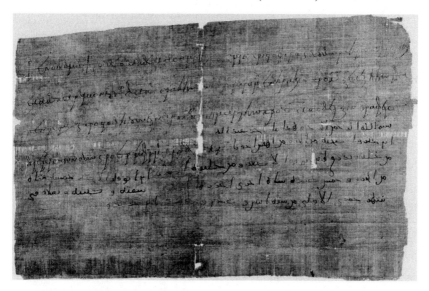

FIGURE 3.3 Papyrus bought by Archduke Rainer from Egypt, dated 643 AD. ©
Vienna National Museum.

Arabic inscriptions on coins, tombstones, buildings, and rocks (for graffiti)
from Egypt to Iraq.

Second, the papyrus is written in Greek and Arabic. This is surprising
because we have no documents written in Arabic prior to 643. We knew
that it was used before this on the evidence of a few inscriptions in Arabic
from the preceding centuries, but now we can infer, given that papyri like
no. 558 are written quite competently, that an Arabic administrative tradition
existed before the seventh century. It was evidently a tradition nurtured by the
Byzantine world, for it shares the same notions of contract, surety, and mutual
guarantee. It also follows the practice, established by edict of the emperor
Maurice (580–602), of beginning with an invocation to God: the Arabic *bismillah* is an exact translation of the Greek *en onomati tou theou* ("in the name of
God"). The obvious candidates for practitioners of such a tradition would
have been the various Arab tribes allied to the Byzantine and Persian empires
in the fifth and sixth centuries AD whom we know were using Arabic already in
the sixth century and who would have had at least a rudimentary bureaucracy.

CARL A. RUDISILL LIBRARY
LENOIR-RHYNE UNIVERSITY

A third revealing feature of Papyrus 558 is its designation of the conquerors as *magaritai* (also written *moagaritai*), which is how they are most commonly referred to in Greek documents of the seventh century. A clearly related term is found in Syriac literary texts from the 640s onward, namely, *mhaggre*. Both terms are intended to convey the Arabic term *muhajir*, which is the word used in Muhammad's foundation agreement to specify those who had left Mecca with him to find refuge in Medina and begin the war against the infidels. Evidently the word had become applied since then to all those who left their homeland to join in the battle against the empires. A crucial component of its meaning was settling, for it is often contrasted with the word *ta'arrub*, which meant "to return to desert life"; as one early governor of Iraq said: "a *muhajir* is never a nomad." In the Qur'an it is often linked with jihad, both being conducted "in God's path." The word has the meaning, then, of both soldier and settler, but to the conquered peoples it simply served as a label for the conquering armies, and in the rare cases that *magaritai* features in a bilingual Greek-Arabic document it is rendered in Arabic by the word *juyush*, that is, troops.[41] Since it is the most common word for the conquerors in the seventh century, employed by themselves and by the conquered, we should really speak of the conquests of the *muhajirun*, rather than of the Arabs or Muslims, which only become popular terms in the eighth century. At the very least, we should recognize this primary impulse of the movement after Muhammad's death, namely, to conquer and settle, a message that must have originated in the early drive to recruit the nomadic tribes of Arabia and the Syrian desert.

CARL A. RUDISILL LIBRARY
LENOIR-RHYNE UNIVERSITY

Chapter Four

THE PUSH FOR CONSTANTINOPLE (652–685)

here was very little expansion of Arab territory during these three decades. This was partly because the Arabs became bogged down in two civil wars (656–61 and 683–92), and partly because the caliph Mu'awiya felt it prudent to direct some of his efforts to establishing administrative control over what had already been taken lest it slip out of Arab hands. Moreover, he was convinced that if he could just capture Constantinople then the rest of the Byzantine Empire would crumble, as had happened with the Persian Empire after the successful Arab siege of its capital. As he was forever fond of saying to his confidants: "tighten the noose around the Byzantines and the other nations will follow."[1] To this end he dispatched regular campaigns into Anatolia from northern Syria in order to place a constant drain on Byzantine resources and then, at opportune moments, launched combined sea and land assaults on the imperial city itself.

The first major land and sea expedition against Constantinople, initiated in 654, came to an abrupt end when a large part of the Arab fleet was destroyed by a storm. This loss diminished the reputation of the caliph 'Uthman somewhat and contributed to the outbreak of civil war that plagued the Arabs from

656 to 661. They began to fight among themselves, observed the contemporary Armenian chronicler Sebeos: those in Egypt and Arabia united; they killed 'Uthman, plundered the treasury, and installed another king, namely, 'Ali, Muhammad's son-in-law. Then, when Mu'awiya, who was at that time the commander-in-chief in Syria, saw what had occurred, he mustered his troops and joined the fray. Eventually, "after the blood of the slaughter of immense multitudes flowed thickly among their armies," Mu'awiya fought and killed 'Ali, and brought all the Arabs into submission to himself "and he made peace with all."[2] Whoever ruled the new Arab empire wielded enormous power and so it was inevitable that there would be competition for the top job. Moreover, the spoils of war were enormous and there was fierce contention over how they should be shared out. Veterans of the early battles felt that they should get more than those who signed up later, and the nascent state wanted to cream off revenue to a central treasury whereas regional governors and generals in the field clamored for it to be distributed where it was acquired.

In order to have a free hand to deal with the infighting, Mu'awiya had been obliged to beg a truce from Byzantium and to pay heavy tribute for the privilege. This was a godsend for the emperor Constans, who wisely used the period of respite to reorganize the military defense of what remained of his empire. Anatolia needed to be reinforced so that it could withstand the constant Arab incursions from northern Syria. It was divided into four sectors and each had its own standing army, made up in part from what was left of the eastern field armies combined with troops from Thrace (the region to the west of Constantinople), Armenia, and what was called the Obsequium, a collection of units that had been dedicated to the protection of emperors on campaign. Constans then sought to strengthen his alliances, first in Caucasia, where he toured in 660–61, and then in Italy, where he won the support of a leading Lombard prince. After a ceremonial visit to Rome in 663 he traveled to Syracuse in Sicily, where he spent the next six years raising money and overseeing the construction and manning of a large fleet by means of which he hoped to maintain Byzantine dominance over the Mediterranean and keep Africa in Byzantine hands. These measures served well his son, Constantine IV (668–85), who was able to draw upon them to defend Constantinople when the Arabs launched a new offensive in 668–70, not long after his accession.

One initiative that Mu'awiya instituted to try to bring about the stability of the empire ended up having precisely the opposite effect, in the beginning at least. When he nominated his own son as his successor, widespread fury erupted at what was interpreted as an attempt by the Umayyad family to monopolize power. There were other families, such as the Zubayrids and 'Alids, who thought they had an equal if not better claim to rule. And then there were those who opposed any move by a single family to assert their dominance, preferring that the sovereign be elected on the basis of merit and be bound by the dictates of God rather than by his own clan interests. Mu'awiya's inauguration of dynastic rule provoked a second civil war that was even more destructive than the first—as one early Christian chronicler succinctly noted: "Waging countless great battles against each other, an innumerable multitude of men fell from each army in their communal warfare"[3]—and the slaughter continued for almost a decade (683–92). This gave a number of parties around the edges of the Arab empire the opportunity to throw off their allegiance, and it was a boon for Byzantium, since it gave them a further respite and obliged the Umayyads once more to make a truce so that they could wage war against their internal opponents.

Attempts on Constantinople

The Byzantines easily repulsed Mu'awiya's exploratory foray in the direction of Constantinople in 649, but the thought of the Arabs taking to the waves worried the emperor Constans enough to request a three-year truce (ca. 650–53). We can pick up the story from Sebeos, who gives a particularly detailed account.[4] The death of the Persian emperor Yazdgird in 652 emboldened Mu'awiya to renew hostilities against Byzantium "so that they might take Constantinople and exterminate that kingdom as well." He is even said to have composed a letter to Constans offering to let him remain "the great prince" in his lands and to retain a quarter of the wealth of the realm if he would submit and "abandon that vain cult which you learned from childhood, deny Jesus and turn to the great God whom I worship, the God of our father Abraham." For the next two years, Mu'awiya threw himself into preparing a huge naval and land attack force. He levied troops from all the garrisons throughout the lands the Arabs had conquered. They constructed warships in Levantine ports and in Alexandria, and this is reflected in contemporary papyri, which depict a scene of frenzied activity as carpenters, caulkers (joint-sealers), blacksmiths, and oarsmen were press-ganged into service and supplies were commandeered for the soldiers and crew. There were the usual large troop-carrying vessels, numbering some 300, which were able to transport a thousand elite cavalry on each one, and they also bore various items of military hardware, such as catapults and towers, which would enable them to breach walls or to scale them. In addition, however, there were special light ships, with only a hundred men aboard, "so that they might rapidly dart to and fro over the waves of the sea around the very large ships," which would, it was hoped, give the Arab fleet a tactical advantage.

The plan was that Mu'awiya would march by land as far as Chalcedon, which lay across the Bosphorus from Constantinople, while the general Abu l-A'war would command the Arab armada and sail up to the Byzantine capital (Map 4.1). There was some delay because of a minor incident in Levantine Tripoli. Two men broke down the gates of the city prison and liberated numerous Byzantine captives, and together they slew the governor of the city along with his retinue and burned all the ships moored in the port before escaping in a small boat to Byzantium. Mu'awiya was furious but refused to let his plans be derailed. He went ahead to Chalcedon while Abu l-A'war oversaw the completion of the shipbuilding before he too set off, probably in the summer of 654. When they were approaching Phoenix, off the coast of Lycia, south of modern Antalya, they encountered a Byzantine fleet led by the emperor Constans himself and his brother. That both of them accompanied the fleet in person is a measure of how seriously they viewed the threat. In the event the light vessels of the Arabs easily outmaneuvered the large cumbersome Byzantine ships. It looked like the emperor himself might be captured, but one foresighted soldier whisked his master onto another ship in time to make a fast getaway, while another man courageously put on the imperial robes and "stationed himself bravely on the imperial ship, killing many of the enemy before giving up his life on behalf of the king." The emperor and his brother sailed as swiftly as they could back to Constantinople, while the rest of the Byzantine fleet was cut to pieces "on a sea so violent that it was said that dense spray ascended

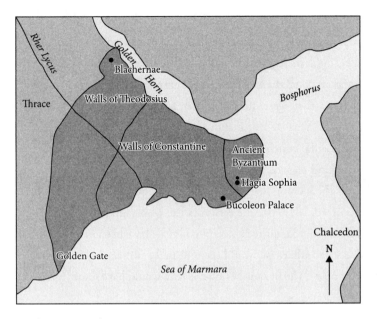

MAP 4.1 Constantinople.

among the ships like dust from dry land and that the sea was dyed with blood."
Abu l-A'war ordered that they fish out the corpses of the Byzantines and their
number was estimated at some 20,000.

The Arab fleet continued toward Constantinople, chasing the surviving
Byzantine ships as far as Rhodes. The capital's inhabitants were now nervous,
since they knew about the Arabs' approach by land and by sea, and were
shaken by the naval defeat at Phoenix. The emperor entered the church of
Hagia Sophia and implored God to aid the city; he lifted the crown from his
head, put aside the purple, donned sackcloth and sat on ashes, and ordered a
fast to be proclaimed in Constantinople. As the Arabs drew near in the early
autumn of 654, Abu l-A'war ordered the ships to be deployed in lines and
to attack the city, but out of nowhere a storm brewed, a miracle worked by
God to save the Byzantine capital, said its inhabitants. The sea was stirred
up from the depths; its waves piled up high "like the summits of very high
mountains," and, together with the raging wind, broke up the Arab ships
and sent their war machines and sailors plunging headlong into the seething
ocean. When the Arabs encamped at Chalcedon saw the power of the storm

and the destruction it wrought, they slipped away by night and began the long march home. A contingent that Mu'awiya had left near Cappadocian Caesarea, modern Kayseri, to safeguard his rear attempted to salvage some honor and attacked the local Byzantine garrison, but even here the Arabs were defeated and they were obliged to flee to safety in northern Mesopotamia. Muslim historians do not mention this defeat, focusing instead on the victory at Phoenix, which is called in Arabic the Battle of the Masts. However, there are good reasons to give Sebeos's narrative credence. He was a contemporary of these events, writing in the early 660s, so less than a decade after they occurred. Moreover, he recounts the whole affair with such a wealth of detail that it is difficult to believe it could all have been manufactured. It also explains what otherwise would seem to make no sense, that is, why the Arab fleet, having got the Byzantines on the run, would have simply given up at this point and gone home.

Byzantium enjoyed a period of relative calm while Mu'awiya was distracted by civil war at home, but then in 667 the Byzantine commander of the Armenian army, a man named Shabur, rebelled against Constans and sought the aid of the caliph Mu'awiya in his bid to win the rule of the Byzantine Empire for himself. This event is narrated very vividly and at great length by a near contemporary Syrian author.[5] The drama takes place at the court of Mu'awiya in Damascus. An envoy of Shabur named Sergius arrives there to plead his master's case before the caliph. On receiving news of this mutiny, Emperor Constans dispatches his chamberlain, the eunuch Andrew, to appeal to Mu'awiya not to become involved in this plot. Sergius is portrayed as weak and fawning; he initially prostrates himself before his superior, Andrew, but then, goaded and mocked by Mu'awiya for his cowardly obsequiousness, he taunts Andrew for his lack of the appurtenances of manhood. Andrew is the hero of the story; he does not tremble before the caliph, but upbraids him for failing to distinguish between a legitimate sovereign and a perfidious insurgent, and he sternly warns the rebel's messenger of the consequences of his disrespectfulness. All works out well for the hero, for Sergius is captured on his return to Armenia and killed with his testicles placed next to him—a fitting punishment for one "so proud of his private parts"—and Shabur has his brains dashed out when his horse rears up as he was passing through a city gate.

This left Mu'awiya in something of a quandary, for he had already sent troops to Shabur under the command of the highly respected Fadala ibn 'Ubayd al-Ansari. When the latter learned of the death of Shabur, he wrote to Mu'awiya asking what he should do. The caliph determined to take this opportunity to launch another major assault on the Byzantine capital. He ordered Fadala to winter in Melitene, in southern Anatolia, and dispatched his son Yazid with a large body of cavalry to catch up with Fadala and then for the two of them to march on toward Constantinople. This they did and by the summer of 668 they had reached Chalcedon. In the meantime, a fleet was readied and dispatched. The emperor Constantine IV, on being informed of this major expedition advancing toward Constantinople, had large bireme boats built and ordered them to be stationed at the city's eastern harbor. In the following year, the Arab fleet set sail and came to anchor in the region of Thrace, to the southwest of the capital, on the European shore. "Every day there was a military engagement from morning until evening, with thrust and counter-thrust," and this went on from spring until autumn. Neither side landed a fatal blow on the other, and so, as the weather deteriorated, the Arabs looked for somewhere to spend the winter. They captured the ancient city of Cyzicus, just across the Sea of Marmara from Constantinople, and there made secure their fleet. The following spring they set out once more and the naval jousting match recommenced.

For two years, in 668 and 669, the blockade of the imperial city continued. We know this from a contemporary archivist who went to retrieve some documents during a council at Constantinople in 681 and found a synodical letter of the patriarch Thomas (667–69) to the pope, which was still sealed and which he had not been able to send for the two years that he was patriarch "because of the prolonged incursion of the impious Saracens and their siege."[6] It is not certain what led to the end of this blockade, but one early chronicle says that the Arabs maintained it "until they could no longer bear the pain of hunger and pestilence," at which point the land force returned, plundering Anatolian towns along the way. Two other factors might have tipped the balance in favor of the Byzantines. The first is that the emperor Constantine had ships brought from the central Mediterranean, still outside the control of the Arabs, then along the coast of Greece and finally driven on rollers overland across the Gallipoli peninsula—an arduous task, but presumably the only way to bring in naval reinforcements while the Hellespont was blocked by the Arabs. The second is that the Byzantines had invented a new weapon, namely, Greek fire. Its discovery is attributed to a certain Callinicus, an architect or carpenter from Baalbek in Syria, who had come from there as a refugee to the Byzantine Empire; he concocted a flaming substance, called naphthalene, which could be directed at enemy ships by means of a long metal siphon (Figure 4.I).[7] This weapon the Byzantines were to put to good effect time and time again. In 673, for example, an Arab raiding party reached Lycia by boat, but those who disembarked were routed by a substantial Byzantine force headed by three generals, and those who escaped by sea were treated to a dose of Greek fire administered by some Byzantine skiffs that had managed to catch up with them.[8]

FIGURE 4.I An example of the use of Greek fire from illustration in Ms Matritensis gr. Vitr. 26-2, fol. 34v. © Madrid National Library.

Caucasia

The emperor Constans also had to worry about Byzantium's eastern flank because of the pact that had been concluded in 653 between the Armenian commander Theodore Rshtuni and the Arabs. Not only was Armenia a long-standing and close ally, but also it was an important source of military manpower and a crucial bulwark against any attack from the east. Constans had written a number of letters to Theodore urging him to reinstate the long-standing alliance between their realms, but received no answer.[9] He decided then to go in person, and in the summer of 653 he set off with a huge military escort, a display of strength evidently intended to impress, heading for Karin, now called Erzerum in modern eastern Turkey. On the way, an Arab delegation brought Constans a message from Mu'awiya warning him: "Armenia is mine, do not go there; but if you do go, I shall attack you and shall make sure that you cannot escape." However, Constans dismissed it contemptuously, saying that it was for God to judge such matters. Once at Karin, he stayed for a few days to meet and talk with those Armenian princes still loyal to him, who explained the intentions of Theodore and "the frequent coming and going to him of envoys from the Arabs." Constans then sent back the majority of the army and continued with a smaller retinue to Dvin, where he stayed with the head of the Armenian church, celebrating the liturgy with him so as to emphasize the closeness of the Byzantine-Armenian relationship.

At this point news came from Constantinople that the Arabs were planning an attack on the capital itself and Constans was obliged to cut short his trip and return in haste. He gave command of the Byzantine army in Armenia to the patrician Maurianus with orders that he keep nudging the Armenian princes back into allegiance with Byzantium. However, Theodore Rshtuni received reinforcements of 7,000 Arab soldiers and was easily able, once the winter had passed, to put the Byzantine troops to flight, driving them back to the Black Sea coast. This, plus the rumors circulating about the huge assault being unleashed upon Constantinople, impelled the rest of the Armenian princes to submit to the Arabs. Theodore now went in honor to Damascus to offer Mu'awiya presents and to receive from him robes of gold and a banner of his own colors and, most important, the rank of prince of Armenia along with oversight of Georgia, Albania, and Siunik. These three principalities had been allied to the Persian Empire, but with the latter now defunct, Theodore could hope to bring them back into the fold of the Greater Armenian Kingdom that had existed before AD 428.

News of the devastating defeat of the Arab expeditionary force to Constantinople began to filter through to Caucasia in the autumn of 654 and it had the double effect of weakening the morale of the Arabs campaigning there and stiffening the resolve of those opposing them. The Arab unit stationed by Dvin, headed by the general Habib ibn Maslama, "a merciless executioner," thought to attack Georgia, whose inhabitants were warned that "they should either submit or abandon their country." The Georgians ignored these threats and vowed to fight to the last man, but in the end they were spared the trouble, for the Arab advance was beset by heavy snow and forced to retreat. The patrician Maurianus and his men, who had spent much of 654 lying low in Trebizond, now felt confident enough to attempt once more to carry out the instructions imparted to them by the emperor Constans, namely, to recapture Armenia for Byzantium. First they harried the retreating Arabs, who were unaccustomed to the extreme cold and unwilling to fight; rather than return to their previous quarters at Dvin, they crossed the Araxes River and kept going south to the plains around Lake Urmiah. Maurianus took the opportunity to sack the fortress of Dvin and to attack the stronghold of Nakhchawan some seventy miles to the southeast. On top of all this the inhabitants of Media, northwest Iran, threw off their submission to the Arabs and "killed the chief of the tax-collectors." Seeking to further his northern alliance against the Arabs, Constans at once sent an emissary "to the prince of the Medes and made peace proposals to him," and received many gifts from him in return.

In order to regain at least some of their prestige and avoid an all-out rebellion on many fronts, the Arabs now needed to make a show of strength, and so two regiments were hurriedly dispatched to the north from Iraq. One contingent, headed by Habib ibn Maslama, had the objective of regaining control of Armenia. In the spring of 655 they moved against the Byzantines, who were besieging Nakhchawan. With relative ease they defeated them, slaying many while the rest fled, including Maurianus himself. The Arabs continued on to Karin. Its inhabitants, ill equipped to offer military resistance, opened the gates of the city, submitted, and yielded up a substantial quantity of gold and silver and other precious goods. Thereafter the Arabs "ravaged all the land of Armenia, Albania and Siunik, and stripped all the churches; they seized as hostages the leading princes of the country, and the wives, sons and daughters of many people." A second Arab contingent was charged with the job of taming the eastern side of Caucasia; according to Muslim sources it was captained by the veteran soldier Salman ibn Rabi'a al-Bahili and their goal was the Khazar forward base of Balanjar, in modern Dagestan. They headed for the coastal region of the Caspian Sea and then marched northward "towards the people by the Caspian Gates." They passed the fortress city of Darband, called by the Arabs the "Gate of Gates" (Bab al-Abwab), a reference to its location at the start of the east-west wall constructed by the Sasanians as part of a trans-Caucasian barrier to keep out the barbarians to the north (Figure 4.2). At first they encountered only a local defensive force, "the guards of that place," but

FIGURE 4.2 Walls of Darband (Bab al-Abwab) in Dagestan (Russia), by the Caspian Sea (ca. 1890). Photo from ca. 1890 by Dmitry Yermakov.

then a large army of nomads appeared on the scene and they caught the Arabs in a classic pincer movement. One branch attacked them from the front, while another came up behind them cutting off their retreat. The only escape was up through the difficult terrain of the Caucasus Mountains and only a very few, "naked and unshod, on foot and wounded, reached the area of Ctesiphon, their own homeland." These nomads were almost certainly the Khazars, who were at this time establishing themselves in the southern Russian steppe and northern Caucasia and beginning to flex their muscles.

Theodore Rshtuni died in 655 and he was succeeded as prince of Armenia by his son-in-law Hamazasp Mamikonean, "a virtuous man in all respects. . . but he was not trained and experienced in the details of military skill." The major Arab defeat plus the outbreak of civil war among the Arabs in 656 emboldened Hamazasp, who sought to live up to "the valiant character of his ancestral house," to abandon submission to the Arabs and resume ties once more with the Byzantine Empire. This change of allegiance was warmly welcomed by Constans, who gave him silver cushions and the rank of prince of Armenia. There was a high price to pay for this policy, though, for a furious Mu'awiya rounded up all the hostages that had been brought from that region and had them all put to death, "about 1775 people." All the princes of Siunik and Albania followed suit with the Armenians and pledged allegiance to Emperor Constans. This meant that there was a Christian pro-Byzantine coalition across Caucasia, and Constans took full advantage of the respite granted him by the Arab civil war to try to strengthen this bulwark against the Arabs. In his nineteenth regnal year (659–60) he set off on a grand procession through the region, meeting local lords and handing out gifts and titles. Juansher, prince of Albania, came to meet him in Media, which Constans hoped also to wrest from Arab control. He took the Holy Cross and cut off a piece in Juansher's presence and gave it to him, saying: "Let this be a tower of strength for yourself and your sons against the enemy."

By 661, however, the Arab civil war was at an end and Mu'awiya was reasserting his authority over the conquered lands. Juansher observed how the emperor of Byzantium had been rendered powerless and weak by the Arabs, "who had consumed the former's populous markets and cities like a flame," and he became worried that they might do the same to his lands. He therefore determined to switch sides and join the Arabs. In the year 664 he prepared magnificent presents and took them "to salute the conqueror of the world." Mu'awiya received him with great pomp and ceremony and set his seal to a treaty of sincere and perpetual friendship between them. On his return, Juansher met with a number of Armenian nobles who apparently received him with honor, and so it is likely that they had made a similar decision and that Byzantium's Caucasian bulwark had already crumbled. To reinforce his writ Mu'awiya had appointed Gregory Mamikonean, who had been a hostage in Damascus, to be the prince of Armenia and returned him to his country with great honors. During all the time that he served in this capacity, 662–85, Gregory was able to maintain Armenia free from all marauding and attack, and this perhaps explains the many churches that were constructed there in his time. For the moment then, though they had "to submit to the yoke of vassalage of the king of the South," these Caucasian princes did at least retain their status and exercised a free hand within their realms. And the second Arab civil war (683–92) gave them further respite, for during this time the Armenians, the Georgians, and the Albanians ceased to pay tribute to the Arabs. In some ways things had not changed so much for the lords of Caucasia: as before they were torn between two empires; it was just that now the Arabs had taken the place of the Persians.

Northern Iran and the Eastern Frontier (Maps 3.3 and 4.2)

Like Caucasia, northern Iran and Central Asia were endowed with the sort of terrain that impeded easy conquest and they were able to retain a fair degree of independence throughout the seventh century. As well as the mountain ranges of the Elburz in the north, the Kopet Dag in the northeast, the Paropamisus and Hindu Kush in the east, there are a number of deserts that hamper travel: the Kavir and Lut in the center, the Karakum to the northeast, and the Margo and Rigestan to the southeast. It goes without saying, then, that the conquest of this land by the Arabs proceeded very slowly. By 652 they had a grip on the western central plateau around Nihawand and on the southwest provinces of Khuzistan, Fars, and Kirman, but the north and the east had experienced little more than opportunistic raiding. The only major Arab garrison was at Merv, and even here the troops were not permanently settled but came on rotation from Iraq. Arab rule was still, therefore, very precarious, but the death of Yazdgird and the flight of his sons to the east meant that there was no obvious person to lead a comeback and most of the region's potentates were happy to do deals with the new rulers in exchange for being left alone. For example, when the Arabs approached Merv al-Rudh, in modern northwest

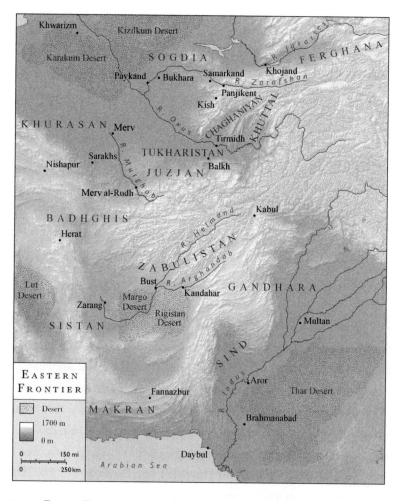

MAP 4.2 Eastern Frontier.

Afghanistan, its local lord sent a letter asking them to respect the agreement that his great-grandfather had made with the emperor Khusrau I "after killing the serpent that used to eat people," which had exempted his family from tax and guaranteed its hereditary governorship of the region.[10] The Arabs mostly accepted these requests, since it gave them the time they needed to gradually establish an administrative infrastructure and to win over or strike down individual nobles and cities one by one rather than en masse.

Northern Iran

There are three distinct sectors in northern Iran. On the west side is Azerbaijan, extending southwest from the western shores of the Caspian Sea. Its governor, based at the capital of Ardabil, had initially opposed the Arabs, but when the latter promised not to kill or enslave anyone or to destroy any fire temples, and to allow them to maintain their observance of Zoroastrianism and their "traditional dancing festivals," he agreed to a treaty. In return, the Arabs received yearly tribute and the right to station a garrison in the capital. In the center are the Caspian provinces, separated from the central Iranian plateau by the Elburz Mountains and blessed with a rich and varied flora due to the humidity of the Caspian Sea. This isolation favored strong local identities and willful petty rulers, who are celebrated in a large number of local histories drafted in medieval times. "They would demand a treaty one time," complained one Muslim author, "but then refuse to pay the tribute the next time, continually starting war and suing for peace." The ruler of Tabaristan (also known as Mazandaran) was particularly independent-minded and it was known even to the Chinese, to whose court he sent emissaries, that he refused to submit to the Arabs. Arab generals did every now and then have a go at asserting their authority over these regions, but most left with a bloody nose. In 674, for example, Masqala ibn Hubayra headed for Tabaristan with 10,000 men seeking to take charge of the land assigned to him, but when they began to ascend the steep valleys the locals rolled down rocks onto their heads, wiping out much of that army. Masqala was obliged to make peace with the people, recognizing their autonomy, in return for "payment of 500,000 dirhams, 100 shawls and 300 head (of slaves)."

Finally, on the east side, are the fertile plains of Gurgan and the steppe lands of Dihistan, sandwiched between the Caspian Sea and the Karakum Desert, where the Persian emperor Peroz met his end in AD 484. These were the preserve of the Turkish Chol (Arabic: Sul) dynasty, which had already made its home there before the Arab conquests. The region was left alone until the reign of Sulayman (715–17), who dispatched the redoubtable general Yazid ibn al-Muhallab to seek its submission. He besieged the incumbent monarch for several months, but was not able to obtain his surrender and agreed to leave on condition of payment of tribute. As soon as he had gone, the locals threw off their allegiance and killed the agent of the government who had been left behind. This provoked a furious reaction from Yazid, who fought them for months until they finally surrendered, and this time "he gibbeted their warriors" and, in fulfillment of an earlier threat, he made bread from their blood and ate it. Thus this country reluctantly became part of the Arab Empire, though like the other Caspian provinces it retained its distinctiveness and detachedness from the central government for many centuries to come.[11]

The Northeast Frontier

The eastern frontier of Iran effectively fell into a northern sector and a southern sector, which lay on either side of the imposing Hindu Kush mountain range. The northern sector was dominated by the upper reaches of the Oxus and Jaxartes Rivers, and was bounded to the west by the Karakum desert and to the north by the Kizilkum desert. It was a world divided into numerous micro-regions by these mountains, rivers, and deserts, and this topographical diversity was matched by political diversity, with a bewildering array of princes and lords ruling over discrete locales. The most important principalities were Tukharistan (ancient Bactria), centered around Balkh in the very north of modern Afghanistan, and Sogdia, which comprised the cities that were strung out along the Zarafshan River, together with their agricultural hinterlands, in particular Bukhara and Samarkand in modern Uzbekistan. This northern sector was much richer than its southern counterpart, especially Sogdia, the inhabitants of which had managed to establish themselves in the pre-Islamic period as the chief middlemen in the overland trade between China, Iran, and Byzantium. This means that it is also better documented than its southern counterpart, both attracting more attention from the world powers, especially China, and even providing us with some local sources in the native languages of Bactrian and Sogdian. These help to bring out the diversity of this land, for whereas Muslim authors tended only to see infidels, contemporary texts make clear that Islam had to jostle for position with Zoroastrianism, Buddhism, Manichaeism, and Christianity for a good while. And where Muslim authors tended to label everyone as Turks or Persians, other texts can help to bring out the rich tapestry of local identities that existed in this region.

The Chinese pilgrim Xuanzang traveled through this region in the early seventh century and he reveals something of this complex mosaic. The country was divided, he tells us, into twenty-seven states, each with separate chiefs but all subject to the Turks. He had arrived shortly before the empire of the western Turks disintegrated under pressure from a resurgent China. Nevertheless, their khagan (leader) still seemed an impressive figure to Xuanzang, who paid him a visit in the year 629-30 in the vicinity of Lake Issykul, in modern Kyrgyzstan: "He was surrounded by about two hundred high-ranking companions (tarkhans), all clothed in brocade, with their hair braided. On the right and the left he was attended by troops clad in furs and fine-spun hair garments, carrying lances, bows and standards, and mounted on camels and horses." They sat in "a pavilion adorned with golden flower ornaments which blinded the eye with their glitter." The officers, kitted out in resplendent garments of embroidered silk, had spread out mats and all the while the khagan's bodyguard stood behind in readiness. Food, wine, and conversation followed, and the pilgrim was sent off with warm regards and commendations, bearing gifts of red satin vestments and fifty pieces of silk.[12] But not long afterward this khagan was killed in a revolt against his authority and the regime he headed faltered, its last leader dying a prisoner in China in 659. The Arabs thus arrived at a time when there was something of a power vacuum at the top. The Chinese emperor Gaozong (650–83) claimed the area formerly overseen by the Turks, since he regarded the latter as vassals of China, but in practical terms this meant little given the difficulty of the terrain and its considerable distance from the imperial heartlands. Circumstances would change at the end of the seventh century when the Turks reasserted their authority and posed a serious threat to the Arabs, but until then the latter had no option but to deal with all the myriad chiefs of this region individually, whether by force or by diplomacy.

The first Arab to tackle the subjugation of this northern sector was 'Abdallah ibn 'Amir, the energetic and capable governor of Basra (649–56, 661–64).[13] He had first set about obtaining the submission of Merv and the smaller settlements of Khurasan, such as Nishapur and Sarakhs, then moved eastward into what is now western Afghanistan. Usually treaties were agreed that guaranteed life and property in return for an annual cash payment, though sometimes slaves, animals, and foodstuffs were given as well or instead; the apportionment of the tribute among the population was the responsibility of the local grandees (*dihqans*) and the Muslims had only to take receipt of it. An expeditionary force entered Tukharistan, in modern north Afghanistan, and agreed to terms with Balkh, a rich agricultural oasis and a renowned center of Buddhism, but did not cross the Oxus River. Ibn 'Amir himself negotiated with the leaders beyond this watery boundary, agreeing not to go over to their side as long as they gave tribute of cattle, male and female slaves, silk, and garments. During the first Arab civil war (656–61), however, all these gains were reversed, for all of northeast Iran took the opportunity to throw off its allegiance. When Ziyad ibn Abi Sufyan took charge of the whole of Persia for Mu'awiya in 670, he was able to bring some order and consistency to the Arab approach to their eastern frontier lands. He centralized the administration at Merv and settled in and around this city 50,000 families from Iraq, presumably with promises of lucrative rewards for those campaigning in this gateway to the east. This meant that there was now a local base of operations and a pool of military manpower, which made it much easier to launch sorties into Transoxania (the lands beyond the Oxus River) than before, when troops had to be drawn from faraway Basra. Subsequent governors of Khurasan took advantage of this resource to try to advance Arab control in the region. Ziyad's own son 'Ubaydallah (673–76) was "the first Arab to cross the river (Oxus) to Bukhara," marching against and defeating the Bukhar Khuda ("the lord of Bukhara"), who ruled the wealthy emporia of Paykand and Bukhara.

At this point the local historical tradition focuses on the person of the Bukhar Khuda's wife, referred to simply as the Khatun ("the lady") and celebrated for her wisdom and capable management. Her husband died leaving an infant son, and so she assumed control, acting as the regent of the country for fifteen years and making deals with various Arab leaders in the best interests of her subjects. Every day, it is said, she would ride out of the fortress on a horse and, halting at the gate of the forage-sellers, she would sit on a throne while before her stood slaves, eunuchs, and nobles. Standing at a distance were "two hundred youths from the landowners and the princes ready for service, girded with gold belts and bearing swords." As soon as she appeared, "all made obeisance to her and stood in two rows while she inquired into the affairs of state and issued orders and prohibitions." In 676 she provided a contingent of Bukharans to support an Arab assault against that other jewel in the crown of this land, Samarkand, the capital of the Sogdians. Though the latter resisted, they quickly submitted when the Arabs, aided by a local guide, targeted "the castle in which were the sons of their kings and nobles," fearing that all of them might be killed. The Arabs were, then, making solid, if slow, gains during Mu'awiya's reign, but the debilitating civil war that erupted upon the death of Yazid I in 683 reversed this process and it was another two decades before they were able to recuperate their losses.

The Southeast Frontier

The core part of the southern sector of the Arabs' eastern frontier equated roughly to the eastern and southern parts of modern Afghanistan and the northwest of modern Pakistan and comprised cities such as Zarang, Bust, Kandahar, Kabul, and Kapisa. These were difficult lands to traverse owing to the prevalence of harsh deserts and high mountains, but in the southwest the Helmand and Arghandab Rivers made agriculture possible and in the east rich seams of precious metals, especially the silver mines of Panjshir, provided a good living for its inhabitants. The Arabs established reasonable control over Zarang and its hinterland, especially in the time of the long-serving governor 'Abd al-Rahman ibn Samura (654–56, 661–70). This was in the west of the province of Sistan; to the east, separated from Zarang by the Margo desert, the going was much harder, especially in the Hindu Kush Mountains. Here there were a number of local rulers, such as the Rutbils in Arrukhaj (ancient Arachosia) and Zabulistan, and the Kabul Shahs and Khingals in the area of Kabul and Gandhara (around modern Peshawar in northwest Pakistan), who, as we can see from their coinage, maintained their rule and distinctive artistic and religious traditions. At the western end of the Hindu Kush was the province of Badhghis, which, with its capital Herat, was one of the last holdouts of the Hephthalites, the people that had dominated pretty much all of Central Asia in the mid-fifth to the mid-sixth century before losing out to the Turks. These various local lords were very jealous of their independence and were protected by rough terrain, and so, though they sometimes signed truces and treaties for a time, they reneged repeatedly whenever the circumstances were propitious. For example, in 654 Herat and Badhghis threw off their allegiance and ejected the agent of the Arab government, apparently acting at the instigation of a member of the noble Persian Karin family. Zarang reneged three times and in 671 successfully resisted an order from Ziyad ibn Abi Sufyan to kill their Zoroastrian chief priest and extinguish their sacred fires. And upon the death of 'Abd al-Rahman ibn Samura the Kabul Shah rallied a force sufficiently strong to expel the Arabs from Kabul and its environs, and the Rutbil reasserted his control over Zabulistan and Arrukhaj as far as Bust. A treaty was renegotiated, but about the time of the death of the caliph Yazid I (680–83) "the people of Kabul treacherously broke the compact" once again and routed the army sent to re-impose it, and throughout the second Arab civil war the Rutbil maintained his authority by playing off the different Arab factions against one another.[14]

Africa (Map 4.3)

Arab troops in North Africa also found further expansion very slow going. The core of Byzantine Africa, and subsequently of Arab *Ifriqiya*, consisted

MAP 4.3 Western Mediterranean.

of the provinces of Zeugitana or Africa Proconsularis (modern northern Tunisia), Byzacena (southern Tunisia), and Numidia (eastern Algeria). To the west was Mauretania (western Algeria and northern Morocco), dominated by the towering Atlas mountain range. The Vandals had captured this region in the 430s and it remained in their hands for a century before being retaken by the Byzantines in the 530s. The Vandals had ruled with a light hand and had kept mostly to the fertile agricultural areas near to the coast, and so the residents of the interior—in the mountains and deserts—had begun to establish their own polities, which often exhibited an interesting blend of Byzantine and Moorish features. For example, an inscription of 508 from Altava, in modern western Algeria, commemorates the construction of a fort on behalf of a certain Masuna, "king of the peoples of the Moors and the Romans." From about the same time, but farther to the east, in the Aures Mountains of modern eastern Algeria, we have the inscription of Masties, "chief and emperor" (*dux et imp[e]r[ator]*), who "never broke faith with the Romans or with the Moors."[15] Moreover, many of these leaders and their subjects were Christian, as is shown by the numerous Christian tombstones of the fifth to seventh century that are found scattered about these regions. Having retaken the area, the Byzantines naturally wished to reassert their authority, but the locals had got used to running their own affairs. When the new governor of Tripolitania refused to listen to the complaints of some Moorish leaders about pillaging by Byzantine troops and had one of their leaders killed for grabbing his sleeve, a full-scale revolt ensued. It took the Byzantines four years to quash this uprising (544–48), but this was no grand triumph; resentment simmered on and Byzantine rule was thereafter largely confined to the coastal plains, and the Moorish polities mostly retained their autonomy.

It was therefore principally with Moorish peoples, or Berbers as they called them, that the Arabs had to contend once they had deposed Gregory, the Byzantine governor of Africa, in 647. After this there would seem to have been no real threat from Byzantine troops, which perhaps explains why the Arabs left the western portion of North Africa alone for a long time. The next reference in a Christian source to raiding there is not until 670, when an army of Arabs invaded the region, "led away about 80,000 captives and returned to their country." The same notice is found in Muslim sources, where it is speci- fied that it was led by Mu'awiya ibn Hudayj, a general of the powerful south Arabian tribe of Kinda, and was targeted against Jalulah, ancient Cululis, in modern Tunisia. We know from a ten-line poetic inscription in Latin that a lot of restoration work, including the erection of ramparts, was carried out here around the year 540. On the lintel of one of the new city gates, accom- panied by lavish ornamentation, was inscribed a poem that recorded how, "by the hand of Justinian," the "terror of the Moors" had been replaced by sound administration, the rule of law, and the protection of strong walls. It is likely that Jalulah still accommodated Byzantine troops in the seventh century and so was an obvious target for an Arab attack. Mu'awiya brought catapults to weaken the sturdy fortifications, and once they were breached he entered the city, quickly overwhelmed the fighters within, and left again with a number of captives.

At about this time the settlement of Qayrawan was founded, in inner Byzacena, about 100 miles south of Tunis (Figure 4.3). The usual date given in Muslim sources for this event is 670, which is the same year as the establishment of a permanent garrison at Merv, and so we should perhaps view these acts as a policy decision of the caliph Mu'awiya himself. As in the case of Merv, such a move was a big step forward in entrenching and stabilizing Arab rule. With a forward base in Africa, the Arabs could keep troops and supplies there and use it as a launching pad for further conquests without having to return to Alexandria, some 1,200 miles to the east as the crow flies. Mostly likely Mu'awiya ibn Hudayj was responsible for initiating its construction after his

FIGURE 4.3 Mosque of Qayrawan (Kairouan) in Tunisia, founded ca. 670 and expanded in the ninth century. Photo by anonymous German Orientalist from ca. 1900.

siege of Jalulah, which lies twenty miles northwest of Qayrawan. However, other candidates have been proposed. One early source states explicitly that Abu al-Muhajir, a freedman who had risen through the ranks of the administration in Egypt, was "the first to reside in Africa," whereas everyone before him just led raiding expeditions and then returned to Egypt. Other sources favor his rival, 'Uqba ibn Nafi', who bore Abu al-Muhajir a grudge for replacing him as the governor of Africa. As a junior contemporary of the prophet Muhammad as well as the nephew of the conqueror of Egypt, 'Amr ibn al-'As, 'Uqba tends to come off better. He is portrayed as a larger-than-life, swashbuckling character, and subsequently gained a cult following as the man who almost single-handedly conquered most of modern Algeria and Morocco in the name of Islam (there is still a shrine dedicated to him in central Algeria). "I have sold my soul to God Almighty," he said as he set off westward at break-neck speed, defeating army after army, finally reaching the Atlantic Ocean where he railed against the enforced curtailment of his onslaught, bearing witness to God that if he could find a way to cross the sea and continue his conquests he would surely do so.

The Failure of Byzantium and Persia to Recover

In many ways the initial success of the Arab conquests is not so surprising. With their mobility and manpower, steppe and desert tribes have frequently demonstrated their ability to strike hard and fast and make rapid gains. For instance, a fourth-century Saracen queen by the name of Mawiya led her troops into Phoenicia and Palestine as far as the regions of Egypt notching up victories wherever she went so that in the end the Romans found it necessary to send an embassy to her in order to solicit peace. And the Mongols were able to capture more landmass than any settled power in just seven decades (1206–79). But once the military machinery of empire has finally been put into motion, it is normally able to halt the invaders in their tracks by virtue of its superior organizational capability or to neutralize the threat by diplomacy and a range of incentives. So what went wrong for the empires in the seventh century or, to look at it the other way, what went right for the Arabs? The total collapse of the Persian Empire seems particularly shocking given that the Sasanian dynasty had managed it successfully for some 430 years.

Persia certainly did not give up without a fight—Christian and Muslim historians allude to uprisings across Iran at different times in different cities. Rayy, for example, reneged on its peace treaty with the Arabs on a number of occasions, and in 654–55 there was a widespread rebellion across northwest Iran, which involved the murder of the Arab agent responsible for tax collection.[16] The insurgents of this rugged mountainous region made use of "the deep forested valleys, the precipices and the rocky peaks" to lead furtive guerrilla-style raids against their overlords. They assembled the surviving militia and organized into battalions initiating a resistance movement that they hoped would free them "from the teeth of the dragon." Their grievance was in part high taxes and in part the abolition of the cavalry and the traditional office of prince of their country. Their tactics evidently bore fruit, at least for a while, for many Arabs perished in the rough terrain, and many were wounded from arrows in the impenetrable fens, which prompted them for a time to flee these lands. However, these and other revolts did not lead to a sustained reversal of Arab gains. The problem for Persia was that its extensive mountain ranges and deserts made large-scale coordinated action very difficult, and so the revolts remained local affairs rather than countrywide. It also meant that Iran was divided into numerous regions, each governed by different noble families and local lords. These had been bound together in a close alliance with the ruling Sasanian dynasty, but the disastrous defeat of Khusrau II in 628 and the ensuing years of civil war loosened that alliance, and the death of Yazdgird led to its complete dissolution.

The Byzantines were better placed than the Persians to withstand the Arab onslaught. In particular, whereas there was no natural barrier and very little distance between Arabia and the Persian capital, Seleucia-Ctesiphon, the steep Taurus Mountains and some 600 miles separated the Byzantine capital from even the northernmost tip of the Syrian desert. Every year the Arabs would send expeditions into Anatolia, but they would be forced to withdraw once the long, hard winter had set in, losing any gains they had made in the summer. On the downside, however, it was similarly problematic for the Byzantines to march an army all the way across Anatolia to Syria. All they could do was initiate sabotage operations along the southern and eastern Mediterranean littoral. The most successful of these missions was carried out in the late 670s and early 680s by the emperor Constantine IV in response to a series of Arab sorties against Constantinople. He dispatched a guerrilla force, dubbed the "insurgents" (*mardaites*), which sailed to the coast of Tyre and Sidon. After disembarking they made their way up into the Lebanese mountain range. There they won over to their cause the Jarajima, who were longtime residents of the Mount Amanus region around Antioch, described by a near contemporary as "the armed men who from olden times had practised banditry in the mountains of Lebanon." They had initially tried to stay out of the Arab-Byzantine wars, but when pressured by the Arabs they grudgingly agreed to act as spies and frontier guards for them as long as they paid no taxes. They had no love of Arab rule, though, and so when the *mardaites* encouraged them to revolt they willingly agreed. In addition, many runaway slaves and Aramaean peasants joined them so that in a short time their ranks swelled to many thousands. Once they had attained sufficient numbers they spread from the mountains around Antioch in the north to the peaks around Galilee in the south, and from these heights they launched raids against the settled lands all around them.

They were evidently very successful and a real thorn in the Arab side, for when ʿAbd al-Malik, faced with a major civil war at home, sought to renew the peace agreement made by his predecessors with Byzantium, one of his key requests was that "the emperor should remove the host of the *mardaites* from Lebanon and prevent their incursions."[17] The Byzantines could therefore inflict losses on the Arab regime, especially on the settlements of the Mediterranean coast, but they could not translate this into a full-scale recovery of their former possessions. To march an army all the way from the coast across the mountains to Damascus was beyond their capacity, and once the Arabs had moved their capital to faraway Baghdad, the Byzantines' chances of a comeback were even slimmer.

Muʿawiya's Rule

What one might have expected to happen, though, was not that Byzantium and Persia would simply march in to take back their lands, but that the

Arab Empire would fragment into warring factions, as happened to many conquerors from the margins, such as the Turks in the late sixth century. Civil war did indeed afflict the Arabs on a number of occasions, but somehow they managed to stay together and maintain their hold over their newly acquired territories. To understand this achievement it is crucial to bear in mind that though nomadic tribes contributed essential raw fighting power, the conquest leadership was not drawn from men innocent of civilization. They were principally from Yemen, which had a history of statehood stretching back more than one and a half millennia, and from the oasis towns of central and northern west Arabia, which had had close ties with the provincial Roman/Byzantine world for centuries. Muhammad himself had participated in trading journeys to Syria and his tribe of Quraysh had numerous links to the Arab Christian tribes of that land. The conquerors were therefore no strangers to the business of government, even if they had not expected to find themselves in the driving seat.[18]

The first Arab ruler whose name is attested on coins, inscriptions, and documents, as well as in contemporary chronicles, is Mu'awiya, the founder of the Umayyad dynasty (661–750). So what do these sources tell us about his reign? In the first place, as one observer put it: "He refused to go to the seat of Muhammad," that is, Medina, home to the Arab rulers before him, but preferred to make his capital at Damascus, where he had already been directing military operations for twenty years. Evidently he recognized that it was not feasible to rule such a far-flung empire from such a remote location. This sounds like an eminently practical decision, but it was very likely a contentious one, given that Medina was where Muhammad had established his community. One of the key promises of 'Abdallah ibn al-Zubayr, the principal challenger to the Umayyads in the 680s, was that he would place Mecca and Medina once more at the heart of the Arab Empire, a pledge that won over many to his cause. Mu'awiya's decision might not, however, have been solely a pragmatic one. He perhaps regarded his rule as a new beginning, and his son Yazid would certainly appear to have held that view, for he took the surprising step at the outset of his reign of stamping on his coins "year one of Yazid" rather than using the *hijra* era that had become standard by his day, counting from the year in which Muhammad founded his community in Medina. It is very much in the tradition of ancient Middle Eastern kings and suggests that he did not see himself as a mere deputy of Muhammad.[19]

Second, Mu'awiya paid attention to the problem of asserting central control over the vast lands to the east of Syria, which would be a thorn in the Umayyads' side for a long time to come and eventually bring about their downfall. His solution was to entrust them to a couple of men who were very close to him: 'Abdallah ibn 'Amir, who was of the same tribe and was married to a daughter of his, and subsequently Ziyad, who was the son of a concubine of his father and whom Mu'awiya formally adopted as his brother. The names of these two men appear on the coinage of the east for the years AD 661–74 (AH 41–54). Ziyad's writ would seem to have extended particularly far, for he was able to have his coinage of 670–74 struck at more than twenty-four mints spread right across Iran, confirming the report of Muslim historians that he acted as Mu'awiya's viceroy over all the eastern territories. He was also the first to add religious slogans in Arabic to the coinage, inscribing the phrase "in the name of God my lord" (*bismillah rabbi*). His sons followed in his footsteps and between them this family ruled over a large portion of the east on behalf of Mu'awiya and his son Yazid for almost two decades.[20]

Third, Mu'awiya followed a laissez-faire policy toward the conquered peoples—"he allowed everyone to live as they wanted" as one contemporary noted—and sought to reassure them that he was not hostile to their religions. For example, in recognition of the fact that the majority of his new subjects were Christian, he made the deliberate decision to have a number of Arab chiefs swear the oath of allegiance to him as leader in Jerusalem, and while there "he went up and sat down on Golgotha and prayed there; he also went to Gethsemane and then went down to the tomb of the blessed Mary and prayed in it." Moreover, Mu'awiya made efforts to win over the Christian Arab elite of Syria (the likes of Sharahil ibn Zalim whom we met in Chapter 1), who had invaluable experience of government. Many of them served as his senior advisors and administrators, such as the Mansur family of Damascus; Christian poets were frequent visitors to his court and quite a number of his tribal backers were Christian. He himself married Maysun, the daughter of the powerful

Christian chief of Kalb, and she bore him the future caliph Yazid. The latter went on to marry two noble women of Ghassan, one of them allegedly the daughter of the last Christian Ghassanid king.[21] Mu'awiya did endeavor to implement a few pro-Muslim policies, in particular to remove the symbol of the cross from the coinage and to incorporate the church of St. John the Baptist in Damascus within the mosque, but when the Christians protested he apparently backed down.[22]

Finally, Mu'awiya gave some thought to the economy. The conquests had given the Arabs access to large amounts of cash from taxes, tribute, and booty, but most of it was simply recycled directly to the army in the form of stipends, which were paid not only to the soldiers but also to their families and dependents. In an account of the annual revenues and expenditure of southern Iraq in 670 we are informed that 60 million dirhams was collected in tax, of which 52 million went on stipends and rations to the military and their families. This amounts to 87 percent of total expenditure, which seems very high (modern estimates for Late Roman military expenditure range from a third to a half of state revenue), but certainly papyri from Umayyad Egypt give no indication of money being sent to the central treasury. So how did Mu'awiya cover the expenses of his household and how did he pay for the running of the state: the repair and maintenance of roads, bridges, and canals; the construction and manning of siege engines and ships; the manufacture and transport of equipment and goods? He had access to manpower from captives, slaves, and compulsory labor, but the papyri that record the requisitioning of labor for building projects and military campaigns show that in general wages were paid and that the raw materials were bought with cash too. So the question remains: how could Mu'awiya raise money? One source tells us that he posed exactly this question to his financial controller in Iraq, who, on consulting the local nobles, advised him to exploit the former Persian royal agricultural estates. These had not been subject to the standard land tax; rather those who managed them had paid a percentage of their yield directly to the Sasanian family. Mu'awiya decided to copy this practice and these properties, after the irrigation systems had been repaired, provided him with substantial revenue.[23]

He did the same with lands elsewhere that had been abandoned by their former owners, who in most cases had either fled or been killed or taken captive during the conquests. He either appropriated them for his own family or handed them out as rewards to kin and allies on the understanding that they would develop them. Contemporary Christian writers inform us about a few such ventures, like the one at Clysma in eastern Egypt where Christian captives worked under a Jewish foreman and another near the Dead Sea in the region of Zoara and Tetraphrygia, where public estates were worked by Cypriot captives, very probably those who had been taken prisoner in the raids on their island in 649–50. But it was not just the Umayyads and their supporters who were enriched by the conquests. In some seventh-century Arabic apocalypses Muhammad is made to predict that "wealth will abound among you to such an extent that were a man given a hundred gold coins he would be displeased and count it as little." A good proportion of this wealth was directed toward conspicuous consumption, stimulating the wider economy, and this is recorded by a number of contemporary Christian writers, who say that trade doubled, prosperity and peace reigned, and public buildings, even churches, were restored.[24]

Many regions, however, would have had little day-to-day contact with the conquerors, for in the first few decades of Arab rule they were either on campaign or confined to the garrison towns; only in inland Syria, where there was already a substantial Arabic-speaking population, and in Khurasan were the newcomers settled among the indigenous people. For example, the contemporary papyri from Egypt show that during Mu'awiya's reign the village headmen, regional administrators (*pagarchs*), and even the provincial dukes were all Christians and very likely all native Egyptians. Only the governor, a few members of his senior staff, and the military were drawn from the ranks of the conquerors. In the archive of Papas, an aristocratic landowner and regional administrator in Upper Egypt of the 670s, there is little overt sign of the presence of the Arab rulers. His correspondence is conducted in Greek with secretaries (*notarioi*) of the same class and upbringing as himself. They share the same language of refined politeness: "my brother, admirable in all ways," "my God-guarded master and brother," "your honourable and admirable Friendship." As a member of the curial class, which traditionally filled town councils, Papas often intervened to solve local disputes, and in a private capacity he dealt with basic legal matters, such as leases, mortgages, and loans against security. But behind the veneer of normality and continuity with the old, there is always in the background the shadow of the new regime, manifest in some of the letters to Papas in phrases like "I cannot disobey the order of our lords" and "the implacable command of our lord the emir." Three complaints against the new rulers crop up time and time again. The first concerns taxes and delivery of goods for the upkeep of the Arab armies, which appear to have been very diligently enforced from on high. The second is about the requisition of men to serve on the Arab fleets, as carpenters, caulkers, oarsmen, and the like. The work was paid, but maritime travel was dangerous, and being involved in a battle at sea even more so, and few were keen to risk their lives in such a venture, especially against their Christian brothers from Byzantium. And the third relates to the phenomenon of enslavement. Church authorities received numerous enquiries from worried members of their flock: "How can one redeem one's sins if, having been reduced to servitude or captured in war, one can no longer attend church, fast or observe a vigil freely and at will? What is one to say regarding Christian women who, as slaves and captives, have given themselves up to prostitution?"[25] Being wrenched from one's homeland and forced to serve foreign masters in a faraway land was a painful experience, and so unsurprisingly, stories about its importunities and hardships abound in our sources.

Mu'awiya's Religion and Mu'awiya's Image

As well as having served in public office for forty years as commander-in-chief of Syria and as head of the Arab Empire, Mu'awiya was a brother-in-law of the prophet Muhammad and had allegedly served as his scribe, and yet he has a rather negative image in ninth-century Muslim histories. His opposition to 'Ali in the first civil war, during which many prominent Muslims died, and his nomination of his own son Yazid as his successor were perceived as unforgiveable acts by later generations. Even Mu'awiya's success in putting in place a framework for governing the lands that the Arabs had newly acquired was criticized. Later scholars were unanimous that whereas the caliphs in Medina (Abu Bakr, 'Umar, 'Uthman, and 'Ali) had ministered to their subjects in fairness and piety, Mu'awiya had transformed this just rule into dynastic and autocratic dominion after the fashion of the Byzantine and Persian emperors. "He was the first to have a bodyguard, police-force and chamberlains. . . . He had somebody walk in front of him with a spear, took alms out of the stipends and sat on a throne with the people below him. . . . He used forced labour for his building projects . . . and confiscated people's property for himself. . . . He was the first to turn this matter [the caliphate] into mere kingship."[26]

The anguish and bloodshed occasioned by the first civil war and the grow- ing concentration of power in the hands of a small elite certainly tarnished Mu'awiya's image. Yet 'Uthman had already inaugurated a nepotistic style of government and 'Ali had been complicit in the first civil war, so why were these two labeled divinely guided, along with Abu Bakr and 'Umar, whereas Mu'awiya and his successors were depicted as tyrants? The answer is that it was the result of a later compromise made by religious scholars. The lat- ter struggled in the course of the eighth and ninth centuries to demonstrate that they, and not caliphs, were the true heirs of the prophet and so had the sole right to serve as guardians of Muhammad's laws and to make new laws. However, Abu Bakr and 'Umar had been very close to Muhammad and had transmitted many of his rulings, and the scholars did not want to alienate moderate pro-Umayyads and pro-'Alids by damning the names of 'Uthman and 'Ali. Thus a caesura was introduced into Islamic history: the four caliphs before Mu'awiya were deemed divinely guided and their time in office regarded as a golden age when Islam was practiced properly, while Mu'awiya and those who succeeded him were reviled as oppressors who diminished the dictates of Islam.

This idea of a golden age of just rule followed by tyranny gained traction only very slowly, but by the mid-ninth century it had become widespread and it entered the mainstream when the highly respected Baghdadi scholar Ahmad ibn Hanbal (d. 855) was won round to it.[27] Those who accepted this historical vision called themselves Sunnis (those who held to the *sunna*/prescribed path), and those who rejected it formed distinct sects outside of this "orthodox" mainstream. Moderate pro-'Alids were won over by this compromise (i.e., they accepted that the other three Medinan caliphs were legitimate as well as 'Ali), but those who were more hard-line continued to insist that 'Ali and his descendants were the only ones qualified to rule the Muslim world. The adherents of this latter view now split off irrevocably from the mainstream Sunnis and formed a group apart, namely, "the party of 'Ali" (*shi'at 'Ali*) or Shi'is, and it is from this time (the mid-ninth century) that the classic Sunni/Shi'i rivalry begins. In Mu'awiya's day, however, there were no distinct sects with clearly defined doctrines (as opposed to loose coalitions reflecting specific grievances), and many of his contemporaries would have regarded him as a legitimate, divinely approved ruler on a par with his predecessors.[28]

Modern historians have also called into question Mu'awiya's commitment to Islam, though in a different vein. On coins and official documents Mu'awiya only ever used the titles "servant of God" and "commander of the faithful" and referred to his rule as "the jurisdiction of the faithful" (*qada' al-mu'minin*).[29] The term "the faithful" had been used by Muhammad in the foundation agreement of his community to refer to all those who pledged loyalty to the new community, its aims, and its leader whatever their monotheist persuasion, and presumably Mu'awiya was just continuing this practice. However, the lack of any explicit reference to Islam or Muhammad in his public proclamations has prompted some to argue that either he was a Christian or he adhered to a "non-confessional" or "indeterminate" form of monotheism that was ecumenical in its outlook.[30] There is probably some truth to the idea that Muslims did not initially see their faith as totally distinct from other monotheist confessions. The Qur'an operates with the notion that there has been only one true religion since the dawn of time, namely, submission (*islam*) to the one God, and that those who divinized Jesus (i.e., Christians) and Ezra (i.e., Jews) were just deviating from this pure monotheism. From this perspective there are not separate monotheist religions, just one true one and a number of warped versions of it. However, the Qur'an does not take a non-confessional or ecumenical position, but rather devotes much effort to polemicizing against Christians and Jews; they can renounce their false belief and return to the true monotheism, but otherwise they remain in a subordinate and erroneous position. Mu'awiya clearly held to this uncompromising view too, as we can see from his challenge to the emperor Constans: "Deny [the divinity of] Jesus and turn to the Great God whom I worship, the God of our father Abraham."[31]

We might best understand Mu'awiya's stance by looking to the Persian emperor Khusrau II, who has also been suspected of converting to Christianity. This is very unlikely, since he promulgated a decree forbidding all his subjects from leaving their ancestral religion. Rather, he sought to show, especially once he became the sovereign of large numbers of Christians in Syria, Palestine, and Egypt in the 620s, that he—and not the Byzantine emperor—was now the principal recipient of God's favor, as was surely illustrated by his success in battle. Accordingly, he sought a blessing for his war against Byzantium from the head of the eastern Christians, he prayed at the shrine of Saint Sergius in northern Syria, and he had a special storeroom built to house the fragment of Christ's cross that his armies had captured and brought back from Jerusalem.[32] And it is in this spirit that we should probably regard Mu'awiya's tour of the Christian sites of Jerusalem—not an ecumenical impulse, but a demonstration of the fact that he, and not the Byzantine emperor, was now God's representative on earth.

An inscription in west Arabia, which commemorates the construction of a dam, adds weight to this argument. It contains a request from Mu'awiya to God for forgiveness, strength, and support, and a plea to let "the faithful profit by him" (Figure 4.4). This implies that Mu'awiya stood between God and the faithful, and the latter needed him for their wellbeing. He evidently did not consider that he had to refer to Muhammad to bolster his legitimacy. Certain Umayyad documents concerning the designation of royal heirs make the same point: after God "took back His prophet and sealed His revelation with him," He entrusted His caliphs to implement His decree and to enact His regulations. Umayyad ideology evidently rested on the notion that the era of prophets was at an end and that caliphs now acted as God's agents on earth. Muhammad's practice and legislation was of course important to his community: the Arabs "kept to the tradition of Muhammad, their instructor, to such an extent that they inflicted the death penalty on anyone who was seen to act brazenly against his laws," says

FIGURE 4.4 Arabic inscription of Mu'awiya from Ta'if in western Saudi Arabia.
© Karl S. Twitchell.

the seventh-century monk John of Fenek.[33] But new laws, the Umayyads
would argue, were the business of caliphs. Religious scholars soon began
to challenge this view, as we have said, and some did this by claiming that
the doings and sayings of Muhammad had been accurately transmitted to
them. It was rare in the first couple of generations after Muhammad: "I
spent a year sitting with 'Umar I's son 'Abdallah (d. 693)," said one legal
scholar, "and I did not hear him transmit anything from the prophet." Not
much later, though, the idea had won some grass-roots support, as we learn
from another scholar, writing around 740, who observes: "I never heard
Jabir ibn Zayd (d. ca. 720) say: 'the prophet said. . .' and yet the young
men round here are saying it twenty times an hour."[34] A little later again
Muhammad's sayings would be put on a par with the Qur'an as the source
of all Islamic law. In Mu'awiya's time, though, this was still far in the future,
and for the moment caliphs made law, not scholars.

Chapter Five

THE GREAT LEAP FORWARD
(685–715)

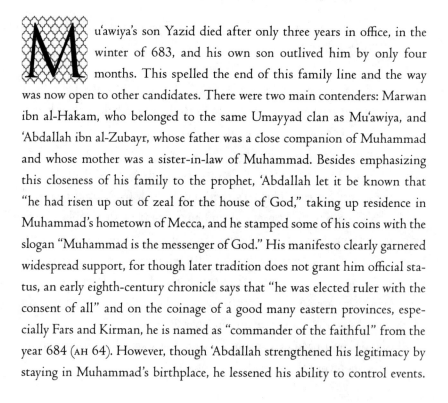

u'awiya's son Yazid died after only three years in office, in the winter of 683, and his own son outlived him by only four months. This spelled the end of this family line and the way was now open to other candidates. There were two main contenders: Marwan ibn al-Hakam, who belonged to the same Umayyad clan as Mu'awiya, and 'Abdallah ibn al-Zubayr, whose father was a close companion of Muhammad and whose mother was a sister-in-law of Muhammad. Besides emphasizing this closeness of his family to the prophet, 'Abdallah let it be known that "he had risen up out of zeal for the house of God," taking up residence in Muhammad's hometown of Mecca, and he stamped some of his coins with the slogan "Muhammad is the messenger of God." His manifesto clearly garnered widespread support, for though later tradition does not grant him official status, an early eighth-century chronicle says that "he was elected ruler with the consent of all" and on the coinage of a good many eastern provinces, especially Fars and Kirman, he is named as "commander of the faithful" from the year 684 (AH 64). However, though 'Abdallah strengthened his legitimacy by staying in Muhammad's birthplace, he lessened his ability to control events.

By contrast, Marwan, though he had the weaker moral case, based himself in Damascus where he could draw upon the formidable power base that Mu'awiya had built up in Syria over the previous decades. As the aforementioned chronicle puts it: "With the consent of a good many from the army, Marwan was carried forward to power, with God turning a blind eye."[1]

To reinforce his position Marwan quickly concluded a peace agreement with the emperor Constantine IV so as to prevent attacks from the north and he obtained allegiance to his eldest son, 'Abd al-Malik, to ensure a problem-free succession in the event of his death. This turned out to be a wise move on Marwan's part, for he died only nine months later, but though 'Abd al-Malik's accession in Syria was smooth, he faced a very bumpy ride to acceptance elsewhere. Some fought to put a son of 'Ali on the throne, believing that his marriage to the prophet's daughter Fatima had made him and his offspring the heir to Muhammad's prophetic charisma. Others, designated Kharijites (literally: "rebels"), opposed all dynastic government, arguing that the leader should simply be the one most competent to enact God's will as manifested in the Qur'an and the practice of Muhammad. Their rallying cry was "rule belongs to God alone" (la hukma illa lillah), which was very likely a response to the move by 'Abd al-Malik to designate himself "deputy of God" (khalifat Allah), implying that he ruled on God's behalf (Figure 5.1). Many of these rebels lived as bandits in the countryside and carried out small-scale attacks on government targets, but some achieved more substantial gains. One of their number carved out for himself a large swathe of central and eastern Arabia in the 680s, and another held portions of western and central Iran from 689 to 696 and minted coins on which he was acclaimed as "commander of the faithful." 'Abd al-Malik very astutely allowed these competing groups to wear one another down and then used his loyal Syrian troops to push home the final victory, killing 'Abdallah ibn al-Zubayr in 692 and bringing to a close almost a decade of turmoil.[2]

This second Arab civil war had been hugely divisive and 'Abd al-Malik realized that he needed to try to bring some unity to his fractious community and to demonstrate to his conquered subjects and those beyond his reach that the Arab regime was still a force to be reckoned with. He made a couple

FIGURE 5.1 Silver coin of Qatari ibn al-Fuja'a, Bishapur, dated 75 AH (694–95), bearing bust of Sasanian emperor and the Arabic legend "rule belongs to God alone." (SICA I/198). © Visitors of the Ashmolean Museum, University of Oxford.

of far-reaching administrative changes that were aimed at harmonizing the different systems in his realm: creating a single uniform coinage and decreeing that there should be a single official language of the bureaucracy, namely, Arabic. He also elevated the status of Islam so that it would play a greater role in public life. Out of deference to the large numbers of Christians among the subject population and among the ranks of the Arab warriors, this had not been done before. However, 'Abd al-Malik had observed how much popular support his rival Ibn al-Zubayr had gained by setting himself up as a champion for the primacy of the sanctuary in Mecca and of the prophet Muhammad, and he was determined to usurp this role for himself. He therefore devised a new Islamic creed—"There is no god but God and Muhammad is His messenger"—and had it placed on all public documents and stamped on his new coinage (Figure 5.2). He renewed Mu'awiya's policy of having a viceroy of the east who would be allowed a free hand to enforce allegiance to Umayyad rule and crush dissent in the former Persian territories, appointing the famously tough and ruthless Hajjaj ibn Yusuf (693–714). Finally, he gave new impetus to the conquests, beginning with Africa and the southeast frontier of Iran.

FIGURE 5.2 Gold coin of ʿAbd al-Malik, dated 77 AH (696–97), bearing image of the caliph and the Arabic legend "there is no god but God alone, Muhammad is the messenger of God" (SICA I/705). © Visitors of the Ashmolean Museum, University of Oxford.

His son Walid continued this policy and in only two decades their generals won the submission of Spain and North Africa in the west and of Sind and Transoxania in the east.

In the same year that ʿAbd al-Malik came to power, a new Byzantine emperor acceded to the throne, the young Justinian II (685–95, 705–11). He also had ambitions of restoring his empire's prestige, perhaps wishing to emulate his earlier namesake, Justinian the Great (527–65). He visited Armenia now that it had reverted to Byzantine control as part of the peace deal concluded with ʿAbd al-Malik, eager to demonstrate that he was back in charge in this part of the world. He then turned his attention to the Balkans where he repulsed the Bulgars, who had been seeking to extend their authority in the region, and advanced as far as Thessalonica, taking back with him a large number of Slavs to repopulate parts of Anatolia and to serve in the military. He selected 30,000 of them, whom he armed and named "the special people," intending to use them as an elite force to combat the Arabs. He soon had an opportunity to do so, for in 692 the peace treaty concluded by his father with Mu'awiya and renewed by Marwan and 'Abd al-Malik was dissolved amid mutual recriminations. The two sides marched out to meet each other at Sebastopolis, in the Pontus region of Anatolia. The Arab side seemed initially to be losing, but the general Muhammad ibn Marwan, brother of 'Abd al-Malik, persuaded the Slavs to defect, and when they saw this the Byzantines fled. For his failures, Justinian had his nose cut off and was banished to the Crimea. A decade later he managed to escape and with Bulgar aid recaptured the throne. However, his vengefulness toward his enemies blighted his attempts to reform his realm's defensive strategy and the Arabs were able to score a number of victories deep inside the Byzantine heartland of Anatolia.[3]

Africa

One achievement of the reign of Justinian II, according to the biographer of Pope John V (685–86), was that "the province of Africa was subjugated and restored to Roman rule." No explanation is given in this or any other Christian source, but there is a possible allusion here to the success of a Berber chief called Kusayla. We only know of him from Muslim sources, which give a very confused picture of his career, complicated by his later image as a heroic defender of his native lands and people. The earliest writer simply says that he was a Christian and that in 683 he fought and killed two of the Arab heroes of the conquest of Africa: 'Uqba ibn Nafi' and Abu al-Muhajir. The next source chronologically adds a few important details: Kusayla's army consisted of "Byzantines and Berbers," it won a victory at Tahuda, ancient Thabudeos, in Numidia (eastern Algeria), and it then went on to capture Qayrawan. Muslim sources tend to say that Kusayla was defeated very soon afterward, but the notice from Pope John V's biographer implies that Kusayla achieved something more lasting. Moreover, it is unlikely that the Arab governor in Egypt would have had troops to spare during the civil war years. A later historian makes the reasonable observation that Kusayla was in charge of Africa and resided in Qayrawan until 'Abd al-Malik's rule was consolidated, and then, in 689, he sent the general in charge of the frontier at Barqa to regain control of Africa. As this Arab general advanced on Qayrawan, Kusayla withdrew from the city, since it did not yet have defensive walls, and took up position at nearby Mammis, which allowed easy escape into the Dorsal Mountains. It was the site chosen by the Berber leader Cusina to confront the Byzantines in 534 and unfortunately for Kusayla he suffered the same fate as Cusina: defeat by his enemy after a long and hard-fought battle.

The next major task for the Arabs was to capture Carthage, the last substantial Byzantine stronghold in Africa. Successive Arab generals had left this city alone, feeling it necessary to first pacify the Berber tribes of the interior and also aware that its strong walls and the fact that it could be constantly supplied by sea would make its siege a drawn-out affair. However, its loss would undoubtedly deal the Byzantines a crippling blow, since it would deprive them of the rich harvests and tax yields of Africa. ʿAbd al-Malik picked for this job Hassan ibn Nuʿman, a member of the tribe of Ghassan that was formerly allied to Byzantium, and granted him a large number of troops, some say 40,000, to ensure his success. When the inhabitants of Carthage saw the size of the forces arrayed against them, they decided to abandon the city, leaving for Sicily and Spain, and so Hassan was able to enter it with relative ease. Emperor Leontius, who had just ousted Justinian II in 695, was furious at this cowardly action and at once dispatched a well-armed fleet, which sailed into the harbor, forcing its way through the chain that guarded it. Its troops swiftly disembarked, decisively routed the Arabs stationed in the city, and liberated a number of neighboring towns. This in turn enraged ʿAbd al-Malik, who sent an even more powerful fleet and forcibly drove the Byzantine ships out of the harbor, which meant that by 698 Hassan was back in charge of Carthage and its hinterland.[4]

There was one remaining task for Hassan to accomplish in Africa, namely, to remove the last Berber challenger to the Arabs, a woman most often referred to simply as "the prophetess" (*kahina*). Kusayla is sometimes referred to as "son of the prophetess," which may mean that this enigmatic Berber woman who takes up his mantle was actually his mother. It is extremely difficult, however, to get any sense of whom she represented and what she stood for, since the earliest sources are very brief and the later ones tend to be imbued with a sense of legend and mystery. Our earliest Muslim source notes only that in 692 Hassan ibn Nu'man raided and conquered the Aures and that in 694 "the prophetess was killed," while a tenth-century Christian chronicler places under the year 697 the notice: "Hassan ibn Nu'man engaged in battle the queen of the Berbers and she defeated him and all his men." Possibly Hassan twice fought this queen of the Berbers—the first time he was defeated and the second time he was victorious and killed her; but given the confusion, all one can do is assign a loose date to her rebellion of the mid-690s. The Aures, the mountain range of eastern Algeria, is the place where a Berber leader named Iaudas had held sway in the 530s and 540s, and it is possible that an independent Berber polity had survived in this region from the early sixth to the late seventh century. Besides these meager scraps of information, there are lengthy tales of the prophetess's gift of second sight, which allowed her to foresee her defeat at the hands of Hassan, and of her tragic aspect, riding heroically into battle, her long hair splayed out behind her, doomed to fight to the last all the while aware of her fate. Yet she is not just a symbol of the old, but also of the new, for she commends her two sons to the care of an Arab she had captured, who did as she predicted and ensured that these boys received a guarantee of protection from Hassan and posts in the new conquering armies. Not just her immediate family, therefore, but also her people survived and continued to prosper, enjoying a new future marching alongside the Arab conquerors.[5]

Having achieved both his objectives, Hassan returned to Qayrawan and set about the task of establishing a functioning government in this large and unwieldy province. He built a congregational mosque, set up a chancellery, and fixed the tax to be paid by "the Africans and the Berbers who were, like them, devotees of Christianity." Muslim sources at this point make the casual but curious remark that "most of these Christian Berbers were *baranis*, with only a few from the *butr*." Unfortunately it is never explained what is meant by this and the Romans/Byzantines before them never made such a distinction, but rather spoke simply of Moors, occasionally of barbarians (whence, one assumes, comes the Arabic word "Berber"), and otherwise of individual tribes. The literal meaning of *baranis* is "hoods" or "cowls," which suggests that there was some difference in appearance; this is less obvious for the word *butr*, which means "cut off/removed," though some Muslim sources state that the *butr* Berbers cut off their hair, explaining it as an indication of their commitment to the Muslim cause. We cannot be sure how this distinction relates to the people themselves, but it is likely to be connected with the fact that the *butr* Berbers hail from Cyrenaica and Tripolitania in the east (modern Libya), where the desert predominated, Romanization was weak, and paganism lingered on, whereas the *baranis* were principally in the west, which had greater agricultural wealth and was more thoroughly Romanized and Christianized. During the great Berber revolt of the 540s the Byzantines had striven to pacify and win over those in the western interior, but those in the east—especially the Luwata tribe, whose ferocity and barbarity was recalled with horror—had to be "banished beyond our borders." In the time of the Arab conquests it was the east that saw peaceful acquiescence, especially from the Luwata, whereas in the west there were the major insurrections of Kusayla and "the prophetess" involving Byzantine and Berber troops. Plausibly, then, the less Romanized/Christianized easterners were more willing to collaborate with the Arabs than their western neighbors, and the Arabs may have noticed the hooded/shaven-headed distinction between some of the Berbers and applied it as a rough-and-ready way to distinguish between the many.[6]

The last notice in a Christian source about the conquest of Africa concerns the subjugation of ancient Mauritania, corresponding to modern western Algeria and Morocco. This was achieved by Musa, whose father, Nusayr, had been captured during the early Arab conquest of southern Iraq and put to work in the new administration. He had shown himself to be a capable man and, upon his conversion and manumission, had quickly risen up the ranks. His son followed him in this career and served in Damascus, Basra, and Fustat as a senior bureaucrat on behalf of the Umayyad family. In the latter city he attracted the attention of the governor of Egypt, 'Abd al-'Aziz, who selected him to replace Hassan ibn Nu'man as governor of Africa. Musa went there in 698 and spent the next few years campaigning in the westernmost reaches of the continent, earning the gratitude and admiration of the caliph 'Abd al-Malik and his son and successor Walid. Musa crowned his achievements with an assault on Tangiers, the most important settlement in the far west. Once he had captured it, certainly by 708, he installed a garrison there commanded by his Berber freedman, Tariq ibn Ziyad, and then returned to take his ease in Qayrawan.[7]

Spain (Map 4.3)

In 710, Witiza, head of the Gothic kingdom of Spain, died and though he had adult sons, a nobleman named Roderick seized the kingdom, allegedly at the instigation of the senate. Numismatic evidence reveals a divided Spain: Roderick's coins are found in the southwest and central regions while those of a certain Achila are encountered in the northeast. Tariq ibn Ziyad decided to take advantage of this division and crossed the straits from Tangiers to Spain in the early summer of 711 with a substantial force of Arabs and Berbers. Our earliest source, a mid-eighth-century Spanish Christian chronicle, says that the force was sent by Musa, but Muslim sources have Tariq act on his own initiative and say that Musa only arrived the following year. He is portrayed as being at first disgruntled by Tariq's failure to consult him before acting, but he was quickly won over once he learned of the profitability of the venture. The first major encounter between the two sides took place in the summer of 711 to the east of Cadiz, and in the course of the battle, relates our Christian chronicler, with some hyperbole, "the entire army of the Goths, which had come with Roderick, treacherously and in rivalry out of ambition for the kingship, fled and Roderick was killed."

Late Muslim sources describe various encounters at sundry locations between the invading Arab-Berber forces and the local populace, but earlier writers are much more reserved. Baladhuri (d. 892), for example, just notes very briefly the capture of Cordoba and Toledo. The aforementioned Christian chronicle mentions only the conquest of Toledo, though it states that Musa imposed on the adjacent regions "an evil and deceitful peace," and he devastated not only Hispania Ulterior (the south and west), but also Hispania Citerior (the northeast) up to and beyond the prosperous city of Zaragoza. Possibly the details of the conquest were unpalatable to him, for he limits himself to a general lament: "Musa ruined beautiful cities, burning them with fire; condemned lords and powerful men to the cross and butchered youths and infants with the sword," culminating in the hyperbolic observation that "even if every limb were transformed into a tongue it would be beyond human capability to express the ruin of Spain and its many and great evils."

The reference to a "deceitful peace" offers a clue to why the country (or at least the western two thirds of it, since the northeast remained independent) fell so easily to the invaders, namely, local lords made agreements with the Arab-Berber generals. This is certainly the impression that late Muslim sources give, the most well-known example being the treaty drawn up between Musa's son and a certain Theodemir, who controlled a portion of southeast Spain around modern Murcia. In conformity with agreements made in the east, which, as we have said, followed ancient traditions about the proper conduct of war, Musa's son pledged to protect life, property, and the Christian religion in return for submission, tribute, and a promise not to shelter fugitives nor to aid the enemy. In this way a proportion of the Visigothic aristocracy managed to retain some of their lands and customs. It would seem that their ancestry continued to count for something long after the conquest, for a number of writers boast of their links with the old regime, such as the historian Ibn al-Qutiya ("son of the Gothic woman"; d. 977), who proudly advertised his descent from Sarah, granddaughter of the last legitimate king of the Goths.

The Arab-Berber conquest of Spain is very poorly documented and this has led some to question the traditional narrative of how it happened. Perhaps, they say, it occurred slowly by steady immigration and social interaction, as in the rise of Saxon England, rather than suddenly by large-scale invasion.[8] It is certainly likely that the conquest was more piecemeal than our sources would have us believe, and without doubt the Islamization of the region proceeded chiefly by social rather than military means. For example, Pope Hadrian (772–95) laments that in Spain it is common for Catholics to marry their daughters to heathens (meaning Muslims). However, coins minted in the name of Arab authorities in Arabic and Latin from the year 716 onward make it abundantly clear that a new regime was in place and that the Arabs were in command of it, even if the majority of the troops may have been Berbers (Figure 5.3). In the end, the reason for the lack of interest in Spanish affairs by Muslim writers from the central Islamic lands simply reflects the fact that Spain was for them

FIGURE 5.3 Gold coin, Spain, dated 98 AH (716–17), legends in Latin and Arabic. © Tonegawa Collection.

a remote country that had a negligible impact on their lives. Consequently, they either said very little about it or concentrated on the fantastical—the locked house that could only be opened by the conqueror of Spain, the city of brass with leaden domes—and on the very few occasions when Spain impinged on the east, such as when Tariq and Musa appeared before the caliph Walid in Damascus and argued over which one of them had discovered in Spain the table of the Israelite king Solomon.[9]

Northeast Iran and Transoxania

As in the west of the Arab Empire, the east experienced a new expansionary drive in the early eighth century that brought great political change to the region. When the Chinese monk Xuanzang traveled through eastern Khurasan, Tukharistan (modern north Afghanistan), and Transoxania (modern Uzbekistan and Tajikistan) in the period 629–44, he encountered no Arabs at all; Turkish chiefs and local lords made up the authorities in charge of this region. The story was very different when the Korean monk Huichao passed through in the 720s.[10] He found that Balkh was "guarded and oppressed by Arab forces." Sogdia was divided into cantons, principally a city and its hinterland, such as Bukhara and Samarkand, and though each still had its own ruler they were all under Arab authority. Also Khuttal, in southern Tajikistan, and Ferghana, in southeast Uzbekistan, were under the control of the Arabs, and the king of Wakhan, on the Afghan-Chinese border, paid to them annually 3,000 rolls of silk. This had not yet impacted on the religious situation, however: Sogdia, for example, still served "the Fire Religion" (Zoroastrianism) and in Tukharistan the king, the chiefs, and the common people respected "the Three Jewels" (Buddhism) and "do not profess any other religions." In the southeast frontier region, however, Huichao saw only non-Arab rulers, and this is confirmed by the coins, which bear the names of local kings. The position of the northeast region on the major overland trade routes from China to Iran and Byzantium and the wealth that accrued from this meant that the Arabs were more eager to capture this region than the southeast and put greater resources into achieving this end. Moreover, the Iranian province that adjoined the northeast frontier, namely, Khurasan, was much richer and had been the focus of much greater Arab settlement than the Iranian province that adjoined the southeast frontier, namely, Sistan, and this meant that more troops were available at not so great a distance.

Conquest of this northeast frontier zone was nevertheless slow going for the Arabs. Although some victories had been won in the early decades, they had led to no permanent conquest before the outbreak of the second Arab civil war in 683. The disorder that this conflict entailed, lasting almost a decade (683–92), was not conducive to reconquest and neither the resources nor the right leader to direct such a venture were found for some time afterward. Moreover, the Arabs were not the only power interested in this wealthy region and the first half of the eighth century saw the involvement of a number of new or revitalized actors. The Tang dynasty of China was at its height under the long-lived Xuanzong (712–56), based in the world's most populous city of the day, Chang-An. In the 660s, the Tibetans had moved into the Pamir region, which lay across the routes passing between the Tarim basin in the east to Sogdia and Tukharistan in the west, and this marked the beginning of an involvement in the area that endured throughout the eighth century. Finally, a number of Turkic groups strove to assert their influence: in particular, the Eastern Turks reestablished their autonomy in the 680s, breaking away from their Chinese overlords, and the lands of the Western Turks fell under the control of a new confederation known as the Turgesh. Alliances and confrontations between these powers—China, Tibet, the Turks, and the Arabs—as well as with local lords shifted to and fro in a rather intricate political dance in the early decades of the eighth century. We are fortunate in having sources from each of the main actors, but they are so varied (Arabic and Tibetan chronicles, Turkic inscriptions, Chinese annals, Bactrian and Sogdian documents, etc.), complex, and fragmentary that scholars have yet to work out a clear and detailed narrative of these events.

The caliph Walid (705–15), who succeeded his father 'Abd al-Malik, favored an expansionist policy and ordered the viceroy of the east, Hajjaj ibn Yusuf, to find the man to establish his writ over Transoxania. Hajjaj chose the stern but capable Qutayba ibn Muslim, who was not from an influential tribe but was as a consequence wholly dependent on the support of Hajjaj for his position as governor of Khurasan, and so he was unlikely to rebel. The region he had to contend with was not so huge—Sogdia, for example, was only about 200 miles in length and its settlements were strung out in a thin line along the Zarafshan River. However, as Huichao noted, each country had its own king and so there was no single target, as there had been in the case of Sasanian Persia (i.e., the emperor); rather, the conquest had to be accomplished in a piecemeal fashion, dealing with each potentate in turn. Yet this disunity could also be an advantage to invaders, since quarrels between local lords could be exploited. Thus the ruler of Chaganiyan, who wanted an ally in his struggle against the neighboring territories of Akharun and Shuman, invited Qutayba into his realm. And the lord of Khwarizm, an oasis near the Aral Sea, promised to pay tribute to Qutayba on the condition that he rid him of his rebellious younger brother.

Besides playing divide and rule, Qutayba simply picked off the main settlements in Sogdia proceeding from west to east: Paykand in 706, Bukhara in 709, and Samarkand in 712. In each case, the conquest was only achieved after a hard struggle and many reverses. Paykand, for instance, had to be recaptured, and on this occasion, to warn against such backsliding, Qutayba destroyed the great mud-brick walls of the city by tunneling underneath them, slaughtered all its fighting men and plundered its immense wealth. Only in the fourth season of hard campaigning was Bukhara overwhelmed. And there were a number of revolts, such as that led by Nizak, a Buddhist prince from the region of Herat, who strove in 709–10 to rouse the various leaders of Tukharistan against Arab domination. Although they initially responded positively to his call, they quickly reaffirmed their allegiance to the Arabs on hearing that a strong Arab force was marching toward them, and Nizak, his plans in tatters, was obliged to flee for his life. The inability of the region to present a united front was in the end its downfall, for the Arabs could always count on some groups willing to fight with them against others. As Ghurak, lord of Samarkand and king of Sogdia (710–37), said to Qutayba: "You are fighting me with my brothers and my own people."[11]

Southeast Iran and the Kabul Region

In contrast with their northeast frontier, where substantial gains were made after the cessation of civil war in 692, the Arabs made little headway in the southeast, and indeed suffered a series of setbacks.[12] The ruler of Zabulistan, in modern central Afghanistan, who bore the title of Rutbil, was killed in the course of an Arab raid in 690, and his successor quickly offered his submission and one million dirhams in tribute. However, the governor of Sistan refused, reckoning that he could extort an even greater sum and humiliate the people of this truculent region. He proceeded up the Helmand River, leading his men ever deeper into the mountainous lands beyond. The new Rutbil allowed him to advance and then, on a particularly tortuous path, he made a surprise attack, taking out many of his men and obliging him to retreat. The governor had to accept the paltry sum of 300,000 dirhams in tribute and the harm done to the Arabs' reputation ensured his swift dismissal from his post.

The next person to have a go at subduing this recalcitrant frontier was 'Ubaydallah ibn Abi Bakra, son of a slave freed by the prophet Muhammad, who had already served as governor of Sistan once before, in the years 671–73. He was sent by Hajjaj ibn Yusuf in the spring of 697 with the instruction: "go out against the Rutbil with your force of Muslims and do not return until you have laid waste his land, destroyed his strongholds, killed his warriors and enslaved his people." With a combined force of Basran and

Kufan troops 'Ubaydallah marched into Zabulistan, seizing livestock and reducing forts as he went. However, lured on by hopes of booty and glory he entered far into enemy territory and found himself without sufficient provisions for his army or their horses. He had repeated the mistake of his predecessor and, like him, was obliged to sue for peace on unfavorable terms. His second-in-command refused to accept the humiliation of begging before infidels and fought on, losing his life and many of his men in the process. Once a peace had been agreed and hostages left behind, 'Ubaydallah was permitted to leave with his men, but many had perished of hunger and cold and it was a bedraggled bunch, labeled by contemporaries "the army of perdition" (*jaysh al-fana'*), that returned to their base. 'Ubaydallah died soon afterward, in 698, chagrined by his failure.

Hajjaj decided that a show of strength was needed to restore Arab prestige and to warn the obdurate Rutbil that such impudence would no longer be tolerated. For this mission he picked a man from one of the great Arab noble families, a descendant of the kings of Kinda, 'Abd al-Rahman ibn al-Ash'ath. To him was assigned an army of 20,000 men from Basra and Kufa, many from influential clans, and all were paid in advance and equipped with the best horses and weaponry, attracting the label of "the peacock army" (*jaysh al-tawawis*) from observers. Ibn al-Ash'ath arrived with his army in Sistan in early 699 and at his first Friday prayer session he called for support from local Arab warriors against "those enemies of yours who have been devastating your land and raiding your precious possessions." Many joined him and at this point the Rutbil, alarmed at this massing of troops, offered to pay tribute at the old rate and to return the hostages left with him by 'Ubaydallah ibn Abi Bakra. But Ibn al-Ash'ath's orders were to punish and not to conciliate, and so he refused the offer and began his march eastward. Rather than risk getting marooned in enemy country like his predecessors, he established a base at Bust, where the Helmand and Arghandab Rivers meet, and built watchtowers, stationed troops at strategic locations, and appointed agents to collect taxes and deliver messages. He sent his brother up the Arghandab River, into Arrukhaj, but found that the Rutbil had withdrawn and left none behind bar the elderly and a few Arab corpses.

Satisfied with his progress for that year, Ibn al-Ash'ath informed Hajjaj that he intended to suspend his advance for the time being. Furious at what he perceived as cowardice and vacillation, Hajjaj fired off three letters ordering Ibn al-Ash'ath to recommence his campaign against the Rutbil or else be demoted to the rank of a simple soldier. Stung by such abuse, Ibn al-Ash'ath roused his troops to revolt, playing on that ancient grievance of soldiers: being sent to serve on remote frontiers for long periods. "If you obey Hajjaj's orders," he urged, "he will condemn you to stay in this country perpetually, and will keep you quartered here just as Pharaoh kept his armies in distant garrisons, and you will never see your loved ones again before most of you have been killed." He made peace with the Rutbil on the condition that he be given asylum if his revolt failed and then marched westward with the majority of his troops and a number of men from Sistan to confront Hajjaj in Iraq. As he passed through Kirman and Fars, many more joined him and coins struck in his name for the year 701 show that the aim was no longer just to chastise Hajjaj for his intransigent stance but to overturn Umayyad rule. He fought and lost a series of battles in Iraq before returning to take up the promise of the Rutbil to give him shelter. Hajjaj sent a powerful army in his pursuit and finally, in 704, Ibn al-Ash'ath killed himself rather than surrender to his archenemy. The Arabs reestablished their authority in Zarang and Bust, but this was the eastward limit of their territorial expansion.

After Ibn al-Ash'ath's revolt, the Arabs mostly left this region alone and the various local potentates enjoyed a high degree of autonomy. Muslim sources say that the Rutbil refused to pay tribute to any of the tax agents of the Umayyads, and Chinese annals report that in 710 and 724 he sent an emissary to the Chinese court and received in return a confirmation of his kingship from the emperor himself as well as a gift of silk. Probably the same Rutbil is responsible for the erection of a Buddhist stupa in 714, which is commemorated in a recently discovered inscription that refers to the "lord of Ghazni," the capital of Zabulistan, lying to the southwest of Kabul. From 700 to 738 the ruler of Kapisa, northeast of Kabul, struck his own coins on which he inscribed the title "king of Khurasan" or, even more boldly, "king of the East." His son went further, portraying himself as "Caesar, noble lord, who smote the Arabs," using the local Bactrian language to signal his cultural allegiance. The Korean monk Huichao confirms this pugnacious spirit, commenting that Kapisa, Zabulistan, and Bamiyan harbored many Buddhist monasteries and monks and that their kings were strong and independent. Of the king of Bamiyan, famous for its twin standing Buddhas that were recently destroyed by the Taliban, he goes as far as to say that "his cavalry is so strong and numerous that other countries do not dare invade this land" (Figure 5.4). Thus matters stood until the coming of Persian dynasties like the Saffarids (861–1003) and Turkish dynasties like the Ghaznavids (975–1187), which furthered the eastward spread of Islam.[13]

Caucasia

The Arabs encountered the same sort of obduracy in the lands to the north of their realm. In 699, Muhammad ibn Marwan, who was the brother of 'Abd al-Malik and responsible for these northern territories, decided to change the

FIGURE 5.4 Giant Buddha, carved into rock face at Bamiyan, Afghanistan. © Western Himalaya Archive Vienna.

prevailing system of indirect rule via a local Armenian prince in favor of direct rule via an agent appointed by Muhammad himself. However, for this proud mountain people any move to reduce their independence and ancient privileges was regarded with hostility, and Armenian sources accuse the appointee of plotting to destroy the nobility of the land of Armenia and their cavalry. Smbat Bagratuni, who had been chosen as the new chief prince of Armenia in 693, roused the nobles against the Arabs and rallied an army, and in January 703 they marched down the river Araxes near to Nakhchawan, where an Arab garrison some 5,000-strong was stationed. The Armenians crossed the river and camped at Vardanakert, pursued all the while by the Arab garrison. It was now nightfall and so the Armenians barricaded the streets of the town and assigned guards to keep watch until dawn. As the sun arose, they performed mass and received communion, and then they organized themselves into units and readied themselves for the attack. Although the Armenian warriors numbered only 2,000, they had the advantage of surprise, launching themselves on the Arabs just as they were waking. Those who escaped the sword fell into the river Araxes, and soon drowned or froze, since it was a cold winter. Some managed to flee, "naked, barefoot and wounded," and they sought refuge with a local princess. "She bandaged their wounds, healed them and gave them clothes to wear," and sent them back to their country, earning the gratitude of the caliph himself. Smbat reported the victory to the Byzantine emperor and sent him some of the choicest booty, for which praise was heaped upon him and he was awarded honors and high rank.[14]

Another assault was targeted against a small Arab unit quartered in the region of Vaspurakan, to the southeast of Lake Van. Once the Armenians realized how few in number the Arabs were, they threw themselves upon them and slaughtered them mercilessly. Only 280 Arabs got away, and they sought sanctuary in a church. The Armenians did not want to harm the church and so they besieged the Arabs inside. One of the latter tried to appeal to the compassion of the Armenian leader, but he replied: "We were taught by our Lord that merciful treatment is due to the merciful. You, however, are a merciless nation and do not deserve mercy." At this the Arab returned to his men and encouraged them to act as true soldiers and to go out fighting. All were slain by the sword, except for this one man, who, it turned out, had done a deal with the Armenians that he should not be slain if he got his companions out of the church, and so instead they threw him into the sea. The Armenians, however, would come to regret their action, for a similar one was subsequently visited upon them.

On hearing of the double defeat of Arab troops, 'Abd al-Malik dispatched his brother Muhammad to reassert his authority over the Armenians. The latter feared a violent reprisal and so they sent the head of their church, Patriarch Sahak, to negotiate with Muhammad. The plan was for the two of them to meet at Harran in northern Syria, now just across the border in modern south Turkey. Unfortunately, Sahak fell sick and died just days before Muhammad arrived, in late 703, but he did leave a letter imploring Muhammad to show compassion to his people. Muhammad respected the man's dying wish and gave his oath that he would leave Armenia in peace for three years. As the expiry of this term drew near, the prince of Armenia, Smbat Bagratuni, wrote to the Byzantine emperor requesting troops, since he was afraid that the new Arab ruler, Walid, was likely to authorize a revenge attack. Muhammad donned his armor once more and marched to counter the Byzantine contingent, which had been reinforced by Armenian troops led by Smbat. The two sides met near Kars, in modern eastern Turkey. Muhammad, a skillful and experienced general, won with relative ease, and he then returned with his army to the Arab base at Dvin. However, Walid had evidently decided that it was time to teach the Armenians a lesson. The Arab commander of the district of Nakhchawan was ordered to summon a number of the Armenian nobles under the pretext of including them in the official register and to distribute payments, which is explained as "the official maintenance given to the Armenian nobles and their cavalry," indicating that the old Sasanian system of granting subsidies to the nobles had been continued by the Arabs. However, once they were assembled "he confined them in a great church and set fire to it, thus incinerating them, and he allowed their women to be taken as spoil."

News of this massacre evidently circulated widely, for it was recorded in Armenian, Byzantine, and Muslim sources. It prompted many Armenian nobles to flee their country. Smbat Bagratuni left with his clan to Phasis on the Black Sea coast, where the Byzantines allowed him to establish a safe haven. However, when Walid felt that his point had been made, he recalled Muhammad and dispatched a certain 'Abd al-'Aziz ibn Hatim as governor of Armenia (706–9), who receives a surprisingly positive write-up in the Armenian sources: "He had poor hearing, but was a man of prudence, full of earthly wisdom, a teller of stories and proverbs. . . . He pacified the country by protecting it from all unjust attacks." He issued an oath in writing guaranteeing the lives and property of the nobles and thus persuaded them to return to their ancestral seats. Prudently, though, he fortified the city of Dvin to give greater protection to the Arab garrison stationed there, installing new gates and a moat around the city walls. Possibly the reason for the more favorable attitude toward Armenia, which extended also to the other Caucasian polities, Georgia and Albania, was that the Arabs now faced a growing threat to the north, namely, the Khazars, and so it made sense to keep their southern Caucasian vassals loyal.

The Mixing of Arabs and Non-Arabs

For the first fifty years or so after the death of Muhammad there was a quite clear demarcation between the conquerors and the conquered. The former were mostly Arabs and mostly Muslims, though not as uniformly so as later histories suggest, and the latter were mostly non-Arabs and very few had converted to Islam.[15] The conquerors were mostly soldiers, who received stipends and lived in garrisons, while the conquered were civilians, who paid taxes and lived in villages and cities. Given that the conquerors were enormously successful and enjoyed many privileges and access to power, it was inevitable that some of the conquered would want to join them. This was not so easy initially, but the situation gradually changed as a result of policy decisions of 'Abd al-Malik and his immediate successors, and a great mingling of peoples and traditions from North Africa to Central Asia was set in motion that resulted ultimately in the emergence of a new civilization, what we call Islamic civilization. It was a complex process, which involved the adoption by the conquered people of the religion (Islam) and identity (Arab) of the conquerors. This did not happen in a passive manner, but rather the two ingredients of Islam and Arab identity were refashioned and reformulated by those who took them on.

This last point is worth emphasizing, since both medieval Muslim and modern Western histories often give the impression that the Arabs conquered and imposed their values and identity on a passive native population, whereas in reality the latter over time absorbed the Arabs and reshaped their values. To understand this, it is worth thinking about numbers. It is very difficult to estimate pre-modern populations, but the order of magnitude we should think of is about 250,000–300,000 Arab conquerors settling among some 25 to 30 million conquered residents, so approximately one Arab to 100 non-Arabs. Since for the first half-century the Arabs mostly lived apart in garrisons rather than settling among the conquered, they were not immediately assimilated. However, they brought back to their garrisons huge numbers of prisoners-of-war from all the lands that they had conquered, in part to remove able fighting men from potentially rebellious regions,[16] and in part to use them as personal valets and household servants, as tutors and scribes, as wives and concubines. This inevitably eroded the barriers between the conquerors and the conquered, and it was facilitated by the fact that the generation of Arabs that had emigrated from Arabia and the Syrian steppe to join the jihad were now mostly dead, and a large proportion of their descendants had grown up far away from their parents' native lands, in garrisons in the urban landscapes of Egypt, Syria, Iraq, and Iran. In short, it was not long before blood was mixed, boundaries were blurred, and religion and society were fast transformed.

Conversion of Non-Arabs to Islam

A crucial aspect of this transformation was the conversion of the conquered population to Islam. Thus, Islam acted as a medium whereby non-Arabs could join the conquest elite and consequently could play a role in shaping its culture and ideology. The Arab conquerors do not seem to have expected or planned for this to happen. God had ordained that the conquered people would be the Arabs' booty, not their equals. Later Muslim historians maintained that the conquerors had offered their opponents the opportunity to convert before fighting them, but this is never mentioned in earlier sources. As John of Fenek observed: "Of each person they required only tribute, allowing him to remain in whatever faith he wished."[17] However, since neither the Qur'an nor Muhammad had put up any bar to conversion, it is not surprising, given that it offered the chance of partaking in the privileges of the conquerors, that many aspired to it.[18] The only snag was that to convert one had to have an Arab patron, in the early period at least. The Arabs initially thought along tribal lines and so required that those who were joining the ranks of the Muslims become affiliated with a tribe. This was in some ways a practical measure, for being a member of a tribe meant that if you fell on hard times or were the victim/perpetrator of a crime your fellow tribesmen would take responsibility for you. But it also meant, ostensibly at least, that non-Arabs were taking on aspects of the conquerors' world (Arabizing), such as an Arab name and the genealogical outlook of the tribal system. Many non-Arabs who had status in their own community balked at having to submit themselves to an Arab patron. However, this issue did not arise for those who had been taken captive, for they were assigned as booty to an Arab. They were wrenched away from their family and friends and their homeland and taken off to the garrison towns to perform a variety of jobs. In this predominantly Muslim milieu there was a strong inducement to convert to Islam. Conversion was no guarantee of manumission, but many would have built up good relations with their masters, who often agreed to free them to deepen the bond between them or in return for a fixed period of service or monthly payments. This transformed them from a captive into a freedman.[19]

Many of these captives ended up in Arab households, supplying services of various kinds. For example, one papyrus preserves a register for the maintenance of the household of 'Abd al-'Aziz ibn Marwan, brother of the caliph 'Abd al-Malik and the governor of Egypt (685–704), and there we find numerous freedmen acting as secretaries, physicians, messengers, tailors, saddlers, sailors, and laborers. There are also free Christian Egyptians on the register, among them Athanasius bar Gumaye, a nobleman from northern Mesopotamia, who is described as being "responsible for general affairs in the various provinces" and is assigned a team of forty-four secretaries. He joined the Arab government of his own volition, as a free man (who had never been enslaved), but more commonly former captives staffed the higher echelons of the regime. A good example is Raja' ibn Haywa; he was originally from Mayshan province in southern Iraq, where he was captured by a warrior of the tribe of Kinda and settled with him in the Palestine-Jordan region. His manifest abilities brought him to the attention of the caliph 'Abd al-Malik, whom he served in a number of capacities: as tutor for his son Sulayman, as a financial manager for the construction of the Dome of the Rock on the Temple Mount in Jerusalem, and as an emissary on certain important diplomatic missions (Figure 5.5).[20]

Contemporary evidence for conversion among non-Arabs in the early decades of Arab rule is very rare. There is the report of the Egyptian chronicler John of Nikiu that when the Arabs' invasion began to succeed, some of his countrymen "apostatised from the Christian faith and embraced the

FIGURE 5.5 The Dome of the Rock completed ca. 692 by 'Abd al-Malik in Jerusalem. Photo (EA.CA.1406) by K. A. C. Creswell © Ashmolean Museum, University of Oxford.

faith of the beast," but it is not until the reign of 'Abd al-Malik that reports about conversion to Islam start to become common in our contemporary sources. The phenomenon evidently worried some Christian authorities, who censured any who abandoned their community and their faith, especially when they did so "without being subjected to any compulsion, lashings or blows."[21] Others were pragmatic, such as Jacob, bishop of Edessa (d. 708), who issued advice to his flock on this matter. For example, he ruled that penitent apostates close to death may receive the eucharist; Christians who become Muslim and then return to Christianity do not need rebaptism, but they should observe a period of penance; and Christian wives of Muslims who threaten to convert to Islam unless given the eucharist should be granted it, but with an appropriate penalty.

The rate of conversion varied substantially from community to community. The Jews had long before adapted to living as a minority under foreign rule and so probably fared best. The Christians had a history of resistance against the pagan Romans which they could draw upon for strength and inspiration, and the anti-Chalcedonians among them had already established their own independent hierarchy in the period before Islam, which meant that they were well placed to take advantage of the virtual self-rule that the Arabs expected of them. Zoroastrian communities survived in mountainous and remote areas quite well, but in the cities, where they had in any case been losing ground to Christianity in the sixth century, they seemed to founder after the loss of state patronage, and so more readily renounced their faith. The speed of conversion was also linked to the potential for interaction and intermarriage with Muslims, for the children of mixed marriages were always counted as Muslims by the state. In Egypt, where the Muslim presence was light for the first two centuries of Arab rule, conversion was very slow, and Islam only became the majority religion around the fourteenth century. In Iraq and Khurasan, however, which bore the brunt of early Muslim settlement, opportunities for social intercourse were numerous and conversion correspondingly more frequent, with Muslims being a majority by the tenth century if not before.

Non-Arabs and the Evolution of Islam

Inevitably, many of these converts—and even more so their descendants, who had been born into Islam—wanted to explore and expound their new religion and to reconcile it with their former faith and culture. Additionally, scholarship was a way for newcomers and the lowborn to attain respect and status; "if it were not for [our expertise in] the sayings of Muhammad," observed one non-Arab religious authority, "we would be on a par with greengrocers."[22] Since Islam had no clergy and in its early stages had no colleges to restrict accreditation, scholarship was open to all who had the time, inclination, and ability to pursue it. Numerous converts availed themselves of this opportunity and dedicated themselves to elaborating a new worldview. There are too many to even begin to list them, but here are a few of the most famous: Muqatil ibn Sulayman (d. 767), a captive from Balkh, author of the earliest extant Qur'an commentary; Yazid ibn Abi Habib (d. 746), son of a captive from Nubia, the top legal authority in Egypt of his generation; Ibn Ishaq (d. 767), grandson of a captive from 'Ayn al-Tamr in Iraq, author of the most famous biography of Muhammad; Ibn Jurayj (d. 767), grandson of a captive from Anatolia, a prolific collector of sayings of Muhammad; Abu Hanifa (d. 767), grandson of a captive from Kabul, eponymous founder of a law school; and Hammad al-Rawiya (d. 772), son of a captive from Daylam, an expert on ancient Arabic poetry. Although all of these men attained maturity later than the period treated in this chapter, they were all born during the reign of 'Abd al-Malik or Walid and were in effect the product of the Islamizing policies of these two rulers.

The conquerors themselves realized that non-Arab converts were starting to ascend the social ladder of their society, as is illustrated by a number of contemporary anecdotes. One relates how the scholar Ibn Shihab al-Zuhri went to see the caliph 'Abd al-Malik, who asked him about who was the top religious authority in the key regions and cities of the empire—Arabia, Egypt, Syria, the Jazira, Khurasan, Basra, and Kufa—and whether they were Arab Muslim or non-Arab Muslim. In every case except for Kufa they were non-Arab Muslims. This prompted the caliph to exclaim that the non-Arabs "are going to predominate over the Arabs to such an extent that they will preach to them from the pulpits, with the Arabs down below listening." "But commander of the faithful," retorts Ibn Shihab, "it is all a matter of religion; whosoever assimilates it will be in charge and whoever neglects it will lose out."[23] The story is quite possibly apocryphal, but it nicely illustrates that the definition of what it meant to be Arab was changing. 'Abd al-Malik is holding to the old definition, what we might call an ethnic Arab: a person who is (and whose parents and grandparents were) a full member of an Arabian tribe, not one who has become (or whose parents or grandparents became) an affiliated member of such a tribe (a freedman/*mawla*).[24] More and more, though, this ethnic qualification for being an Arab, in which genealogical and geographical elements predominated, became irrelevant and a cultural definition began to take hold: someone who spoke Arabic, had an Arab name, and signed up to the evolving cultural and moral norms of the conquest society.

Soon it became difficult to tell these cultural Arabs apart from ethnic Arabs. When the question was posed, for example, about Ibrahim al-Nakha'i (d. 713), who went on to become an accomplished Muslim jurist, whether he was a "real" (i.e., ethnic) Arab or not, no one was sure, and so they had to check in the military register under the tribe of Nakha', and he was found to be inscribed there as a non-Arab client of this tribe. In another case, a soldier of the Tamim al-'Ijli tribe encountered on the north Iranian frontier a man whose family he knew and who asserted that he was directly descended from the tribe's forebear al-'Ijl. "Your father did not try to trace his descent among the Arabs," he said to him, "but rather among the Persians, so how can you claim that al-'Ijl is your ancestor?" to which the man replied: "My mother told me so." Of course, prejudice and backbiting about who was a "real" Arab went on in some quarters, especially on the part of Arabs of good pedigree who had a vested interest in preserving the old definition of Arab identity and who were worried about being swamped by the newcomers. Gradually, however, this new definition of Arabhood took hold, as is evident from a number of sayings put into the mouth of the prophet Muhammad that espoused an inclusive definition of being an Arab; the most liberal of which simply stated that "whoever speaks Arabic is an Arab."[25]

One could say that the Arab Empire became an immigrant society, but people were not migrating from one country to another (though some were doing that as well), but from the ranks of the conquered to the society of the conquerors. And quite quickly we pass from a conquest society composed mainly of ethnic Arabs to a cosmopolitan immigrant society where Muslims are from everywhere, even though many, and especially their descendants, become labeled Arab. So Arab becomes a term like "American," applied to people with very different roots but who have shared cultural values and a common language. Already by the end of the Umayyad period we find Muslims of non-Arab origin in all walks of life and at all levels of society below that of the caliph himself. It was initially frowned upon for them to marry Arab Muslims, and only those with high status and good connections managed it. For instance, the caliph Yazid I's maternal aunt married a freedman, but only his brother dared joke openly that she had been given away to a slave; and Qahdham ibn Sulayman, grandson of a captive from Isfahan, was able to marry an Arab woman of the Banu al-Jarud because of his position as a senior financial secretary in the Umayyad administration and the high status of the Arab family that he was affiliated to. However, these restrictions began to lapse over time, especially when the Umayyad dynasty was overthrown in 750 by men from east Iran and Transoxania, a majority of whom were non-Arabs.[26]

Non-Arabs in the Army

It was not only in the religious sphere that non-Arabs made their mark, but also in the military world, although this was at first harder for them to break into. The conquering armies had initially consisted principally of Arab tribes. Except for certain groups with recognized martial qualities, such as the Luwata Berbers, the Daylamis, elite Sasanian cavalry units, and so on, non-Arabs served in the military only in an ancillary role, as craftsmen, laborers, guides, personal assistants, and the like. The tribal nature of the army made accommodating non-tribal recruits difficult, and it was only done for special cases—the Sasanian cavalry, for example, were repackaged as a unit of the east Arabian tribe of Tamim. However, tribes were unwieldy to mobilize and keep in the field, and they became caught up in political issues, as the second civil war showed. ʿAbd al-Malik's right-hand man, Hajjaj ibn Yusuf, decided therefore to professionalize the army. Chiefs and tribes were gradually replaced with generals and regiments. He also took the opportunity to reform the expensive remuneration system, replacing stipends as a reward for past participation in conquests with a regular salary for continuing military service. In effect, he created a professional standing army, and those Arabs who did not want to be full-time soldiers dropped out and became civilians.

The way was now open for non-Arabs to enter the army and there were two particular factors driving their enrollment. On the demand side, the intense and bitter confrontations between various Arab groups, beginning with the second civil war, prompted the various contenders to try to gain a numerical advantage by employing non-Arabs. For example, when more and more slaves of the Muslims began escaping to join the Byzantine-led insurrection in the mountains of Lebanon ʿAbd al-Malik had a herald go out and proclaim that any slaves who returned would be freed and would have his name inscribed in the army register, a promise that he fulfilled and placed them in a unit of their own. Mundhir ibn al-Zubayr complained to his brother ʿAbdallah, who was competing with ʿAbd al-Malik for the caliphate, that in the course of fighting his opponents he had to face "Aramaean peasants." And this became a frequent criticism of the Syrian troops, namely, that alongside them fought a medley of non-Arab groups. As the rebel Yazid ibn al-Muhallab said to his followers before they marched against an oncoming Syrian army in 720: "There have come against you Berbers, Slavs, Jaramiqa, Copts, Aramaean peasants and a motley assortment of folk." Such statements were of course intended as insults, but there was enough truth in them to make them credible, and it is in line with what one expects from a successful imperial army. This development reached a peak in the time of the early Abbasids, whose armies, as someone who watched them in action in the Jazira in the 760s reported, consisted of "a mixture of all nations; they were called 'the clients of the caliph' and they included Sindis, Alans, Khazars, Medes, Persians, Kufans, Arabs, Khurasanis and Turks."[27]

On the supply side, the Arabs found that there was no shortage of non-Arab volunteers. It was well known that "you only have to let a herald announce that whoever converts will be freed of taxes and 50,000 Muslims will come to you" ready to serve on your behalf. Not only did you not pay taxes in the army, but you also received wages, and so there were many among the conquered people who were willing to sign up. This availability, when combined with the frequency of revolt among the Arabs, meant that caliphs, governors, and even some powerful and/or wealthy individuals began to acquire whole retinues of freedmen and occasionally of slaves. And it was not only Arab potentates: during the second Arab civil war Persian noblemen are recorded as fighting alongside Arab generals using their own freedmen and slaves. Many such retinues were presumably of mixed provenance, but some were derived from a specific location—such as the Qiqaniyya (from modern southwest Pakistan) and Bukhariyya (from Bukhara)—or recruited by a specific person, who presumably commanded the retinue on behalf of its master. The Waddahiyya, for example, were led by a Berber freedman of the Umayyads named Waddah, and this office passed to his descendants. One is reminded of the late Roman *bucellarii*, private armies that were equipped and paid for by various magnates and that acted like personal bodyguards or elite units. However, a more likely model is the pre-Islamic Central Asian institution of *chakars*, professional soldiers recruited from the general population by Turco-Sogdian nobles to whom they were personally loyal and to whom they were bound, at least on some occasions, by a concept of fictional adoption. "These were men of ardent valour," wrote the seventh-century pilgrim Xuanzang, "who looked upon death as a return to their kindred and against whom no foe could stand."[28]

Initially, non-Arabs were only found in the rank and file of the military, but gradually they managed to work their way up into the officer grades. The career of Hayyan al-Nabati (d. 720) is instructive. The general Masqala ibn Hubayra picked him up either while a governor in Fars or on campaign in Tabaristan, or else in one of the slave markets of Basra or Kufa. We do not know about Hayyan's early career, but we find him as commander of the non-Arab forces in Khurasan in the early eighth century. He was particularly esteemed as a negotiator of truces and treaties with rulers in Iran, presumably because he himself had belonged to the Persian nobility and spoke Persian. His son Muqatil became one of the most famous scholars of Balkh, and because of the respect he gained thereby various eastern governors employed him as a messenger and mediator on their behalf. In 747 he commanded the pro-Umayyad forces at Balkh, illustrating how integral to the Arab army non-Arabs had now become.

Non-Arabs in Revolts

The non-Arab Muslims that we hear most about in our sources are those who joined the Arab Muslim establishment, but there were some who decided to oppose it, teaming up with a variety of different rebels, both Arab and non-Arab, Muslim and non-Muslim. There were many such movements, and it is worth looking at a couple of illustrative examples. The first concerns an insurrection that occurred during the second Arab civil war in Nisibis, a strategic town on the modern Turkish-Syrian border. Byzantines and Persians had fought over it in the past, and now, according to the monk John of Fenek, who lived nearby, it was being claimed by both the ruling Umayyad clan and by anti-government rebels.[29] The latter were led by Mukhtar ibn Abi 'Ubayd, who claimed to be acting on behalf of a son of the caliph 'Ali. Angry with the Arabs of Kufa when they lost a battle to the Umayyads, he gave orders that all their slaves should be liberated and go into battle in their masters' stead. These slaves then rallied round Mukhtar in the thousands, and "all that they had in their hands was either a sword or a spear or a stick." They were, says John, "slaves of captive origin" and "include among themselves all the peoples under heaven." In August 686 they participated in a battle on the river Khazir, near Mosul, on the side of Mukhtar and against the Umayyad governor 'Ubaydallah ibn Ziyad. The latter was defeated and the slaves then entered Nisibis and held it, and drove off all who tried to take it from them. They slew the general appointed over them by Mukhtar's right-hand man, along with all his comrades, for "they preferred to have someone from their own ranks as commander" and not one who "belonged to the Arabs." Others of captive origin collected together and joined those who were in the city of Nisibis. Every day more would turn up from every quarter and join them. They captured a number of fortresses, and "the fear of them fell on all the Arabs."

The Muslim sources confirm that a kind of slave revolt was taking place, though they are only concerned with the Arab reaction to this: "Our slaves are rebelling against us," complained the Kufan notables, "yet they are our booty which God has granted us together with these lands." John makes it clear that we have here a rebellion of men removed from their homelands and forced into a life of servitude in the strange environment of the Arab garrison towns, and who have now seized the opportunity afforded them by Mukhtar to rebel against their masters. Not all in Mukhtar's forces were slaves as opposed to freedmen still serving their masters (the Arabic sources usually refer to "slaves and freedmen"); but those in possession of Nisibis were clearly all prisoners-of-war, resentful against their Arab captors and seeking their freedom. The guerrilla troops that the emperor Constantine IV let loose in the Lebanese mountains in the 670s evidently tapped into the same well of resentment, for their ranks were likewise swelled by runaway captives. The Arab conquests had led to the capture and displacement of huge numbers of people, and now that the Arab Empire seemed to be unraveling, many of these prisoners-of-war were seizing the opportunity to escape their servitude. It is interesting to see just how many and how susceptible to recruitment they were: within fifty years of the conquests they had been enrolled as participants in Arab power politics, a harbinger of things to come. However, in the end, because they were neither well equipped nor well trained, they were no match for the experienced Arab troops once the latter had patched up their differences and ended their civil war.

A second example is provided by the exploits of Musa ibn 'Abdallah ibn Khazim, who, upon the assassination of his father, gathered round him some of his own Arab tribesmen and a number of local toughs (sa'alik) and crossed into Transoxania in search of adventure. They were generally moved on by nobles nervous of their intentions, but the lord of Tirmidh, a fortified town on the river Oxus, gave them hospitality. He was to regret this, for

Musa decided to make this his home and ousted his host in unceremonious fashion. He and his followers ran what was effectively a little city-state, and their ranks were soon swelled by men of diverse backgrounds, all with a grudge against the Umayyads and their governors. The most illustrious guests were the brothers Hurayth and Thabit Qutba, local aristocrats who had converted to Islam and attached themselves to an Arab tribe, but had been insulted by Yazid ibn al-Muhallab, the governor of Khurasan (702–4, 715–17), and now offered their services to Musa. Arab and Turk armies tried at different times to wrest Tirmidh from Musa, but all were repulsed. He only met his demise when the coalition of Arabs and locals that he had forged began to come apart and the two sides ended up by destroying each other. Musa was successful for a long time at binding together the different groups in part because he himself was a product of two worlds. His father, 'Abdallah ibn Khazim, of the tribe of Sulaym from west Arabia, had grown up in an Arab tribal setting and fought in Arab armies in numerous campaigns on the eastern frontier, but Musa's mother was the daughter of the ruler of Azadawar, near Qumis in north Iran, and Musa had spent most of his time in the east. In the epic account of his exploits he comes across as someone who transcended the black-and-white categories of Arab/non-Arab, Muslim/non-Muslim, and high-born/low-born, and illustrates how shifting, ambiguous, and complex were the relations between these various groups. [30]

Chapter Six

RETRENCHMENT AND REVOLT
(715–750)

he period up to 715 witnessed a huge expansion of the Arab Empire, as far as North Africa and Spain in the west, and as far as Sind and Transoxania in the east. The caliph Sulayman (715–17) had hoped to extend these successes and to crown them with the capture of the ultimate prize, Constantinople, but a two-year siege in 717–18 ended in a total failure and the loss of most of the invasion force. This not only drew to a close the dream of adding Byzantium to the list of defeated enemies, but it also encouraged other peoples to challenge Arab suzerainty and contributed toward the stalling of the conquest juggernaut. Substantial defeats at the hands of the Franks, Khazars, Turks, and Indians in the 730s put limits on the extent of Arab rule. Then, in 740, Berber revolts erupted across North Africa, which resulted in the secession of segments of that region from Arab control and the emergence of local dynasties, a phenomenon that would spread across the empire in the ninth century.

The position of Byzantium had looked a little precarious following the loss of Carthage in 698 and a string of defeats in Anatolia in the ensuing decade. However, the competent emperor Leo (717–41) managed to keep the resolve of the Byzantines steady in the face of the Arab siege of their capital and, buoyed up by this success, he was able to complete the process begun by Constans and Constantine IV of ensuring that Byzantium had the strength and resources to survive and to some degree flourish for another few centuries. Leo capped his achievements with a victory in 740 against a large Arab army, comprising 20,000 cavalry, which had advanced into Phrygia, west central Anatolia, under the command of the renowned warrior 'Abdallah al-Battal. The Arabs were surrounded and massacred to a man; as one Christian observer noted, "such a disaster had never befallen the Arabs before."[1] After a century on the defensive, Byzantium had now regained its confidence and was willing once more to engage Arab armies in the field rather than just to cower in their fortresses. The Arabs were thus obliged to acknowledge, albeit tacitly and grudgingly, that the Byzantines, along with the Khazars, Franks, and Indians, were not, for the time being at least, going to be subjugated.

Yet this was no doom-and-gloom time for the Arab rulers. They were now beginning to feel comfortable with their newfound wealth and set about spending it on visual displays of their piety and power. Walid I (705–15) inaugurated this activity by erecting the elegant and beautiful mosque of Damascus (Figure 6.1) so that Muslims could feel proud that they had a prayer place to rival the splendid churches of the Christians.[2] His successors followed eagerly in his footsteps, commissioning an impressive number of public and private structures. Sulayman "built palaces, gardens and mills" by the spring of Jericho, and contemporary Christians marveled at the many "villas, shops, hostels and gardens" constructed by the caliph Hisham (724–43).[3] Many of these monumental edifices are still standing or have been recovered archaeologically and attest to a major building program by the Umayyads and their associates, a dramatic demonstration in stone of their earthly might (Figures 6.2 and 6.3). Their detractors would say, however, that too much power and wealth was in the hands of this one family: Walid, Sulayman, and Hisham were all sons of 'Abd al-Malik, as was Yazid II (720–24), and 'Umar II (717–20) and Marwan II (743–50) were his nephews. This narrow concentration of power ensured a stable succession for a while, but it also stoked increasing resentment, which

FIGURE 6.1 Courtyard entrance to prayer hall of the Umayyad Mosque of Damascus, commissioned ca. 706. © Alain George.

culminated in a whole series of revolts in the 740s and the overthrow of the Umayyad family in 750 together with their network of Syrian supporters.

Constantinople and Anatolia

When Sulayman came to the throne in 715, the Muslim year 100 (AD 718) was fast approaching and this was trumpeted as the year when Muslim rule would triumph across the known world. Hoping to fulfill this prediction, Sulayman pledged: "I shall not cease from the struggle with Constantinople until either I conquer it or I destroy the entire dominion of the Arabs in trying."[4] The caliph's brother, Maslama, was to mastermind the expedition. He mustered a huge army and built 5,000 ships, which he filled with troops and provisions. He assembled 12,000 workmen, 6,000 camels, which he loaded with

FIGURE 6.2 Wall paintings from the Umayyad palace of Qasr al-Hayr al-Gharbi, northeast of Damascus, showing court musicians and mounted archer in Persian style. © National Museum of Damascus.

weaponry and catapults, and 6,000 mules for transporting provisions. On top of this, 3,000 volunteers signed up to supplement the regular soldiers; they belonged, according to a Syrian source, "to the class of Arabs without possessions," and presumably they went along in the hope of gaining divine credit and earthly spoils. Arab financiers provided mounts for the troops on the basis of hire or sale in the expectation of being recompensed from the booty to be extracted from the imperial city. As with previous attempts on

FIGURE 6.3 External view of the Umayyad palace of Qasr al-Hayr al-Sharqi in the Syrian desert, east of Damascus. Photo (EA.CA.549) by K. A. C. Creswell © Ashmolean Museum, University of Oxford.

Constantinople, the attack was to be two-pronged: Sulayman ibn Muʿadh was to proceed by land and ʿUmar ibn Hubayra by sea.

After an extended march to the city of Amorium in west central Anatolia, Sulayman encountered there the Byzantine general Leo. He reached an understanding with the Arabs, leading them to believe that he would help them capture Constantinople, and in return Maslama gave orders that no one should do any harm in Leo's region, "not even taking a loaf of bread." For his part, Leo commanded that a traveling market should be loaded up for the Arabs, and the Byzantines bought and sold in good faith and without fear. Leo's real aim was to seize the imperial office for himself, as he thought that he was best qualified to protect Byzantium from the Arabs, but inevitably Byzantine citizens who saw him in the company of enemy troops were very nervous of his intentions. At Amorium, he went right up to the walls and spoke with the leaders and the foremost men of the city, explaining to them that his objective was not at all to betray the Byzantines and that his relationship with Maslama was a pretense designed to save his country from destruction. Perceiving that Leo was indeed the man best suited to be emperor they exchanged with him oaths of allegiance. Troops dispatched by Emperor Theodosius happened to arrive shortly thereafter with orders to kill Leo, but when they reached the latter's camp and the two armies met, the Byzantines on Leo's side and those who had been sent by Theodosius agreed unanimously to crown Leo. Then they all marched to the imperial city where the citizens welcomed them with a festive escort and deposed Theodosius in the spring of 717.

In the meantime, the main body of the Arab troops had spent the winter of 716–17 in Anatolia, while Maslama had sent Sulayman ibn Mu'adh with 12,000 men to lay siege to the city of Chalcedon, on the east side of the Bosphorus facing Constantinople, in order to cut off supplies from that approach to the capital and to lay waste and pillage Byzantine territory in general (Map 4.1). When Maslama heard that Leo had become emperor he was overjoyed, supposing that the latter would soon find an opportunity to fulfill his promise and deliver the city to him, and Leo wrote constantly to Maslama, encouraging him in these vain hopes. At the same time, he was fortifying the city, gathering into it plenty of supplies and readying ships for combat. Furthermore, he came to a financial arrangement with the Bulgars so that they would assist in the defense of the city. Eventually Maslama realized Leo's deceit and he made ready his army and his ships, and in June of 717 he crossed over into Europe. Leo, for his part, had received intelligence about Maslama's movements and he sent men to scorch the earth in the whole region to the west of the city and to cut off the roads by which provisions were brought to the Arab army from Syria.

Maslama's army erected a huge camp outside the west walls of the city, opposite the southern (Golden) Gate (Figure 6.4). They dug a wide trench between the camp and the city, and another one behind it, between the camp and the Bulgars, and they protected the whole by building a breast-high parapet of dry stone. On the first of September the naval support arrived: "enormous ships, military transports, and light ships to the number of 1800." However, the wind then dropped and the big ships,

FIGURE 6.4 View of Theodosian walls of Constantinople (as seen ca. 1930). © Ian Richmond.

heavily laden, found themselves becalmed. Leo had prepared for this eventuality and sent against them fire-bearing vessels. The Arab armada was a sitting target: "some ships were cast up burning by the sea walls, others sank to the bottom with their crews, and others were swept away in flames." Unfortunately the winter of 717–18 proved particularly harsh: "so much snow fell that the ground was made invisible for a hundred days." With provisions now in short supply the Arab troops were in a perilous situation, and matters were made worse by the frequent deadly stealth attacks of the Bulgars, whom the Arabs came to fear more than the Byzantines. They dreaded going back without their caliph's permission and in any case the sea was so rough that it prevented them from leaving. "Constrained thus on every side, with the spectre of death before their eyes, they abandoned all hope." As for Maslama, he deluded the Arab army with the promise that very soon the Byzantines would surrender the city and that donations and supplies would arrive from Syria.

The Byzantines had inflicted such deprivation on the Arabs that they had begun to eat dead animals and dung. In the Arab camp, a measure of wheat had reached the price of ten gold coins and a head of livestock was being sold for two or three gold coins. Many of them used to walk down to the ships and tear off a piece of pitch and chew on it all day long. While they were in these dire straits, the caliph Sulayman died, and so did his son, to whom the Arabs had sworn allegiance as his father's successor. Succession passed instead to 'Umar, a nephew of the caliph 'Abd al-Malik, a softly spoken man with a reputation for piety and sincerity. As soon as he became ruler, he put all his energies into rescuing those Arabs trapped in the Byzantine Empire. First, he arranged for fleets to bring them supplies; 400 transporters laden with grain made their way to Constantinople from Egypt and a further 360 transporters came with arms and provisions from Africa. However, on their arrival some of the Egyptian Christian crew sneaked out by night on skiffs, sought refuge in the city, and apprised its inhabitants of the two Arab fleets hidden in the bay. At once Leo dispatched light boats with fire-throwing equipment, and these were able to sink some ships and put the rest to flight. Laden with what cargo they could salvage from the wrecks, the Byzantine crews returned in triumph to Constantinople.

On receiving news of this, 'Umar concluded that he had no recourse but to call off the siege. He sent an envoy bearing a stern letter to Maslama, in which he warned against causing the ruin of the Arab army and ordered him to decamp. Maslama at first tried to conceal the command from the troops, but they came to know what the caliph had ordered and proclaimed it publicly throughout the camp: "Caliph 'Umar has commanded you to leave and to return to your own country." In the summer of 718 they began their long journey home. Some looked to leave by sea and embarked on the remaining ships, but even then they were harried, for a storm overtook them and sank most of the ships. The survivors clung to the wreckage and were driven over to the shores of the country of Thrace while others ended up on remote isles and were marooned there. Caliph 'Umar sent troops with mules and horses to escort those who had come away by land, for all their livestock had either been eaten or perished of starvation.[5] He also sent food

and money, and he issued a call throughout his empire to everyone who
had a brother or other relative in the army under Maslama's command to
accompany him home. "Many went out to meet them and did all they could
do to save them."

France and the Franks

The Arabs initially fared much better in the far west. The decentralized nature
of the Gothic kingdom had made it easy for them to practice divide and rule
and to win over many local nobles with generous terms of surrender, allowing
them to retain their lands and autonomy. Matters were very different, however, in the land of the Franks, and here the Arab-Berber forces faced much
stiffer resistance.[6] In the 720s a series of Arab governors launched campaigns
against the Franks, even besieging Toulouse, but without achieving any lasting success. The last and greatest attack, commanded by the governor 'Abd
al-Rahman ibn 'Abdallah al-Ghafiqi (730–32), began as an attempt to capture
the Berber chief Munnuza, who had gone over to the Franks and married the
daughter of Odo, the duke of Aquitaine. 'Abd al-Rahman besieged him in his
mountain hideout in the Pyrenees. When water became scarce, Munnuza fled,
but, wounded, he could not outrun his pursuers and so he threw himself off
a cliff, impaling himself on the sharp rocks beneath, out of a desperate desire
to avoid being captured alive. 'Abd al-Rahman took the opportunity to raid
deep into Frankish territory. He crossed the Garonne and Dordogne Rivers
and confronted Odo, who slipped away when it became evident that the battle
was going badly for his side. 'Abd al-Rahman pursued him, plundering Tours
on the way. Then, somewhere between Poitiers and Tours, in October 732, he
encountered Charles, the powerful consul of Austrasia, the northeast sector of
the Frankish kingdom. For seven days the two sides nervously eyed each other
and tested each other with probing sorties. Finally, battle lines were drawn and
the fight began. "The northern peoples remained immobile like a wall, it is
said, holding together like a glacier in the cold regions, and in the blink of an
eye they annihilated the Arabs with their swords." The triumph seemed a sign
of divine favor to many Christians and the Anglo-Saxon monk Bede summed

it up with the words: "The Saracens who had wrought miserable slaughter on Gaul . . . were punished for their faithlessness."

There are almost no contemporary descriptions of this battle and concrete details about it are hard to come by; even its location is uncertain, and it tends to go by the name of one of the nearest of the two large towns: the battle of Tours or the battle of Poitiers. Gradually, however, its significance grew in the European imagination. Charles was hailed as a savior anointed by Christ and he was later awarded the sobriquet of "the hammer" (Martel). By early modern times the battle had taken on enormous proportions: one of the most important encounters "in the history of the world," when "the world's fate was played out between the Franks and the Arabs," when Europe was saved from subjection to "Asiatics and Africans." In characteristically vivid prose Edward Gibbon had speculated that were it not for Charles's victory the Koran might be "taught in the schools of Oxford and her pulpits might demonstrate to a circumcised people the sanctity and truth of the revelation of Mahomet."[7] Yet, though this defeat was a substantial one, it was not the reason that the Arabs achieved no further victories of note north of the Pyrenees. In fact, the very next governor after 'Abd al-Rahman undertook a new expedition against the Franks, but before he had even reached Zaragoza he was informed by letter of the outbreak of a major revolt among the Berbers of Africa and he hurried back to Cordoba. At this stage there were mere rumblings of dissent, but in 740 a full-scale insurgency on many different fronts erupted and continued for a number of years as the Berbers "openly shook their necks from the Arab yoke." Arab rule was never fully reinstated in the province of Africa, which witnessed instead the emergence of a variety of dynasties, some of local origin, some from outside. This meant that Arab-ruled Spain, known as Andalus, became somewhat cut off from the central government in Damascus and this was made definitive when a son of the defeated Umayyad family, on the run from the Abbasid revolutionary armies that had toppled their regime in 750, installed himself as the province's new ruler. Losing the support of the caliphs, now based in Baghdad, meant that the Arab sovereigns of Andalus no longer had the manpower to embark upon expansion into other countries, and even in their core territory they had to be careful to cultivate links with the Berber clans and the local Hispano-Roman aristocracies lest these unite to eject them.

North Africa and the Berbers

The Berber rebellion of the 740s occurred in many of the same areas where there had been uprisings against the Byzantines two centuries before, but now the main Berber actors were not just Christians, but also Kharijite Muslims, who adhered to a form of Islam that opposed the monopolization of power by one clan and sought to make the post of caliph open to all and its holder accountable to his subjects. This suited well a people who felt little in common with the remote caliphs of Damascus and their Arab agents, and who were accustomed to chiefs of more humble standing. Their principal motive was probably still regional pride and dislike of domination by outsiders, as it had been in Byzantine times, though control of the lucrative trade in gold and slaves with sub-Saharan Africa also played a part. The Arab conquest was still recent and the Arab presence principally limited to garrisons, and so much of the resident population would have viewed the Arabs as an alien occupying force and resented their meddling in local affairs. Though brief, notices in Christian chronicles do seem to confirm this sense of difference and remoteness: "Many Saracens [i.e., Arabs] were killed by the Romans [i.e., natives/non-Arabs] of Africa" and "the people of Africa rebelled and killed their governor and every Muslim [i.e., Arab] there."

Our earliest Muslim account of the uprising says that the two initiators, one Berber and one Byzantine African, both converts to Islam, led coordinated revolts in August 740, at a pre-arranged time, in the region of Tangiers. At the first major confrontation, in November of that year, the revolutionaries annihilated a large Arab force and killed a considerable number of the local Arab leaders, which led to this engagement being dubbed the Battle of the Nobles. A new governor of Africa was hastily dispatched from Damascus and the following year he led a sortie against the Berbers, now under the command of a chief of the Zanata tribe, who were "naked and wearing nothing but undergarments."[8] Once more, however, the Arabs were defeated and the new governor was slain. A certain 'Abd al-Wahid ibn Yazid of the Berber Hawwara tribe, who had been acclaimed as their caliph, wiped out another Arab force during the autumn of 741. The caliph Hisham appreciated that the situation was becoming critical, and so he sent his most experienced general, Hanzala ibn Safwan of the powerful Syrian tribe of Kalb, to serve as the new governor of Africa with just one mandate: crush the insurrection. He arrived at Qayrawan in March 742 with a huge army and immediately set about arming all adult males in the city so as to bolster his military strength even further. 'Abd al-Wahid approached Qayrawan a couple of months later, but though he and his men put up a fierce fight, killing many of their enemy, they were outnumbered and Hanzala remorselessly pushed home his advantage until all opponents had died or fled.

Although the dream of a unified Berber caliphate in Africa was shattered in 742, the region continued to drift away from central control from this time onward. Numerous local dynasties popped up across the region, some of them very long-lived and many of them incorporating ingredients from Berber culture. For example, the Barghawata polity on Morocco's Atlantic coast endured for over four centuries (744–1058); they allegedly had their own Berber holy family beginning with the prophet Salih, used a Berber version of the Qur'an, and held to a number of Berber dietary and magical practices.[9] This process culminated in the emergence of the two most powerful Berber kingdoms, the Almoravids (1062–1147) and the Almohads (1147–1248), who came closest to realizing the idea of a Berber Empire, at one point holding the entire African littoral from Benghazi to the Atlantic and the southern part of Spain.

Transoxania and the Turks

Over in the far east of the Arab Empire, Qutayba ibn Muslim had conquered much of Central Asia in the course of the caliphate of Walid (705–715). When the latter died, Qutayba seemed to fear that the new ruler, Sulayman, would dismiss him, and so he asked his men to rebel with him. They refused outright and when he upbraided them, they fell upon him and killed him—a sad end for a great general. For the next five years there was a lull in campaigning in the region; Sulayman had concentrated all his resources on Constantinople and the failure of this venture made his successor, 'Umar II, wary of any further expansion. Sensing an opportunity and encouraged by rumors that Arab rule was destined to last only one century, a number of Transoxanian nobles wrote to the Chinese emperor pleading for military support. The most interesting is that from Ghurak, lord of Samarkand and king of Sogdia (710–37), since it also gives an account of the Arab capture of the city:

> For thirty-five years we have been battling constantly against Arab (*ta-shih*) brigands; every year we have sent on campaign great armies of soldiers and cavalrymen without having had the good fortune to receive any military aid from the imperial majesty. Six years ago the chief general of the Arabs, the emir Qutayba, came here with a huge army; he fought against us and we suffered a great defeat at the hands of our enemies, and many of our men were killed or wounded. Since the infantry and cavalry of the Arabs were very numerous and our forces could not resist them, I withdrew into the fortress to protect myself. The Arabs then besieged the city: they set 300 catapults against the walls and breached them in three places. They wanted to destroy our city and our kingdom. I humbly request that the imperial majesty, being now informed, dispatch here a contingent of Chinese soldiers to help me in these difficult times.

The king of the Surkhab valley, southwest of Kabul, also sent an emissary to the Chinese court, complaining that "all that was in my treasury and my storehouses, all my precious objects and jewels, as well as the riches of the people who are my subjects, have been appropriated by the Arabs, who carried them off for themselves." And the lord of Bukhara lamented that "every year we have suffered the incursions and ravages of the Arab brigands and our country has enjoyed no respite" and he asked for an imperial decree ordering the Turks to come to his aid.[10]

Whether in response to a Chinese decree or not, the western Turks did become actively involved in the resistance against the Arabs in Transoxania. Their fortunes were revived by the able leader Suluk (715–38), who was chief of one of their subgroups known as the Turgesh. He is referred to by Chinese sources as Sulu and described by them as a "diligent and moderate" man who "loved and governed his people well." He had to fight on two fronts: the Eastern Turk confederation to the east and the Arabs to the west. By marrying the daughters of the Eastern Turk leader, as well as of the king of Tibet, he placated his east flank. In 720–21 he turned his attention to the west and dispatched an army to campaign alongside some Sogdian nobles; together they engaged an Arab contingent northeast of Samarkand and though nothing decisive was achieved, it is clear that the Arabs were pushed onto the defensive. Emboldened by the entry into the fray of the Turgesh, some Sogdians rebelled against the Arabs, led by a certain Dewashtich, the ruler of Panjikent (Figure 6.5), whom we know of thanks to the chance survival of a portion of his correspondence. There he refers to himself as, and is addressed as, "lord of Samarkand, king of Sogdia," challenging the current holder of that title, Ghurak, who had been nervous of overtly going against the Arabs. We see Dewashtich writing to a number of authorities, especially the Turks and the lords of Ferghana and Shash, beseeching them to support his struggle.

FIGURE 6.5 Wall painting from a palace in Panjikent, mid-eighth century, showing a local nobleman in typical Hu attire. © State Hermitage Museum, St. Petersburg.

Unfortunately for Dewashtich, the new governor of Khurasan was the implacable Sa'id al-Harashi (722–24). Having received intelligence of the vulnerability of Arab rule in the region, Sa'id crossed the river Oxus as soon as he received his posting in late June 722. The Sogdian nobles were divided as to what to do: one group wanted to make a stand and sided with Dewashtich, whereas the majority opted to seek asylum with the king of Ferghana. However, the queen mother of Ferghana was not well disposed to these refugees and informed Sa'id that the Sogdians had already left their land and established themselves at Khojand, which lies 150 miles northeast of Samarkand as the crow flies and is the gateway to the fertile valley of Ferghana. Sa'id advanced upon it at full speed and, after a brief siege, the city's inhabitants surrendered. A postmaster sent Dewashtich a short message about the conclusion of the affair: "Here is the news: Khojand is finished and all the people have left on the guarantee of the emir; whatever nobles, merchants and farmers there were, some 14,000, they have evacuated." If this is a reference just to the Sogdians, and not the locals, then they had evidently undertaken a major exodus to escape from the avenging Arab force. Their fears were justified, for though Sa'id had promised them safe passage, he subsequently executed them, the nobles among them at least. A month later, in the late summer of 722, an Arab contingent dispatched by Sa'id caught up with Dewashtich in his mountain stronghold to the east of Panjikent and brought to an end the revolt of this would-be king of Soghdia.[11]

This was the last Arab success in the region for a while, as Suluk stepped up his offensive; in 724 his forces surrounded an Arab army invading Ferghana and annihilated all bar a few in a battle known to Muslim sources as the Day of Thirst. This prompted a major uprising against the Arabs right across Transoxania, and by 730 only Samarkand and a couple of fortresses were left in Arab hands. In 731 Suluk besieged Samarkand itself. The commander of the Arab garrison in the city sent an impassioned plea for help to the governor of Khurasan, Junayd al-Murri, who was at that time in Balkh. He marched to Kish and then paused to consider whether to take the long way round to Samarkand, via the plains to the west, or to follow the more direct route, which involved crossing a steep ridge of mountains through the Tashtakaracha Pass. He opted for the latter, but as luck would have it he encountered a Turgesh unit in the vicinity of the pass. Junayd's men held out, but it was clear that they would not escape alive without reinforcements. The only option was to turn for help to those they were meant to be helping, that is, to call upon the commander of the Arab garrison in Samarkand to come to their aid. Reluctantly its commander set out with 12,000 soldiers and managed to relieve Junayd, though in the process lost all but 1,000 of his men. Junayd and the remnants of his army made it into Samarkand where they were able to hold out long enough for the Turks to get tired and leave. This Battle of the Defile, as it came to be known, marks a low point in the rule of the Arabs in Transoxania. Had they not managed to hold Samarkand, they might have lost control of the entire region to the Turgesh.

Thwarted in their expansion plans to the west, the Turgesh turned to the east; but this proved no more fruitful for them and in 736 Suluk was soundly defeated by the Chinese in the Tarim basin. He resolved to try one last time to dislodge the Arabs and in 737 he crossed the Oxus accompanied by allies from Sogdia and Tukharistan; their target was the city of Balkh, which the current governor of Khurasan, Asad ibn 'Abdallah, was using as his headquarters. Suluk divided up his troops and dispatched them to raid in different directions. It turned out to be a bad decision, for Asad came out with a very large force and encountered the khagan with only a relatively small retinue. Suluk was obliged to flee, and with this second defeat his reputation was fatally damaged; the next year a rival Turgesh faction hunted him down and slew him. With this threat removed, the new Arab governor of Khurasan, Nasr ibn Sayyar (738–48), was well placed to reassert Arab control of the region. Previous appointees had generally come from the west, with little or no knowledge of this complex land, but Nasr had spent most of his adult life there, in the staff of previous governors and as governor of Balkh. He had some appreciation of the local culture and politics and was sensitive to the fact that there had been more than three decades of continual campaigning, which had caused huge loss of life on both sides. He therefore adopted a conciliatory stance upon taking up office. He wrote to the Sogdian nobles inviting them to return home and promising to fulfill their previous requests, namely: "those who had been Muslims and then apostatised should not be punished, no excessive demands for repayment of debts should be imposed on any of the people, they should not be required to pay any tax arrears which they owed to the treasury, and they should not have to return Muslim prisoners except at the decree of a judge backed up by the testimony of trustworthy witnesses."[12] Many regarded Nasr as weak for caving in to such demands, but his policy of accommodation certainly lowered the tensions in this volatile frontier region and extended Umayyad rule there by a decade or so.

In the end, though, this policy of moderation came too late to save the Umayyads, who faced a number of challenges from the east. Most significant was the insurgency masterminded by the shadowy figure of Abu Muslim, a native of east Iran/Transoxania, who recruited a large army from his homeland, comprising both Arabs and non-Arabs, and dispatched it westward to overthrow the Umayyads. Less reported is the Chinese attempt to reassert their authority in these lands in the wake of the enfeeblement of the Turgesh in 738 and of the collapse of the eastern Turk confederation in 744. This initiative was spearheaded by the celebrated Tang general Gao Xianzhi (also written Kao Hsien-chih), of Korean origin, who scored a number of victories in the Pamir-Himalaya mountain region, particularly against the Tibetan Empire, from which he wrested control of the Buddhist kingdom of Gilgit, in modern north Pakistan, in 747. And when a couple of years later the kings of Ferghana and Shash clashed and sought the backing of their imperial overlords, the Chinese and the Muslims respectively, Gao acted decisively, subjugating the capital of Shash after a short siege and taking many prisoners, including the king himself. Confrontation between the two empires seemed now inevitable. The Muslim garrison at Samarkand was alerted by refugees from Shash and its commander, one Ziyad ibn Salih, marched eastward once he had received reinforcements from Tukharistan, determined to teach the Chinese a lesson. Some 300 miles northeast of Samarkand, at Talas on the modern Kazak-Kyrgyz border, he encountered Gao Xianzhi, who was supported by men of Ferghana and Karluk Turks. The fighting took place over five days in July 751 without any breakthrough for either party, but then the Karluk contingent switched sides and the Tang troops were quickly routed.[13]

Like the Battle of Poitiers/Tours, the Battle of Talas has acquired legendary status, in this case in the Arabs' favor. The great Sinologist Carrington Goodrich ranked it as "one of the decisive battles of history," and the renowned Russian Orientalist Vasily Barthold regarded the Tang defeat as the decisive factor in determining "which of the two civilizations, the Chinese or the Muslim, should predominate" in Central Asia. In reality, as with the Battle of Poitiers/Tours, too much credit has been assigned to a single event. It may have slowed the Chinese advance, but it certainly did not stop it; indeed, only two years later the Chinese successfully dislodged the Tibetans from the Pamir region. The halt to Tang ambitions to the west was actually brought about by the rebellion of An Lushan, commander of all the armies of northeast China, which took seven years to quash (755–63) and caused irreparable damage to the Tang Empire. Provincial governors seceded, distant territories were lost, and the Tibetans and Uighur Turks grabbed most of the western half of modern China and divided it up among themselves. The *History of An Lushan*, composed some fifty years after the uprising, emphasizes the Hu (east Iranian/Transoxanian) background of its subject: his father was Hu, he wore Hu dress, and his close followers were Hu. It also accords him a cult-like status: "He was seated on a double bed while incense was burned before him and precious objects were arranged. . . . The crowd of Hu around him prostrated themselves at his feet to implore the blessings of Heaven, and he had the animals prepared and arrayed for sacrifice, while the sorceresses beat the drums, danced and sang."[14] There are many similarities between An Lushan and Abu Muslim: both hailed from the wealthy, cosmopolitan, mercantile region of east Iran/Transoxania, both proved to be masters of strategy in the planning of their respective insurgencies, and both inspired such fierce devotion in their supporters that they became the object of cults after their death. But whereas An Lushan failed in his aim of promoting Hu ascendancy in the Chinese Empire, Abu Muslim succeeded in winning a bigger role for the inhabitants of east Iran/Transoxania in the future direction of the Islamic Empire.

Caucasia and the Khazars

Another group that caused the Arabs a headache at this time was the Khazars, who had slowly been forging their own identity and establishing their own polity in the wake of the withdrawal of the west Turk confederation from Caucasia in 630. They co-opted many local peoples under their lead, such as the Alans and Sabirs, and from their capital on the river Volga they controlled a large swathe of the Ponto-Caspian steppe in what is now southwest Russia. Taking advantage of the second Arab civil war they launched raids across Caucasia in 685, which brought them into conflict with the Arabs, and in the first half of the eighth century there were numerous confrontations of increasing severity between these two youthful and ambitious powers. 'Abd al-Malik's son Maslama, who took over the governorship of Armenia and Azerbaijan from his uncle in 710, led a number of campaigns into Khazar territory, just beyond Darband, without achieving anything notable, but keeping his opponents on the defensive. In 718, though, encouraged by the failed Arab siege of Constantinople, the Khazars began to take the offensive and to raid Arab lands. They continued this over the next few years and in 722, during a particularly bitter winter, they confronted and wiped out much of an ill-prepared Arab regiment, inaugurating a period of Khazar ascendancy.[15]

In 726 the Khazar khagan sent his son, Martik, who marched southward as far as Azerbaijan and besieged the settlement of Warthan, to the northeast of modern Tabriz, and defeated and killed the Arab governor of Armenia, who had come to lift the siege. Two years later Maslama targeted the khagan himself, but after a few days of skirmishing he almost fell into the hands of the enemy and only escaped by abandoning all the supplies of his camp, the servants, concubines and maids. Muslim sources merely note that "he returned safely," but the lack of any of the usual triumphant claims—God defeated the infidels through him, and so on—lends credence to the Christian reports of Maslama's ignominious flight. Martik returned to the fray once again in 730 and besieged Ardabil, the capital of Azerbaijan. Jarrah ibn 'Abdallah, who had been reappointed governor of Armenia, tried to relieve the city, but failed in the face of superior numbers of enemy troops. He sent an urgent message to the caliph Hisham requesting reinforcements, but even as Maslama marched to his aid with as many troops as he had been able to hurriedly muster, Jarrah and his men were put to the sword. The Khazar cavalry roamed unopposed right across the region, plundering as far south and west as Mosul. The residents of Ardabil, seeing no signs of help forthcoming, submitted, with the result that the Arab garrison was massacred, the women and children were taken captive, and "the Khazars took control of Azerbaijan." A hastily assembled force led by Sa'id al-Harashi, the former governor of Khurasan, was able to rescue the captives and drive the Khazars back, even seizing from them the bronze image that they bore on a standard. It was nevertheless evident that the Khazars had struck a major blow against the Arabs.

Despite harsh weather conditions, Maslama was dispatched in the spring of 731 with instructions to reassert Arab authority. Yet though he was able to inflict heavy losses—"he shed their blood like water on the face of the earth, and sated the birds of the sky and the beasts of the steppe with their flesh"—the Khazars blocked his progress beyond the Caspian Gates, at Darband (Arabic: Bab al-Abwab), and he could do no more than lay the groundwork for a more substantial future expedition. He recruited a large body of craftsmen and laborers and initiated the rebuilding and fortification of Darband, which was to serve as the major Arab garrison in the eastern sector of Caucasia (Figure 4.2), and he sent out a number of units to demand the submission of various strongholds in the vicinity. Command of Armenia, Azerbaijan, and northern Mesopotamia then passed in 732 to the competent Marwan ibn Muhammad, nephew of 'Abd al-Malik, who began by making peace with the Khazar ruler so as to buy time for rallying an army. In the course of 737, supported by Armenian troops, Marwan traversed the Alan Gates (the Darial pass), on the modern Georgian-Russian border north of Tbilisi, and passed through the land of the Alans until he entered the territory of the Khazars. Here he surprised the khagan who was obliged to flee for his life. The following year Marwan visited one by one the local lords in the mountainous region between the Caspian Gates and the Alan Gates, receiving or enforcing their submission. Effectively he was doing what Khusrau I had done two centuries beforehand, establishing a buffer zone between his realm and the steppe peoples to the north.

Though still wary of each other, the Arabs and Khazars had come to realize that neither of them could defeat the other and they moved from conflict to co-existence, consolidating what they already held and demarcating the limits of their territory. This northern limit to Arab Caucasia followed pretty much the same line as had existed between Byzantium and Persia and as exists today between the Caucasian republics and Russia. This is principally a facet of the region's topography, since the high northern Caucasian mountain range forms a natural barrier to north-south movement, bar the Caspian Gates in the east and the Alan Gates in the center. The same three principalities as had existed in Byzantine-Persian times—Armenia, Georgia, and Albania—survived alongside the Arab realm and they managed to maintain a high degree of autonomy. This was easiest for Georgia, which was more remote, and Armenia, which could more easily play the Byzantines and Arabs off against each other. Albania (Arabic: Arran), with its capital at Partaw (modern Barda), suffered greater loss of its independence, for it was easier to enter and traverse due to the wide coastal plain around Baku and the river Kura that ran through it. Moreover, it was the most accessible route for invaders from the north, and so the Arabs maintained a number of garrisons in the region, in particular at Darband, to which they transferred 24,000 Syrian Arabs, again following a policy of the Sasanian Persians before them. The Khazars themselves went from strength to strength, growing rich by acting as middlemen in the overland trade between Scandinavia and the Muslim world. Though tending to side with the Byzantines, they forged their own path, converting to Judaism and creating a distinctive and pluralistic culture.

Sind

The one piece of good news for the Arabs at this time was the conquest of the Indus River valley, known as Sind. The caliph 'Uthman had already shown an interest in this region and had ordered his governor of Basra to send someone to find out whether it was worth conquering or not. The scout reached the arid wastelands of Makran that lead on to Sind and sent back the message: "The water supply is scanty, the dates are inferior, and the robbers are bold; a small army would be lost there and a large army would starve." As a consequence of this intelligence, 'Uthman did not dispatch any army to this region. Some hardy Arab generals ventured in that direction anyway, but they encountered stiff resistance from the tribes of Qiqan in modern western Pakistan, and two of them lost their lives in the 660s. Others tried to march along the coast, but the going is tough, as Alexander the Great had found almost a millennium before, for rainfall is minimal and the craggy Makran Mountains come very close to the sea. Moreover, it was a sparsely populated region, though the rugged valleys and isolated ports harbored a number of Buddhist communities according to the seventh-century monk Xuanzang. In the 670s, a small Arab garrison was established there, but it was a very unpopular posting, a land where "most people are hungry and the rest are depraved."[16]

When Hajjaj ibn Yusuf was appointed viceroy of the East in 694, he resolved to take control of this wayward frontier. What allegedly goaded him on to this decision was a rather strange event that has caught the imagination of scholars into modern times. The lord of the "island of rubies" dispatched to Hajjaj, in the hope of winning his favor, some Muslim girls whose fathers were itinerant traders and had recently died. The reference is obscure, but in any case, the Med people of Daybul, a town in the Indus delta, east of modern Karachi, rowed out in canoes and captured the ship and its female cargo. A desperate plea for aid by one of the Muslim women eventually reached the notice of Hajjaj, who sent two generals, one after the other, to answer this entreaty, but both perished without accomplishing their task. A personal request by letter from Hajjaj himself to the local ruler, Dahir, met with the non-committal answer that "they were captured by pirates whom I do not control." This hard-hearted response and the plight of the Muslim maidens are usually made into the casus belli for the Arab invasion of Sind, though a number of years would appear to have separated the two events.

Hajjaj eventually settled on a kinsman of his as the right man to carry out the difficult job of extending his authority over Makran and Sind, namely, Muhammad ibn Qasim. He made sure his relative was fully equipped, even to the extent of packing for him cotton soaked in vinegar because he had heard that vinegar was scarce there, and then finally dispatched him in 710 with the inducement that "you are governor over whatever lands you conquer." Muhammad marched via Makran, first subduing Fannazbur in modern south-west Pakistan, and then kept going eastward until he reached Daybul. Using catapults he was able to breach the walls of the fort and damage the tower of the Buddhist temple, whereupon the local governor fled and the temple guardians and many residents were slaughtered. He then pressed on up the Indus valley seeking out the local sovereign, the aforementioned Dahir. When he caught up with him, a fierce battle ensued; Dahir was killed and so "Muhammad ibn Qasim gained complete control of the country of Sind." He sent a large proportion of the booty back to Hajjaj, who estimated its worth at 120 million dirhams, which pleased him greatly since he had only expended 60 million dirhams on equipping and transporting Muhammad's troops.

This is the outline of events presented by early Muslim sources, which gives us a fairly colorless picture of the Arabs marching around the country demanding submission, awarding guarantees of life and property to those who agreed and conquering by force those who refused, confiscating huge amounts of gold in the process. The only concrete detail concerns the founding of Mansura in the 730s, the capital of Muslim Sind, the ruins of which occupy some four square miles and lie about forty miles northeast of modern Hyderabad. Later sources, especially the famous thirteenth-century epic known as the *Chachnama*, present dramatically more information, including an account of the events preceding the Arab conquest. It narrates at length how the ruling Buddhist Rais dynasty was ousted in a coup by its Hindu minister, who then married the last Rais Queen. The two of them begot Dahir, who lost the kingdom to the Arabs.[17] Although this information has generally made it into the standard history books, none of it can be substantiated by contemporary sources. However, the monotonous statements of Arab victory in Muslim accounts can be set next to two declarations of success in battle against the Arabs by neighboring rulers in Gujarat. Presumably, some Arab contingents had marched south from Sind in search of more conquest and booty, or perhaps sailed in by boat, looking to seize a share of the busy Indian Ocean trade. Two of their encounters with the local population are described in texts written in Sanskrit on copper plates. These survived well in the wet climate of India and so were commonly used to record important transactions, especially land grants, but in addition to this official business, donors would often take the opportunity to proclaim their heroic exploits and virtuous deeds.

The earlier of the two texts, dated to 736, is from the Gurjara king Jayalbhata IV. Having completed the formal part of the text, that is, the details of the land grant, he proceeds to boast about his victory against the Arabs. "This is the same Jayalbhata," he affirms, "who, with the edge of his sword, has forcibly vanquished, in the city of the lord of Valabhi, the Arabs (*tajikas*), who greatly opposed all people, (and he did this) as a cloud extinguishes with its showers the fire that troubles all people." Valabhi was a celebrated center of Buddhist learning, possessing one hundred monasteries and six thousand priests according to Xuanzang, and it was also a bustling port, on the west side of the Gulf of Cambay, which may have been what attracted the interest of the Arab raiding party. Only a short time later Jayalbhata himself needed to seek help against the Arabs, turning to the more powerful Chalukya kingdom to the south. He gained the ear of a local Chalukya lord, who came to his aid with a contingent of troops. Like Jayalbhata a short time before, this lord makes use of a land grant document to advertise his successes. He vaunts the honors that he has received from the Chalukya sovereign and recounts the battle in which he defeated an Arab army. Since we have almost no such narratives from opponents of the Arabs in this part of the world, it is worth quoting in full:

> The Arabs had destroyed many renowned kings with their piercing, brightly gleaming swords. Hurling arrows, lances and clubs, the Arabs were eager to enter the South and conquer. From the outset they came to subjugate the realm of Navasari. The tough noisy hooves of their steeds kicked up the ground to shroud the earth with dust in all directions. Their bodies were hideous, their armour reddened with torrents of blood from innards that had burst out from the heavy bellies of great warriors who had rushed at them wildly and were mangled by the blades of their spears. The best among hosts of

kings had not defeated them before. Any number of champions' bodies were armoured with hair that bristled in the fury of their battle spirit. These were men who attacked the Arabs full on, giving their own heads in exchange for the extraordinary gifts and honours they had received from their lord. They bit their pursed lips cruelly with the tips of their teeth, their turbans and honed swords reddened by a thick veil of blood that had poured from wounds in the trunks and sloping cheeks of enemy elephants, which had only the nooks and crannies of countless battlefields for a stable. Though the Arabs were mighty warriors, who sliced enemy necks like lotus stalks and launched a hail of arrows tipped with forged crescent blades in a swift barrage to destroy their foes, they did not attain success. Though their bodies were covered with a coat of bristling hair on account of their martial spirit and excitement, they were defeated on the battle front when headless bodies began a circular dance to the accompaniment of the loud noise of drums beaten continuously in joy caused, as it were, by the thought "Today at least we have, by laying down our heads, paid off the debt we owed to our lord in (this) one life!"

Navasari and Valabhi lie either side of the Gulf of Cambay, through which many ships passed on their way to the ancient port of Barygaza, and so it is very likely that the Arabs were trying to extend their control over international trade routes in the Indian Ocean. The two texts cited suggest that they were thwarted in this endeavor. Another copper plate, dated 753 and stamped with an image of the god Shiva, records that a Rashtrakuta king defeated the Chalukyas in 753 and appropriated their territories. This empire of the Rashtrakutas, religiously tolerant and culturally vibrant, dominated a large portion of the Indian subcontinent and lasted until the tenth century, limiting any further Arab military expansion southward from Sind. It did not stop peaceful commerce, however, and we find a few references in Indian sources to such activity by Arab traders, or at least by those who are described as such (tajikas), though whether this meant ethnic Arabs or Muslims (whether Arab or non-Arab) or inhabitants of the Abbasid Empire of whatever religious persuasion is impossible to tell. From ninth-century Kollam, in southwest India, we have a set of copper plates that record in Tamil a land grant in favor of two trading communities. The text sets out the conditions under which they can trade and is signed and witnessed by fourteen persons writing in Persian (in both Pahlavi and Hebrew script)—comprising Zoroastrians, Jews, and Christians—and eleven persons writing in Arabic, both Muslims and Christians. Evidently, then, trade was a very international business and here Arab Muslims rubbed shoulders with all manner of other races and creeds.[18]

A Society of Muslims and Non-Muslims

Before 'Abd al-Malik we have no evidence for the public display of Islam by the state. Possibly caliphs before him thought that Islam was only meant for the conquerors, not for the conquered, or that, as with Muhammad's community, people could keep to their own religion and there was no one official creed, or else they did not want to antagonize their non-Muslim subjects while their rule was still new and fragile. We do not really know, but in any case this situation changed dramatically from the time of 'Abd al-Malik when coins and documents, and even practical objects like milestones and glass weights, became emblazoned with Qur'anic slogans emphasizing God's oneness and Muhammad's mission. Individual believers, too, especially those going on pilgrimage to Mecca, inscribed on rocks and stones their belief in God and His prophets and their desire to join them in paradise and stay out of hellfire (Figure 6.6). Entrances to monumental buildings—mosques and palaces—began to display Arabic texts paying homage to God's power and Muhammad's prophetic status. This change was a response to the need to unify the conquest community after its acrimonious civil war (683–92): it stressed the common faith that the majority of them held and it focused their attention on their chief surviving enemy, the Byzantine Christian empire. Many of the official religious slogans were accordingly chosen for their challenge to Christianity, in particular Qur'an 112: "God the one, God the eternal, He did not beget and was not begotten," and Qur'an 9:33: "Muhammad is the messenger of God whom He

FIGURE 6.6 Arabic inscription of 109 AH (727–28) from Jabal Ramm in southern Jordan, recording the prayer of 'Abd al-'Ala' ibn Sa'id that God accept his Ramadan fast and grant him peace, mercy, and blessings. © Alison McQuitty.

sent with guidance and the religion of truth that He might make it the dominant religion." And the magnificent Dome of the Rock (Figure 5.5), erected on the spot in Jerusalem where Jesus had predicted that "not one stone will be left upon another" (Mark 13:2), was decked out with beautiful tiles inscribed with a paraphrase of Qur'an 4:171: "The Messiah Jesus son of Mary was only a messenger of God, and His word which He committed to Mary, and a spirit from Him. . . . Do not say 'three.' . . . God is only one god; he is too exalted to have a son." This process of elevating Islam to the religion of state was inevitably accompanied by a demotion of all other religions, and in the decades after 'Abd al-Malik, Muslim lawyers gradually worked out a legal framework for incorporating all creeds into Islamic society whereby the non-Muslim faiths would have a subordinate, but protected, status within the new empire. The result was a society that was increasingly ordered along religious lines.

Differential Status

Of course, all states make some distinction between categories of people living within their borders and accord them different rights. Some differentiate between full citizens and resident aliens, the latter facing a number of restrictions. In the Greco-Roman world, such people (called *metoikos* in Greek, *peregrinus* in Latin) were not allowed to hold public office, own land, or marry a citizen (until the time of Augustus in the Roman case). The promotion of Christianity to the state religion gradually changed this situation and increasingly the distinction was between Christian and non-Christian, the latter further subdivided into adherents of a licit religion (Jews), who were—in theory at least—protected, or of an illicit religion (pagans), who faced severe constraints. The same model took hold in the Arab Empire, with non-Muslims being classified either as possessors of a scripture (*ahl al-kitab*), in which case they could pay a tax in return for protection and the right to continue in their religion, or as pagans (*mushrikun*), who faced the stark choice of conversion or death. The Sasanian Persian Empire, by contrast, tended to put more weight on social distinctions (having a caste-like system) than on religious distinctions. The Georgian patriarch emphasized to his Armenian counterpart that Khusrau II, unlike the Byzantines, "permitted every people to have its own religion," and certainly a number of groups that would have looked decidedly pagan to the Byzantine Christians, such as the Mandaeans and Yazidis of Iraq, enjoyed protection. Fortunately, the Muslim government in Iraq left in place this tradition, categorizing most as possessors of a scripture, and as a result such groups have survived until modern times, although in drastically reduced numbers.[19]

Medieval and modern historians tend to assume that the Arabs enforced the distinction between Muslim and non-Muslim as soon as they began their conquests. However, as we have seen, there were many non-Muslims in their ranks initially; what united them was their focus on jihad and so the distinction in the early decades was chiefly between conquerors and conquered. Only later, when most of the non-Muslims in the imperial armies had converted to Islam, did the division conqueror/conquered shift to Muslim/non-Muslim. In any case, it is only with 'Umar II that we begin to have contemporary evidence for discriminatory policies.[20] The stimulus for this seems to have been the ignominious failure of the Arab siege of Constantinople in 717–18 and the huge loss of Arab life. This defeat intensified hostility toward Byzantium, and by association toward Christians, and it also accelerated the professionalization of the army. Many Arab Muslims relinquished their military role and became civilians, but they did not want to rub shoulders on an equal footing with the non-Muslim conquered peoples. Accordingly, restrictions were placed on the latter to keep them in their subject position. The raw material for these restrictions came mostly from Byzantine curbs on Jews (not building new synagogues, not giving testimony against Christians, not defaming Christianity, etc.) and Sasanian Persian regulations for distinguishing between nobles and commoners (not wearing the same headgear, overcoats, belts, shoes, and hairstyles of the superior group, etc.). Gradually there evolved an extensive body of legal rulings governing what non-Muslims could and could not do and how they should behave toward Muslims. Jews and Christians and other non-Muslims became a subordinate class, and yet were integrated within the Muslim legal system and granted protection.

Differential Taxation

The most contentious aspect of this discriminatory policy was taxation. Initially, as one would expect, the Arabs, as conquerors and soldiers/rulers, did not pay any taxes. The (adult male) conquered people, on the other hand, all paid tax, irrespective of their religion or ethnicity, unless they were granted an exemption in return for providing military service or spying or the like. Contemporary Egyptian papyri make clear that there were a number of different taxes, but the main two were land tax and poll tax.[21] The latter came to be regarded as a religious tax, payable only by non-Muslims, but in the beginning it was simply what the conquered people paid to the conquerors, though it may have been perceived as apt that those whom God had evidently forsaken should pay for the upkeep of those whom God had patently favored. The Arab conquerors would probably have wished that things stayed that way: themselves living a life of luxury at the expense of the conquered. Inevitably, however, many of the latter sought to get a share of the immense privileges enjoyed by the conquerors, in particular, release from taxes. Fiscal agents for Hajjaj complained again and again that "the tax revenue has diminished, for the conquered people have become Muslims and gone off to the garrison cities." One group that we hear a lot about in the papyri of the late seventh and early eighth centuries are peasants who had fallen behind with their taxes and left their land in the hope of escaping their plight by conversion. In former times they would have sought refuge in a monastery, whereas now they hoped to find service with an Arab patron or to be enrolled in the army. This situation also left its mark in the Muslim literary sources, which recount numerous tales of ragtag groups of converts who served alongside registered soldiers in the army but received no pay or rations. The authorities did not want such untrained recruits in the military and worried about the depletion of the agricultural labor force, and so they usually had them rounded up and sent back to their villages where they would once again be liable for taxes.[22]

'Umar II, revered as the most pious and devout of all the Umayyad rulers, sought to extend 'Abd al-Malik's policy of promoting the status of Islam as the foundation of the Arab Empire. He was, therefore, angry at this treatment of converts to Islam and he wrote to his governors ordering them to desist from exacting taxes from Muslims, whatever their origin. He reinforced this point in an edict on taxation: "Whosoever accepts Islam, whether Christian, Jew or Zoroastrian, of those now subject to taxes and who joins himself to the body of the Muslims in their abode, forsaking the abode in which he was before, he shall have the same rights and duties as they have, and they are obliged to associate with him and to treat him as one of themselves."[23] His successors, however, obstructed this policy, and some governors circumvented it by agreeing to relieve recent converts of taxes, but only on condition that they could demonstrate the sincerity of their conversion by reciting a portion of the Qur'an and undergoing circumcision, which provoked widespread retraction. The problem might usefully be compared to the attitude of modern wealthy nations toward immigration. Being a citizen of such countries brings many benefits and those who are already citizens tend to be nervous that if the door is opened wide to immigrants those benefits will be diluted. The authorities would ideally like to accept only educated and skilled immigrants, but it can be difficult to justify a selection process on legal grounds and returning failed immigrants is always contentious. The conquerors were in much the same position: the benefits that they enjoyed were very generous, and so there really was no way that these could be extended to all who sought to join them without decimating the economy. The choice before them was either to use increasing force to stem the tide of would-be members of their club or to reduce the benefit package.

Not surprisingly, given their numerical inferiority, the Arabs chose the latter course and from the time of 'Abd al-Malik onward a number of major changes were introduced with the aim of making the financial basis of the Arab Empire more sustainable. First, as we have said before, the incentive to enroll in the army was reduced by commuting payments to soldiers as a reward for past participation into a regular salary for continuing service. One could no longer rest on former glory but had to remain an active and full-time soldier. This not only made would-be recruits pause for thought before signing up, but also prompted a number of existing members to opt out and join the civilian ranks. Second, to stem the reduction in land tax caused by non-Muslim farmers converting to Islam and Muslims buying land from non-Muslims, there was a shift from payment according to category of person (Muslim or non-Muslims) to payment according to category of land. In general, for non-crown lands, there was now a uniform land tax levied on Muslims and non-Muslims alike. The third reform was to provide a Muslim counterpart to the poll tax, which had come to be seen as a specifically non-Muslim tax; the solution was to make almsgiving for Muslims compulsory, collected just like a tax. This policy was probably introduced not long before 730, when we find Najid ibn Muslim, the governor of the Fayum district, south of modern Cairo, both justifying and explaining the new system to an underling:

> God sent his prophet Muhammad, may God praise him, with guidance and the true religion and everything that God approves of for his worshippers. On those belonging to the people of the religion of

Islam (*ahl al-islam*), the upright religion, God has imposed an alms-tax (*sadaqa*) on their property in order to purify them. . . . Give a receipt for everything that you have taken from each person . . . with their name, the name of their father, their tribe and village . . .[24]

By the second half of the eighth century, the island of privilege that the early Arab conquest society had been no longer existed. An average Muslim very likely paid less tax than an average non-Muslim, but it varied according to profession and status, and of course the reality of tax collection was very much more complex than the simple and elegant theories of the lawyers.

Muslim Revolts and the Fall of the Umayyads

Though they may have been necessary, these reforms to the tax system stoked resentment against the Umayyads and, together with the run of defeats experienced by the imperial armies in the 730s, added to the sentiment that the Umayyads were unjust and ungodly rulers. The Iraqi participants in Ibn al-Ash'ath's revolt in 701 first demonstrated their animosity by burning the tax registers, a sure sign of the object of their fury. Many different groups felt that they had lost out, in particular, local elites and recent converts to Islam. The former had been acting as tax collectors for the Arabs: the taxes on many cities and regions were assessed as a lump sum, and these local notables were entrusted with the task of apportioning it among the local inhabitants, a job that gave them autonomy, status, and the means to work the system as best suited them. As a part of the reforms, however, there was a gradual shift from collective to individual assessment, with the actual collection carried out more and more by agents directly appointed by the state, diminishing the role of the local nobility.[25]

Recent and would-be converts to Islam, especially low-status individuals, often encountered hostility from the authorities and were frequently denied the exemption from poll tax that they had been promised when they converted. This situation worsened as the number of converts increased, which happened in the aftermath of the failed siege of Constantinople when military campaigns were often supplemented by missionary activities, presumably in the belief that converts would be more loyal to the regime. For example, 'Umar II dispatched a group of Muslim religious scholars to Africa and Mauritania to disseminate Islam there in 718. Over in the east, Ashras ibn 'Abdallah, the governor of Khurasan (727–30), advertised for "a man possessing piety and virtue whom I may send across the Oxus to call people there to Islam"; the man they hired preached in the environs of Samarkand, declaring that those who became Muslim would be freed of the poll tax, "and the people flocked to him." New mosques were built and instructors taught the neophytes how to pray and recited Qur'anic verses with them in Persian. However, when Ashras realized that a consequence of his policy was a sharp drop in tax revenues, he ordered: "Take the tax from whomever you used to take it from," and so they reimposed the poll tax on those who had become Muslim, prompting many to apostatize.[26]

These and other grievances drove many into the arms of various opposition movements. There were two broad umbrella groups, which came in many local varieties, but represented two very different attitudes toward government. At one end of the spectrum were the Kharijites, who argued that the office of caliph should go to the most qualified and suitable person, irrespective of his ethnicity or ancestry, and that the caliph should be a first among equals rather than an absolute ruler. Charisma and authority rested, they felt, principally with the community, which had a direct relationship with God and did not need a powerbroker to act on their behalf. At the other end of the spectrum were the Shi'ites. Instead of a charismatic community served by the leader, they supported the notion of a charismatic leader served by the community. 'Ali, by virtue of his marriage to the daughter of Muhammad, had inherited the prophet's religious charisma, and it continued to flow through his descendants, whom Shi'ites therefore strove to place at the helm of the Islamic world. Both views of the leadership contrasted with the position of the Umayyads, who stressed that the right to determine political and religious matters had passed from prophets to caliphs and that they were the clan best suited to discharge this office.

Protagonists of these two anti-government movements had already been flexing their muscle during the second Arab civil war, but by the 730s they had become more numerous, largely by winning over many non-Arabs to their cause, and more ambitious. This is apparent in the numismatic record, for many of them were minting their own coins across surprisingly large areas. In northwest Africa, as we have seen, there was a rash of Kharijite uprisings, some of which led to the installation of local rulers at places like Tripoli and Tlemcen (in modern west Algeria). In Yemen one rebel had himself proclaimed caliph in 746, taking the regnal title "seeker of truth" (*talib al-haqq*), and went so far as to seize control of Mecca and Medina, though this prompted a swift response from the Umayyad authorities, who assassinated the pretender in 748. Kharijite revolutionaries were endemic in the countryside of the Jazira, but the disorder of the 740s allowed them to expand their operations, and coins struck at Mosul and Kufa by a local Kharijite leader and scholar show that they had managed to extend their authority to cities.[27]

Shi'ite rebels did particularly well in the former Persian lands at least in part because the idea of a leader belonging to a sacred lineage and endowed with divine charisma gelled well with ancient Iranian ideas of kingship. Also Shi'ism's belief that the gates of prophecy and divine inspiration were still open made it more receptive than other Islamic sects to tenets of the Persian religious tradition, such as messianism, dualism, cyclical time, and indwelling of the divine spirit. A good example is provided by the movement of the freed-man Mughira ibn Sa'id, who supported the imamate of Muhammad al-Baqir (d. 743), a great-grandson of 'Ali, and portrayed him as a savior figure. Mughira preached that God was a man of light, with a crown of light on his head, and that His limbs corresponded to the letters of the Arabic alphabet, and he taught an elaborate Creation myth which rested on a strong contrast between light and dark:

> God wrote with His finger on His palm men's deeds of obedi-
> ence and disobedience. The latter angered Him and He sweated, and
> two seas were formed from His sweat, one salt and dark and one
> sweet and bright. He gazed into the sea and saw His shadow. He went
> forth to seize it, but it flew away. He then plucked out the eye of His
> shadow and from it created a sun. He annihilated the shadow and

said: "There should not be another god besides me." He then made all creation from the two seas. He called forth the unbelievers from the salt, dark sea, and the believers from the sweet, bright sea; and he fashioned the shadows of men. The first shadows he created were those of Muhammad and 'Ali.[28]

Shortly after Muhammad al-Baqir died, 'Abdallah ibn Mu'awiya, a grandson of 'Ali's brother Ja'far, rebelled in Kufa, in October 744. He traveled from Iraq to Iran and traversed that land in search of support for his claim to the caliphate on the basis of his kinship with 'Ali and Muhammad, a message he substantiated by stamping on his coinage the Qur'anic verse "I ask of you no recompense except love of kin," which was understood by Shi'ites as an exhortation by Muhammad to honor his daughter Fatima, her husband 'Ali, and their descendants (Figure 6.7). Among 'Abdallah's most fervent followers were a loose-knit band known as the Janahiyya, who maintained that the spirit of God had first dwelt in Adam, and then passed to the prophets and imams, including 'Ali, his son Muhammad, his son 'Abdallah Abu Hashim, and then from him to 'Abdallah ibn Mu'awiya. Of course the latter may have

FIGURE 6.7 Coin of 'Abdallah ibn Mu'awiya (SICA 2/1370 = Shamma no. 1357).
© Visitors of the Ashmolean Museum, University of Oxford.

been suspicious, if not downright dismissive, of such elements within the ranks of his supporters, and in general the more staid wing of the Shi'ites were wary of those among them whom they saw as extremists (*ghulat*), but nevertheless Shi'ism did come to adopt a number of these Persian-influenced beliefs, especially the notion that their imams were divinely inspired.

Although very popular, these two religio-political movements by no means encapsulated the full range of opposition to the Umayyads and some uprisings had very local coloring. In the region around Balkh, in modern north Afghanistan, a rebel named Harith ibn Surayj managed to defy the authorities for twelve years (734–46) and won to his side a stunningly diverse array of supporters, including the khagan of the Turgesh. Muslim sources say that "he adhered to the doctrine of the Murji'ites," who professed that faith alone was sufficient to be a Muslim without any necessity for virtuous behavior. This was directed against the Kharijites, who said that good deeds were an integral part of being a Muslim and that evil deeds could exclude one from the Muslim community, but it attracted support from those converts who had been told that their conversion was not valid unless accompanied by actions such as memorization of the Qur'an and circumcision.

This region of east Iran/Transoxania provided a majority of the troops who would overthrow the Umayyad dynasty in AD 750 and also many of the scholars who would play a leading role in creating a new Islamic civilization, breaking it away from the more narrow Judaeo-Christian focus that it had had in Damascus and suffusing it with elements from this culturally syncretic world. There were a number of reasons why this region was so pivotal. First, its terrain is difficult for conquerors, and by the time they had got this far east the Arabs were overstretched; so whereas in west Iran they had crushed the local elites, here they worked with them, which meant that the region's culture was to some extent preserved. Second, many of the religions it harbored—Christianity, Buddhism, Manichaeism—placed a high value on literacy, and this was further strengthened by the strong mercantile credentials of the region as a major junction of trade routes between China, India, and the Mediterranean world. Third, the Arabs were commonly settled in cities among the population—at Merv, Balkh (after 726), Bukhara, and Samarkand, for example—rather than in separate garrisons, as happened in Iraq and Egypt. This, plus the missionary efforts initiated by some local governors, meant that there was much interaction and assimilation between the conquerors and conquered, and since the Arabs were relatively few and far from home they, or at least their descendants, took Persian wives, began to speak Persian, and attended Persian festivals like Nawruz. Ethnic and cultural allegiances became blurred and a Persianized Islam became the common idiom for a new elite. Tellingly, when the governor Nasr ibn Sayyar and the rebel Harith ibn Surayj decided to negotiate, they chose to represent them "men mindful of the Book of God," namely, Muqatil ibn Hayyan, a lawyer resident in Balkh, and Jahm ibn Safwan, a theologian resident in Tirmidh, both sons of Persian captives turned Muslim. And the architect of the Abbasid revolution, Abu Muslim, who was also a native of this region, when asked who he was, replied: "I am a man from among the Muslims and I do not trace my descent to any one group to the exclusion of another. . . . My only ancestry is Islam."[29]

People like Muqatil ibn Hayyan, Jahm ibn Safwan, and Abu Muslim are a good example of how quickly many of the conquered people became involved in the religious, cultural, and political life of the world of the conquerors. In the introduction to this book I pointed out how much Western scholars fixated on the speed of the Arab conquests, but what is much more remarkable is the rapid rate at which a new empire emerged from the ashes of the old. If one examines the family histories of some of the main actors of this new regime, both Arab and non-Arab, one can see that in only three generations their whole social situation and cultural orientation has changed beyond recognition. To some degree that is the exciting thing about all empires, and in any imperial capital in history one can find characters who have gone from rags to riches, from obscurity to fame, or from servitude to high office in a single lifetime. But this seems to have happened on a particularly grand scale and at an accelerated rate in the case of the Arab Empire, and it is to this question, of the rapid incubation of Islamic civilization, that we shall now turn.

Chapter Seven

THE MAKING OF ISLAMIC CIVILIZATION

A century or so of fighting and campaigning had seen Arab armies achieve victories from the Atlantic Ocean to the Aral Sea, from the Atlas Mountains to the Hindu Kush. Now, however, they had come up against a combination of natural barriers and well-organized states that impeded further progress. Islam would still spread further, but local dynasties, missionaries, and traders would henceforth act as its standard bearers, not Arab armies. This meant that the easy supply of booty dried up, prompting many more fighters to exchange their military gear for civilian garb. The focus on jihad and acquiring territory gave way to building an Islamic empire and forging an Islamic civilization. The conquests had provided the space for Islam to flourish but had not allowed the time for it to develop. Islamic law, science, philosophy, theology, literature, and art were all as yet in their infancy or still unborn. The large array of cultures that were now under Arab rule meant that there were abundant raw materials available for the task, and the increasing number of converts provided willing hands to do the work. The Abbasid revolution in 750 swept away the tight-knit Syro-Arabian elite and its obsession with tribal politics and opened the doors to the cosmopolitan world of Iraq and east Iran/Transoxania. The conditions were perfect for the reshaping of the cultural landscape.

One might legitimately ask if it were inevitable that Islam would be a feature of this new world order. Since around two thirds of the revolutionaries in the Abbasid armies were natives of the lands formerly a part of the Persian Empire, could they not have swept aside the religion that the Arabs had brought if they had chosen to do so? Yet it was in the name of Islam that they rebelled. The rapid downfall of the Sasanian dynasty must have convinced many in Persia that God was on the side of the Arabs and approved of their faith—success is always a powerful argument. What the rebels wanted, therefore, was not to get rid of Islam but to make it more responsive to their needs and more in tune with their culture and to free it from the control of an alien ruling elite in Syria. Some of the native revolutionaries were only superficially Islamized, as we can see from the extreme actions of followers of the Rawandi sect, who acclaimed the caliph Mansur as the messiah and jumped naked or wearing silk garments from city walls in the expectation of the end of days, but there is no reason to doubt their original sincerity and their hope that through Islam they would achieve a better life. Zoroastrianism's stronghold had been in southwest Iran, which had been hit hard by the Arab conquerors and its noble families slaughtered or dispersed, whereas east Iran and Transoxania had been home to many religions. Islam, made attractive by its link to power and the elite, provided a common religious idiom for all the diverse groups of this multi-faith land. Moreover, unlike Zoroastrianism and Christianity, it had no institutionalized clergy or hierarchy, which meant that it was particularly open to newcomers, despite prejudice from some quarters of the Arab population. There were a number of insurrections by Zoroastrian groups, especially in the mountainous regions of Iran, but these were isolated affairs, and their failure only served to confirm that by the late eighth century Islam was already too well established to be uprooted.[1]

Empire or Commonwealth?

Another feature that one might have expected to endure, at least for a few centuries, was a single unified imperial government over all the lands that the Arabs had conquered, but in the end it proved to be ephemeral. The Umayyad dynasty (661–750) did quite a good job, despite three civil wars, though of course they were as busy acquiring territory as governing it. The Abbasid dynasty that succeeded them, however, watched parts of the empire break away from day one of their rule. Spain was a direct casualty of the revolution, for some members of the Umayyad family fled there and made it their new home, and the implacable hostility of the Abbasid family toward them left them no choice but to secede. The Berber revolt in northwest Africa, though initially crushed, had set in motion an unstoppable exodus, and by the year 800 there were at least five autonomous dynasties in the region. A bloody civil war (809–13) between the sons of the caliph Harun al-Rashid weakened Abbasid rule in Iran and enabled a number of different types of dynasties of local origin to flourish there. Only a short while afterward the political fragmentation of the Arab Empire extended to the central lands, and in 945 Iraq itself was captured, first by Daylamis from northern Iran, who revived the Persian title "shah of shahs," and then in 1055 by Turks from Central Asia, which heralded a long period of Turkish domination in the Middle East. Political unity was never to return and the Muslim world remained a multi-polar one forever thereafter. And yet the societies ruled by these petty dynasties did enjoy a broadly similar culture. We can speak of an Islamic commonwealth or Islamdom in the medieval Middle East just as we can speak of a Christian commonwealth or Christendom in medieval Europe, that is, a loose amalgam of polities where Islam was the dominant (though not necessarily the majority) religion and where the general way of life had a significant number of common features. The Muslim geographers who bravely traversed these lands from the tenth to the fifteenth century present a picture that, although exhibiting numerous local differences, has reassuringly recognizable outlines: Turkish soldiers; Jewish merchants; Christian doctors; the symbiotic triad of mosque, church, and synagogue; lively bazaars; a passion for poetry; Arabic religious texts; Persian epic history, and so on.

Why, then, did a unitary Arab Empire last such a short time in comparison to its predecessors, that is, why did it not enjoy the same sort of life span as the Roman/Byzantine Empire (ca. 830 years until the Arab conquests) or the Persian Empire (ca. 1,100 years)?[2] There are two main answers to this, one topographical/ecological and the other ideological. The former is perhaps the most significant and can be put very simply: the Arab Empire was strung out over thousands of miles across deserts and mountains, which made communication and transportation slow and revolts at the margins difficult to contain. A similar problem afflicted many empires acquired in a rapid and relatively unplanned manner, such as that of the Turks (552–630) and Mongols (1206–94). By contrast, the Roman Empire, acquired much more slowly, was organized around the Mediterranean Sea, which allowed comparatively fast and cheap transportation of goods and troops, and the Persian Empire, though less integrated, was still quite manageable, predicated on control of the rich Tigris-Euphrates river system in Iraq by the adjacent Iranian highland peoples. These two water systems (the Mediterranean and the Tigris-Euphrates) were, however, separated by the stony wastes of the Syrian desert, which greatly hampered the efforts of any one power to dominate both of them (only the Achaemenid Persians and the Arabs ever managed it). Furthermore, a large proportion of the territory conquered by the Arabs consisted of marginal/arid lands, which had two potentially dangerous consequences: their empire was particularly vulnerable to climatic fluctuations and over-exploitation and also to the movements of the large populations of nomads who inhabited these lands, especially the Turk and Mongol tribes of the great Eurasian steppe. The so-called Medieval Warm Period, for instance, which lasted from the tenth to the early fourteenth century, resulted in very volatile climatic conditions in Central Asia, including persistent droughts and cold winters, and prompted the migration of some of these steppe tribes into the eastern part of the Arab Empire and their gradual usurpation of political power.[3]

Inhospitable terrain also impeded internal conquest. For the whole of the Umayyad period the inhabitants of pretty much every upland region within the lands claimed by the Arab regime maintained a high degree of autonomy. Some did so officially, acknowledged as vassals of the Arabs and accorded a treaty; in this position were the Armenians, Georgians, Albanians, and various peoples of the Caspian region. Many did so unofficially, such as the Berbers of the Atlas and Aures Mountains, and the Kurds and other peoples of the eastern Taurus/northern Zagros range in modern southeast Turkey and northwest Iran. This unofficial category we only tend to hear about when they came into conflict with the Arabs. For example, in 751, the Arabs of Mayferqat in northern Mesopotamia rose up against Abbasid rule and caused many problems for the people in the surrounding area. Those in the mountains organized their own militia under a local Christian named John son of Daddi. "From this point on evils increased between the people of the mountains and the Arabs, for they committed murder against each other every day without end. The people of the mountains seized all the passes; not one Arab was seen in the whole mountain region." Soon the affair spread and we hear of Armenians and Urartians (from the area around Lake Van) fomenting trouble in this region.[4] The mountains of the Middle East continued to harbor distinctive tight-knit communities fiercely attached to their identities and native lands, and it was principally in the cities of the fertile lowlands that the Arabs held sway. But of course it was in these cities that mainstream culture flourished, and so even when desert and mountain peoples succeeded not just in holding their own but also in conquering the lowlands, they were not able to impress much of their own culture upon Islamic civilization.

The second answer to the question of why the Arabs failed to maintain durable political unity concerns ideology. In effect, Islam itself became hostile to an imperial style of government, but that of course only raises the question of why it developed in that direction. Jesus had said that his kingdom was not of this world, but that did not stop Eusebius, bishop of Caesarea, from happily endorsing Constantine the Great as a Christian emperor upon the latter's conversion in AD 312 and drawing up a theoretical blueprint for Christian imperialism. The Qur'an, though it offers no detailed instructions on how to govern, does insist on obedience to "those in authority" (*uli l-amr*) and these and similar injunctions could easily have been used in support of an Islamic imperialism. Certainly Umayyad dynasts seemed willing to emulate the emperors of old, as we can see from a fresco in Walid II's palace of Qusayr 'Amra that portrays him receiving homage from past and present world leaders and from a poem of Yazid III that boasts of his kinship ties to the Persian, Byzantine, and Turkish royal families.[5] It was not to be, however, and there are two main reasons for this. First, since Islam, unlike Christianity, had no clergy (especially before the introduction of madrasas in the eleventh century), there was no hierarchy of religious staff to offer ideological support for an imperial Islamic rule in return for political and financial backing.[6] The men who began to lay the foundations of Islamic law in the eighth century were amateurs, either independently wealthy or pursuing their studies alongside their main occupation. They were mostly outside the political establishment and so tended to put into their writings an idealized portrayal of what government should be. This can be seen in their characterization of the caliph 'Umar I, the model statesman, who is presented as virulently opposed to the accumulation of wealth and power by the state. The only persons who did recommend a more imperial style of rule were senior administrators, but they did not have the moral authority to make it a part of Islam. One of their number, Ibn al-Muqaffa' (d. 757), did devise a blueprint for an imperial form of Islamic government, and it is telling that he was executed by the Abbasid caliph Mansur in striking contrast to Eusebius, who was personally honored by the Emperor Constantine.[7]

Second, many of the participants in the early Arab conquests were nomads and they had a nomad attitude toward the spoils of conquest, namely, that they should be redistributed to all directly and not accumulated by the state for apportionment at a later date.[8] "You have appropriated our spoils (*fay'*)" is the most common accusation of rebels against the government throughout the Umayyad period and "equal distribution of the spoils" is the most common pledge of revolutionaries to their followers. Soldiers were paid stipends by the state from the tax revenues that it had collected, but that meant they were dependent on the state, which added to their sense of grievance and made them more determined to reduce the power of the central government so that it could not filch what they felt was due to the rank and file. Arguments over who was entitled to what were legion, and changes to the system were very difficult to implement. The extreme concentration of power—in the hands of a single clan (Umayyads and then Abbasids) from just one tribe (Quraysh)—also exacerbated the situation. In short, a fair proportion of the soldiery of the early Arab army was disgruntled by the center's monopoly of wealth and power and did all they could to constrain an imperial style of government. Their attitude evidently fed into the idealized image of 'Umar I as a Bedouin hero: he wears rough animal-hair clothes, prefers his camel to a horse, is fiercely opposed to affected manners and ostentatious displays of wealth, and favors a simple and austere life over the fineries and fripperies of empire.

Arab Islam or Gentile Islam?

Whatever the exact reason, Arab rule over all the conquered land lasted only about 100 years (ca. 640s–740s), and Arab control of the central portion of their realm for about 300 years (ca. 640s–940s). Yet in this short time the Arabs were able to set in motion two processes that helped to offset their political fragmentation: Arabization and Islamization. These faced limits to their progress, and they happened much more slowly than is usually assumed, but there is no doubt that they were wildly successful even if there were compromises along the way. They tend to be regarded as one-way processes—the conquerors imposing their identity and religion on the conquered—but in reality the conquered were fully involved, especially those who converted to Islam, whose contribution was crucial.

Arabization has two aspects to it that are closely related: language and identity. Many of the conquerors spoke a dialect of Arabic as their native tongue and it had also been used by at least some of the tribes allied to Byzantium and Persia for their own internal administrative purposes in the century or so before the Arab conquests. It is not surprising, then, that the Arabs employed Arabic for certain bureaucratic purposes from the very beginning of their occupation. For the first few decades, local languages continued to be used alongside Arabic, but in the 690s the caliph 'Abd al-Malik, wishing to integrate better the former Persian and Byzantine realms, ordered that Arabic be the sole official language of the government offices. This policy took some time to come into effect, but by the mid-eighth century it was fully in place, and thereafter, if one wanted a good administrative job, it was essential to be well versed in Arabic. Historians of medieval Europe are often surprised by this success, for the Germanic invaders of the West Roman Empire all ended up learning Latin rather than imposing Gothic. In part, the difference is that the Arabs were more linguistically homogeneous than the Germanic tribes and possessed a holy scripture in Arabic, but there is also the practical point that the Arabs acquired not just one empire, but all of one (Persia) and part of another (Byzantium). This meant that they had to deal with not just one imperial language but at least two (Persian and Greek), as well as a whole host of very different regional languages—a situation that cried out for a lingua franca.

The pre-conquest languages of the Middle East had different fates. The lands that lay on the edges of the empire but that avoided direct conquest by the Arabs retained their languages and in many cases they are still spoken today, even if by substantially fewer people: Armenian, Georgian, Caucasian Albanian (spoken by the Udi people of modern Azerbaijan), Nubian (spoken by some tribes in modern Sudan), and various languages of the Hindu Kush region (e.g., Pashto). Within the Arab Empire, language survival was determined by a number of factors, the most important of which was the geography/environment of the area where the language was spoken. In mountain ranges and deserts they could survive more easily, as was the case with the Kurdish and Berber languages, whereas in the Nile valley of Egypt and along the coastal plains of North Africa there was nowhere to hide and their two languages, Coptic (Egypt) and Latin (North Africa), had already lost considerable ground to Arabic by the eleventh century and dwindled fast thereafter.[9]

A second major factor was the degree to which a linguistic community maintained its traditions and elites intacted in the course of the conquests and subsequent political changes. In the difficult terrain of eastern Iran and Transoxania, local potentates had been able to bargain with the invaders to preserve their autonomy. Since they had a political tradition as well as a historical-cultural one, they were also able to take advantage of the weakness at the center of the Arab Empire in the ninth century to establish their own independent dynasties, which permitted the use of the Persian language not only in speech but also, crucially, in writing. Whereas the Islamic religious tradition came to be inimical to imperial government, Persian literature celebrated it, remembering the great days of the Sasanian emperors, and for this reason it was enthusiastically adopted by various imperial rulers in the east, such as the Mongols of Iran (1258–1335), the Timurids of Central Asia (1370–1501) and the Mughals of India (1526–1757), who also all used Persian for their administration (Figure 7.1). The language was then taken up by the Safavids (1501–1736), who made it the official tongue of the whole of Iran, as well as making Shi'ism the official form of Islam in their realm. One might have expected the same thing to happen in North Africa, where independent Berber

FIGURE 7.1 Scene from Firdawsi's *Shahname*: Zal, mythical king of Iran, in the pavilion of Rudabeh, princess of Kabul; done in Indian style for a Mughal emperor. © British Library (Add 5600, fol. 42v, ca. 1616 AD).

dynasties emerged. However, they had no imperial tradition of their own to fall back on and so they based the legitimacy of their rule on strict adherence to Sunni Islam; this, plus the reliance of their economies on international trade, linked them with the central Islamic lands and favored the primacy of Arabic in their dominions. Berber only survived well in places difficult to access (the Atlas and Kabyle Mountains and the Sahara desert), which were unattractive to outsiders and where its speakers were locked into close communities, some of them adhering to different versions of Islam, such as Kharijism.

A third factor is the level and manner of immigration of native speakers of the politically dominant language. Large numbers of Arab troops were stationed in the garrisons of Basra and Kufa in Iraq and Fustat in Egypt, and many more settled in and around the cities of Damascus, Homs, and Aleppo, where Arabophone tribes had already been a familiar sight before Islam. Soon new cities were built, either for troops—like Mosul and Wasit—or for civilians—like 'Aqaba and Ramla. Even if not all who came to live in these centers knew Arabic when they arrived, they soon learned it, for there it was the language of power and everyday communication. By contrast, fewer Arabs settled in Iran and Transoxania and they were dispersed among the population, taking up residence in pre-existing cities rather than in newly constructed garrisons. This meant that over time the Arabs usually became Persian speakers instead of the Persians becoming Arabic speakers. For religious matters it remained important to know Arabic, but at the everyday level and for subjects like literature and history Persian was preferred. As the scholar who translated an Arabic history of Bukhara into Persian in 1128 observed, "most people (in Transoxania) show no desire to read an Arabic book."[10]

The large concentrations of Arabic speakers in Syria and Iraq quite soon had an impact upon the two main languages of the region, Greek and Aramaic. Greek was worst affected, since it was mainly spoken only in the cities and plains and so had no ecological niche in which to entrench itself, and a moderate proportion of the Greek-speaking elite had fled to Byzantium in the course of the Arab conquests. In addition, Greek's appeal came from being a lingua franca and the language of a powerful empire, but Arabic fulfilled these two functions much better than Greek by the eighth century, and by around AD

800 Greek had ceased to operate as a major language of the Levant and Egypt. Aramaic fared much better because it was the language of a number of discrete socio-religious communities that had learned how to organize themselves for survival in the period before the Arab conquests, such as the Mandaeans of southern Iraq and the various anti-Chalcedonian Christian communities of Syria, Iraq, and the Jazira. Some of these had the added advantage of living in mountainous areas, where even today they cling on (in modern Lebanon, southeast Turkey, and northern Iraq). But since these Aramaic speakers had no experience of self-rule in the period before the Arab conquests, having been under the sway of Byzantium and Persia for centuries, it was never likely that they would manage to form their own independent dynasties like the Persians and Berbers. This meant that in the long term their numbers were set to dwindle, given the deleterious effects of enduring inferior status.

Once Arabic had risen to the status of a lingua franca for the whole Arab Empire, it became used not only for administration and the military but also for law, theology, literature, and science. This helped to bring about a cultural boom in the ninth century, as numerous Greek, Persian, Syriac, and Sanskrit texts were translated into Arabic, studied, and made a part of the intellectual worldview of Islamic civilization. Despite this international input, Islam itself retained a strong Arab imprint, and this brings us to the second aspect of Arabization, namely, the imposition of Arab identity: the assumption of an Arab name, the acceptance of Arabian history as the fount of Islamic origins and of the superiority of Arab ancestry to any other.[11] Some non-Arab elites, especially from the lands of the former Persian Empire, disliked this heavy Arab stamp and called for a more open and cosmopolitan Islam. This was not a clash between ethnic groups, though it is often portrayed in our sources in terms of Arabs versus Persians, principally because those were the two main cultural models on offer. Few of those who supported the Arab side and wrote books about Arab culture and history were themselves ethnically Arab; for example, probably the greatest expert on Arabian history was Abu 'Ubayda (d. 825), grandson of a Persian Jew, and one of the most vocal opponents of a gentile Islam was Ibn Qutayba (d. 889), descendant of a Persian family from Khurasan. The question was rather whether one supported a narrow Arab focus for Islam (the "Arab" party) or a more cosmopolitan focus, which was open to alien wisdom and values (the "gentile" party). In modern terms, it was a debate over cultural orientation: how multicultural Islam should be. Those favoring a gentile or multicultural Islam (called *shu'ubis*, which, like "gentiles," is the adjective from "peoples") pointed out that all the marvels of history—scientific inventions, monumental buildings, great works of literature, and so on—had been accomplished by non-Arabs, and all the famous persons of history were non-Arabs, and so Islam should celebrate all these characters and achievements and not stay fixated on the pre-Islamic Arabian past.[12]

In a sense both sides won, or at least they both got something of what they wanted. The fact that the Qur'an was revealed in Arabic and that Islam was preached by an Arab prophet in Arabia was a strong argument in favor of retaining the Arab focus. Moreover, the whole legal system (*shari'a*) rested on knowledge of the Arabic Qur'an and the Arabic sayings of Muhammad, and those scholars who had invested so much effort into acquiring this knowledge, and derived status and income from it, were unwilling to accept the validity of any other legal system in any other language. Yet it became acceptable to recite the Qur'an and write works of Islamic scholarship in languages other than Arabic, to adopt foreign styles of aesthetic representation and storytelling, to recount the past glories of non-Arab civilizations, and so on. This situation accelerated with the rise of non-Arab dynasties. Many of these, in order to mark their difference and independence from the Arab regime, played up their own culture and celebrated it in their own language. The rulers of the various breakaway states of Iran and Transoxania, for example, often claimed descent from Sasanian emperors and magnates, which was a way of reinforcing their own legitimacy, of maintaining some distinctiveness from their Arab Muslim neighbors to the west and of tapping into an imperial tradition that was still widely recognized and revered. They played up the exploits and cultural achievements of their alleged noble ancestors, and they patronized Persian poetry, history-writing, and figural representation.

The Arab imprint upon Islam was, therefore, gradually weakened over time, especially after Turkish groups had taken charge of pretty much all the eastern portions of the Arab Empire and after Islam had spread to ever more

THE MAKING OF ISLAMIC CIVILIZATION 219

distant lands. Yet even now many Muslims will want to go on pilgrimage to Arabia, learn some Arabic, and give their children Arab names. Islam ended up, then, as something of a hybrid religion. It did not lose totally its attachment to the ethnic identity of its founding fathers, as did Christianity and Buddhism, but equally it did not manage to elevate the identity and language of these founding fathers to an exclusive status, as did Judaism (Jews/Hebrew), Hinduism (Hindus/Sanskrit), and Zoroastrianism (Iranians/Persian). The fact, however, that this Arab focus endured so well indicates that it must have been an important aspect of the identity of the prime movers and shakers guiding the initial conquests.

The Ingredients of Islamic Civilization

The second process initiated by the Arabs was Islamization. Again, this consisted of two parts: the spread of the religion of Islam and the evolution and dissemination of a distinctively Islamic way of doing things—not just in the field of religion, but also in art, literature, politics, and so on. Western scholars have tended to focus heavily on the religious dimension, especially in recent times, so much so that we use the term "Islam" for both the religion and the civilization as though they are the same thing. Certainly the religion of Islam was a major part of Islamic civilization, but it was never all there was to it, and non-Muslims, though they could not contribute to Islamic religion (except as examples of what behavior and thinking to avoid), did play a major part in the development of Islamic civilization. They formed the majority of the population of the Middle East for at least the first three centuries after the death of Muhammad, and their status within the Arab Empire as protected peoples was part and parcel of what became Islamic civilization, distinguishing it from medieval Christendom, which offered no such legal protection. This enabled Christians and Jews to make a substantial contribution to the intellectual life of the Islamic world, as we can see from the lists of scholars active in medieval times in cosmopolitan cities like Baghdad, Aleppo, Cairo, and Cordoba.[13]

In a general way, the ingredients for Islamic civilization derived from the conquerors, hailing from Arabia, and from the conquered. Some modern scholars regard Arabia as having been cut off from the wider world in pre-Islamic times and so principally look for these ingredients in the cultures of the late antique settled Middle East: Islamic philosophy in neo-Platonic thought, Islamic law in rabbinic Judaism, Islamic ethics and statecraft in Sasanian Persia, Islamic theology in Byzantine Christianity, and so on.[14] Others believe Arabia, precisely because it was cut off from the mainstream, preserved ancient Middle Eastern traditions, or they accept the view of medieval Muslim sources that most elements of Islamic civilization go back to Muhammad and the caliphs of Medina, and they hunt for these ingredients in pre-Islamic Arabian custom and lore. The truth is probably somewhere in between, but pre-Islamic Arabia was never culturally uniform and it was not as isolated as is usually supposed: the south maintained maritime relations with India and the Mediterranean world, and its northwest and northeast sectors had long been in contact with the frontier zones of the complex societies of the Levant and Iraq. And in these zones hybrid cultures arose that blended imperial and local traditions, as we can see from the Qur'an, where well-known biblical stories about miscreants and prophets are told with a local spin.

By what mechanisms did these ingredients make their way into the newly emerging civilization? Converts are likely to have been instrumental, for they acted as conduits between two worlds, especially as many in the early period were prisoners-of-war who often originated in a very different place from where they ended up. Shared environment is also important, for in the early centuries, and especially in the big cities, people of very different geographical, cultural, and religious affiliations lived in close proximity. Separate quarters for different confessional groups only came much later, and the Arabs themselves did not differentiate between non-Muslims, as the seventh-century monk John of Fenek notes with disapproval: "there was no distinction between pagan and Christian, the believer was not known from a Jew." Such inter-confessional mixing was especially common in the bustling heterogeneous garrison cities of the new rulers, where one was exposed to contact with persons of very diverse origin, creed, and status.[15] In addition, there were the widespread phenomena of mixed marriages and reciprocal festival attendance, of commercial contacts and public debate, all of which promoted the circulation of ideas and information.

As regards who contributed what, the broad answer is that contributions came from a multitude of sources, for the early Muslim community quickly became a very pluralist one; to cite John of Fenek again: the Arab armies "went annually to distant parts and to the islands, and brought back captives from all the peoples under the heavens."[16] However, it is very noticeable when one looks at the origins of converts who became religious authorities or administrators that a high proportion of them were from the former territories of the Persian Empire and from Transoxania. In part, this is because the population of the former Byzantine provinces converted to Islam much more slowly than that of the eastern half of the caliphate, where the total collapse of the Persian Empire left no prospect of a revival of the old regime. And in part it reflects the survival in east Iran and Transoxania of highly literate elites who had the ability and motivation to become senior bureaucrats and scholars. Good examples are the Barmakids, formerly Buddhist leaders from Balkh, and the Sahlids, originally Zoroastrian nobles from Sarakhs, whose families dominated the top jobs in the Abbasid administration in the late eighth and early ninth centuries.[17] Such persons, once the seat of government had moved to Baghdad, a stone's throw away from the former Persian capital, oversaw a large-scale Persianization of Islamic culture, especially in such areas as literature, history, and art. Moreover, it was safe to emulate, even idealize, Sasanian Persian emperors because their rule had been extinguished, in contrast to Byzantine emperors, who represented an enemy power and so could not serve as models. For example, the caliph Mansur imitated Khusrau I in initiating a program of translating foreign scholarship, though Mansur outdid him in the volume and breadth of the works translated. And there was a great appetite for works on Persian statecraft and court etiquette, especially among the secretarial class, who were often criticized for preferring such literature to Islamic texts. A ninth-century satirist, for example, caricatured the novice scribe, saying that he enthusiastically learns the maxims of Buzurgmihr (chief minister of Khusrau I), the Testament of Emperor Ardashir (on good government), the epistles (on how to be a good secretary) of 'Abd al-Hamid, and the wisdom literature of Ibn al-Muqaffa' (two mid-eighth-century bureaucrats). But if anyone in his presence mentions the Qur'an or the prophet "he grimaces and interrupts the conversation to speak of the admirable way the country was run under the Persians."[18]

One aspect of Persia that was more difficult to insert into Islam was its religious thought, for it was quite alien to the monotheist traditions of the Near East. Yet given its richness, distinctiveness, and antiquity, it was inevitable that its adherents would make efforts to preserve at least some of its components within Islam. This happened in particular through Shi'ism and Sufism (Islamic mysticism). Unlike Sunni Islam, which gave preference to book-based knowledge with only limited interpretative powers allowed to scholars, Shi'ism and Sufism granted a substantial role in the elaboration of Islam to living guides with direct access to God. In the case of Shi'ism, this meant imams and their intermediaries,[19] and in Sufism this role was diffused among numerous gurus and teachers. This flexibility meant that such figures could adapt easily to local conditions and ways of thought and this facilitated the evolution of a distinctively Persian strain of Sufism. One of its key features is the notion of "universal manifestation": the divine is everywhere, in rocks and trees as well as humans and animals, and Sufi-minded poets would speak of their divine beloved as pervading existence, "appearing in white and black, in Christians and Jews, in dogs and cats." Another is reincarnation, both the idea that humans return in different forms according to how virtuous they were in their previous life, and the belief that the spirit might migrate from person to person. Again, this could take a poetic form, as in the verse attributed to Rumi that his beloved appears in different garb, sometimes old and sometimes young, as Noah, Abraham, Joseph, Moses, Jesus, in the image of Muhammad, and as the sword of 'Ali. Sufism preached that the truth did not lie in external rules and fixed conventions but in hidden meanings and shifting forms, and this flexibility and ambiguity, coupled with a loose organizational structure, made it an attractive receptacle for the Persian religious tradition, and though it was suffused with beliefs from many other traditions similarly seeking a home, the input from Iran constituted perhaps the richest contribution.[20]

Though a few of the more extreme Sufis rejected all law as mere earthly shackles, the majority, not wanting to exclude themselves from mainstream Islam, accepted it as necessary for the duration of a human's lifetime. This was essential, for Islamic law (shari'a) came to be a defining feature of Islamic civilisation. Its structural similarity with Judaism (a comprehensive religio-legal system regulated by scholars on the basis of scripture and oral tradition from a prophet) betrays its origins in early Abbasid Iraq where Muslim lawyers enjoyed close and sustained contact with the region's large and prosperous Jewish community. Jurisprudential theory, which stressed four principal sources—scripture, practice (of the prophet in the case of Islam), analogy, and consensus—could be Roman, Judaic, or derive more broadly from the late antique Middle East.[21] But where did the raw material for the individual laws come from? They give the appearance of having all originated in Muhammad's Arabia, since they are traced back via a chain of transmitters to Muhammad himself. This is the view put out by Muslim scholars, namely, that the Arab conquerors brought with them from west Arabia a fully formed body of law that was different from that current in the rest of the Middle East and made it the new law of the Muslims, and many modern Islamicists accept this picture without demur.[22] However, Arabia had been in contact with the rest of the Middle East for millennia, and in any case, legal systems are highly resistant to rapid change. The laws that were in place in the Middle East the day before the Arab conquests were still in use the day after, and this pre-existing corpus of laws—a mixture of ancient Middle Eastern and Roman law—remained current in the Umayyad period, supplemented by ad hoc emendations made by caliphs and their agents.

Starting in the early eighth century, though, an emerging body of Muslim scholars began working through this ancient corpus and accepted, rejected, or modified its rulings, giving those that they endorsed a "done/said by Muhammad" stamp, which lent old practices the appearance of being new Islamic ones from Arabia. For example, two sixth-century documents on papyrus from Petra and Nessana in Byzantine Arabia record the division of an inheritance by the drawing of lots (as opposed to applying a set of pre-ordained rules). If we turn to collections of Muhammad's sayings we find it written there that Muhammad was once approached by two men who disagreed about an inheritance and he told them to cast lots and to accept whatever result this yielded. Whether Muhammad had this encounter or not does not really matter; the point is that this pre-Islamic practice (which may well have been current in pre-Islamic west Arabia) now had the prophetic seal of approval and could rightfully take its place in the vast edifice of Islamic law.[23]

The point being made here is not that Islam borrowed from or was influenced by ancient Middle Eastern and Roman law, but that this corpus of law remained current after the Arab conquests and was taken over and reworked by Muslim scholars. Thus, many rulings that we think of as very Islamic, like amputation of the hand for theft and the death penalty for apostates, were applied in the region long before Islam. Some of these items were maintained while others, such as the adoption of children and contracts involving earnest money (non-refundable deposits), were rejected; in both cases the acceptances and rejections were attributed to Muhammad himself.[24] This process was carried out by a large number of religious authorities in different centers of the Arab Empire at a furious pace, and already by the mid-ninth century a number of collections of the sayings and deeds of Muhammad had been compiled, including the celebrated volumes of Bukhari (d. 870) and Muslim (d. 875). There one could find rulings on most aspects of everyday life—marriage and divorce, prayer and ablutions, relations between Muslims and non-Muslims, contracts and partnerships, waging war and concluding treaties, menstruation and shaving, meritorious and criminal actions. This did not set the law in stone—new sayings/deeds were added and judges used analytical reasoning to develop new rulings (fatwas) by analogy with existing rulings—but with the emergence of these collections one could speak of a tangibly Islamic way of doing things, and so they contributed to the Islamicization of the lands conquered by the Arabs. Since many items in these collections were formed from the customs and practices of the pre-Islamic Middle East, we should not see this process as the imposition of an alien legal corpus, but as the consensual construction of a body of law by the new Muslim community, a majority of whom were from the ranks of the conquered peoples.

Some features of Islamic civilization did not derive from adoption of existing ideas but arose in reaction to them. Converts to Islam very often wanted to draw a line between themselves and their former co-religionists, and if they attained a position of religious authority they would commonly encourage their Muslim followers to dissociate themselves from Christian, Jewish, and Zoroastrian practices.[25] An interesting example is that of images. The Qur'an makes no mention of them, presumably because it was not really an issue in the relatively poor settlements of west Arabia. But in the rich cities of the Byzantine and Persian empires they were everywhere: on frescoes, mosaics, manuscripts, buildings, rock faces, metal bowls, textiles, and so on. When 'Abd al-Malik sought to unify the currency of his realm, he initially followed the standard custom of placing his image, as the ruler, on the new coins (Figure 5.2), but a couple of years later he withdrew this type and minted coins with no images on them, bearing only words, principally the Muslim creed and a couple of quotations from the Qur'an. No explanation is given, though not long afterward sayings attributed to Muhammad expressing disapproval of images began to circulate. Since it only affected the display of images in public spaces (they remained common in private settings, especially in elite residences), it seems likely that it was a reaction to the profusion of images that could be seen on non-Muslim artifacts and constructions and was regarded as a very dramatic way of illustrating the difference between Muslims and non-Muslims in the field of public art. The new policy had the unintended consequence of stimulating geometric styles of representation and calligraphy, which are art forms that we think of as very "Islamic" today (Figure 7.2). Thus, an apparently negative decision ended up by promoting what came to be seen as an Islamic aesthetic and Islamicizing the public space of the conquered lands.

Besides elaborating a system of Islamic law, Muslim scholars also embarked upon the Islamicization of history. For the pre-Islamic period this meant linking biblical monotheist tradition with Arabia, which was accomplished by having Ishmael travel to Mecca with his father Abraham, build the Muslim sanctuary (ka'ba) there, and become the progenitor of the Arab people by marrying into the Arabian tribe of Jurhum. In addition, certain key human figures, like Aristotle, Alexander the Great, and Jesus, were repackaged as visionary

FIGURE 7.2 Arabic inscription on a rock face near Mecca, dated 80 AH (699–700), containing the Qur'anic verse 38:26; note the careful proportion between ascendant and non-ascendant letters. © 'Abd al-Rahman Fahmi.

Muslim monotheists. For the Islamic period it meant portraying the birth of Muhammad's community as the dawn of a new age, marked concretely by the inauguration of a new calendar (AH I = AD 622) and morally by the transition from ignorance and barbarism (*jahl*) to knowledge (*'ilm*) and truth (*haqq*). This new dispensation was anchored in the Qur'an, which Muhammad had received from God, and it was spread far and wide by the Arab conquests, which were presented as having been orchestrated by God, leading to the establishment of God's rule (*hukm Allah*). One blot on this otherwise idyllic picture was the unseemly behavior of Muhammad's companions, who squabbled and fought one another, most obviously in the first civil war (656–61). This was a problem for Islamic law, for it was the companions of Muhammad who had passed on his teachings and legal decisions to the next generation and the wider world, and one therefore needed to know that they could be relied upon to have transmitted this material correctly and carefully. They were therefore given a makeover, sanctified by recourse to Late Antique hagiographical techniques, and all came out as models of piety and beyond reproach, headed by the four rightly guided caliphs (Abu Bakr, 'Umar, 'Uthman, and 'Ali). Finally, the religious scholars sought to protect their own status as the guardians of the law by closing the door to any other would-be legislators, in particular the rulers, who had themselves legislated in the past or appointed others to do so for them. The scholars achieved this by positing that only the first four caliphs had the power to legislate, making the period when they ruled (632–60) into a golden age when Islam was perfected and its norms properly practiced and implemented. It is a measure of the success of these scholars that still today it is their Islamicized version of history that is taught in schools and colleges around the world, in non-Muslim as well as Muslim countries.[26]

Conclusion

One of the aims of this book has been to peel away these Islamicizing layers in order to understand better the factors that underlay the success of the Arab conquests and the transformative impact that they had on the political, social, and cultural makeup of the Middle East. In the first place, we have seen that the most commented-upon aspect of the conquests, their rapidity, is a consequence of the drive by the conquest leadership to recruit nomads into their armies. Nomads are much more mobile than sedentary people, more used to fighting in their everyday lives, and their work (herding animals) is less labor intensive than growing crops, so more of them can be spared to fight than in an agricultural society. Nomad conquests tend, therefore, to have an explosive character, and this is most dramatically illustrated by the Mongol conquests, which led to the establishment, in just over seventy years, of the biggest empire of pre-modern times. In the Arab case, non-Muslim sources allow us to perceive an additional advantage, namely, that Arabs had been serving in the armies of Byzantium and Persia long before Islam; they had acquired valuable training in the weaponry and military tactics of the empires and had become to some degree acculturated to their ways. In fact, these sources hint that we should view many in Muhammad's west Arabian coalition, its settled members as well as its nomads, not so much as outsiders seeking to despoil the empires but as insiders trying to grab a share of the wealth of their imperial masters.[27]

In the second place, I have stressed that the Arab conquerors made heavy use of non-military means to extend and entrench their gains. As well as the usual promises to respect life, property, and freedom of worship to those who submitted without a fight, they offered tax exemptions and autonomy to those who lived in difficult terrain and who were willing to provide military service or to act as guides, spies, and informers. They also enrolled groups who showed themselves to be skilled in warfare and agreed to pay them stipends. This was of course a sound policy for any aspiring empire and adopted by many in the past. Around 80 percent of the soldiers in the British imperial army in India were natives of the subcontinent; men of British origin were mainly found only in senior positions. Empires would also move conquered subjects around and deploy them far from their homeland, since they would then have no local sympathies; for example, garrisons in French Algeria were frequently composed, according to an American observer of 1922, of "negro troops... in French uniform, under the French flag and commanded by French officers."[28] These sorts of policies were practiced by the Arabs, too, but it is somewhat obscured by the fact that converts to Islam took Arab names and learned to speak Arabic, making the Arab armies look more homogeneous than they actually were. In reality, it was only by large-scale recruitment of non-Arabs in their armies that the Arabs could maintain their hold over their vast territories.

Third, there is the role of Islam. Whereas a number of recent studies have emphasized the zeal that it imparted to the conquerors, I have preferred to focus on its integrative capacity, which allowed the conquerors and conquered to come together to create a new identity and a new civilization. Islam as outlined in the Qur'an would have been reassuringly familiar to Middle Easterners, drawing on the standard constituents of Abrahamic monotheism: one omnipotent God, prophets, scripture, prayer, fasting, almsgiving, pilgrimage, holy days, congregational buildings, and so on. It was different enough from Christianity and Judaism to make it distinctive, but similar enough to make it palatable, and the lack of any clergy or hierarchy made it particularly easy to convert to (in terms of faith at least, all believers are equal before God). In this respect the Arabs were very different from the Mongols: all that Genghis Khan's chiefs had to offer was worship of the sky god Tengri and this cult was just too alien for the Mongols' new subjects to consider converting to, even if the Mongols had been willing to let them do so. Consequently, Mongol leaders mostly adopted one of the religions of the conquered peoples, which limited the degree to which they could instigate major cultural change.

It is clear why some of the conquered would want to convert to Islam, since it facilitated access to all the benefits that the conquerors enjoyed.[29] What is less evident is why the Arabs would let them do so. Conquerors do not normally grant entry to their ranks so easily, for they want to keep the privileges of conquest for themselves. European imperial powers, for example, were very restrictive; the Romans were much less so, but it was still some four hundred years before they extended citizenship to everyone in their realm. There are hints that the Arabs favored a genealogical restriction (for example, blocking marriage between Arabs and non-Arabs), but they unwittingly found themselves in a Trojan horse scenario. They brought back such huge numbers of captives from their raids into their homes and government offices that it was difficult to keep them separate, especially once they started converting to Islam. Moreover, the right of Muslim males to marry four women and have numerous concubines coupled with access to money and power meant that on average they fathered many more children than non-Muslims, and their political dominance ensured that these children were raised as Muslims.[30] Some Arab governors did reject the conversions of low-status people, but given the lack of any support for such a policy in the Qur'an or the sayings of Muhammad it was difficult to defend as a principle and faced strong opposition from those who felt that the spread of Islam was God's wish and strengthened Arab rule. One Muslim authority advocated "the killing of nine out of ten non-Arab captives," but that was hardly a realistic option. In short, the combination of the ease of conversion to Islam and the numerousness of displaced prisoners-of-war willing to convert resulted in the rapid incubation of a Muslim population and ultimately of Islamic civilization.[31]

But if Islam was just a version of Abrahamic monotheism, like Judaism and Christianity, why did Islamic civilization diverge so much from Roman Christian civilization? A major part of the answer is that the Arabs not only captured large chunks of the Byzantine Empire but also the entirety of the Persian Empire. The Arabs were, therefore, not only heirs to Rome, as has been highlighted by a number of recent studies, but also heirs to Persia.[32] In the former Byzantine province of Syria, Islam had a close affinity to Christianity: Muslims were debating classic Christian questions like the relationship between free will and predetermination, the link between miracles and prophecy, and the ontological status of God's attributes. If they had only conquered Syria and Egypt, the Arabs would probably have partially assimilated to Byzantium in the same way that various Gothic and Frankish polities modeled themselves on the West Roman Empire, especially as many in the upper echelons of the Umayyad elite were descendants of Arab Christian tribesmen who had been citizens or allies of Byzantium.[33] But the Arabs had swallowed the Persian Empire whole, and so unsurprisingly its culture was to have a huge impact on the nascent Arab polity. In particular, when the Arabs moved their capital to Iraq in AD 750, they were exposed to the full cultural weight of this realm. From Basra to Balkh, the grandsons of the aristocrats and bureaucrats of late Sasanian Persia were waiting in the wings to impart this cultural wealth to their new masters. Under their direction, the provincial minimalism of Umayyad Damascus was upgraded to the imperial grandeur of Abbasid Baghdad. In addition, an infusion of scholarship from ancient Greek texts translated into Arabic and the input from talented persons from all over the conquered territories, from Seville to Samarkand, transformed the Arabs' local Abrahamic cult from west Arabia into a world religion and the centerpiece of a thriving new civilization.

> Postscript: In the Qur'an jihad means 'struggle', not only military struggle, but also moral struggle, 'struggle of the self' as it would be called later. Inevitably it was the idea of military struggle that was to the fore while the conquests were in full swing, but as these waned the pacific notion gained ground: the struggle to act in accordance with God's laws and to build a just society.

Appendix

SOURCES AND SOURCE CRITICAL
REMARKS

Muslims came to see the rule of Muhammad and the first four caliphs in Medina (622–60) as the golden age of Islam, a time when the prophet and his companions perfected Islam for its followers and acted justly in full accord with the tenets of God's religion. Muslim history writing both reflected and inculcated this idea, holding up these figures as models of pious behavior and as sources of correct legal practice. Inevitably, once the principle had become accepted in the early ninth century that laws and moral conduct had to be based on the sayings and doings of the prophet Muhammad and his companions, then the period of Islam's founding fathers (the *salaf*) became the arena for legal and pious debates from a later time.[1] This situation creates a problem for modern historians. How can we write about the history of this period without simply regurgitating the religious perspectives and legal controversies of a later age? One way is to give the lead role to contemporary coins, documents, and non-Muslim sources for reconstructing events up to the death of the fourth caliph 'Ali in 660, which is what I have done in this book. Of course, these materials are not without their problems, but they do at least date to the period in question (630–60) or shortly thereafter, whereas extant Muslim accounts do not antedate the ninth century and rely on a long line of authorities, any one of which may have reworded and reshaped the original report (or even invented the report and attributed it to a putative eyewitness).[2]

There is no doubt that some genuine early material has survived. For example, Ibn 'Abd al-Hakam gives the terms of the treaty agreed with the Nubians, taken, he says, from someone who looked at the original, and indeed it accords well with an extant letter dated AD 758 that alludes to the conditions of the earlier treaty (see Chapter 3). Our problem is how we can verify an account for the times—and they are the majority—when we do not have independent testimony. In this situation scholars have tended to take either a guilty until proven innocent approach or an innocent until proven guilty approach, which means that they end up rejecting most of the Islamic tradition or accepting most of it. This has had the effect of polarizing Islamic historians into skeptics/revisionists and traditionists.[3] The former were in the ascendant in the 1970s–80s, but the massively increased public profile of Islam since then has made many academics, who are usually left-leaning liberals, shy of criticizing Islam and this has favored the traditionalist approach while pushing skeptics/revisionists to become more extreme.[4] I have tried to promote in this book another approach, which might help diminish the problem, namely, to situate Islamic history in a broader historical framework. Islamic historians tend to be rather introverted, focusing on their own sources and their own region.[5] Looking to the societies and civilizations around the Middle East would help to relativize and expand their vision. And their complaint that we have no seventh- and eighth-century testimonies could be answered by engaging more with the large number of Christian and Jewish writings produced in that period.[6] If Islamic history is to mean the study of the lands and peoples under Muslim rule, and not just the study of Muslims, then Islamicists who deal with the early part of this history will have to be more open in their attitude toward sources.

Once one moves into the Umayyad period (661–750), one enters upon profane time. Muslim authors switch from writing salvation history to chronicling the mundane business of government and the interminable squabbles between various sectarian and tribal factions. We can therefore have more confidence in the literary evidence and treat it in the usual ways, scrutinizing it for bias, reshaping, selective reporting, and so on. Since our earliest extant sources hail from the Abbasid period, we have particularly to be on the watch for *damnatio memoriae*, that is, character assassination of their predecessors by the incoming Abbasid dynasty. By chance a Syrian source from 741 survives in Latin translation in a Spanish chronicle, and its entry for Yazid I (680–83) runs as follows: "a most pleasant man and deemed highly agreeable by all the peoples subject to his rule. He never, as is the wont of men, sought glory for himself because of his royal rank, but lived as a citizen along with all the common people," though it does add that "he achieved few or no victories." This contrasts starkly with the extant Muslim histories, which portray him as "a sinner in respect of his belly and his private parts," "an arrogant drunken sot," "motivated by defiance of God, lack of faith in His religion and hostility toward His Messenger."[7] The other main problem is selectivity. There are the obvious things that one might expect any victor to emphasize (triumphs) and play down (defeats). In the case of the Muslim sources there is also their blinkered attitude to non-Muslims, generally seeing them only as conquered peoples, servants, and slaves. In the words of one seasoned commentator, "Jews and Christians, Persians and East Romans were allotted 'walk-on parts', but little more. The immensely rich but inward-looking Arabic historical tradition virtually ignored the intimacy and the complexity of the relations between the Arabs and the other cultures of the Near East."[8] Adducing non-Muslim sources helps to bring some balance to the picture, which I hope will have been the achievement of this book.

The Authors

Studies on the Middle East historians of the seventh to ninth centuries are relatively rare and this makes it difficult for the novice to get a sense of what has been written and by whom and how much faith we can place in their version of events. I therefore present here some basic information about the core texts that I have used in this book. All the non-Muslim sources that I have used and many more are examined and discussed at length in my *Seeing Islam* and Howard-Johnston's *Witnesses to a World Crisis*. The best place to start for Muslim history writing is Chase Robinson's *Islamic Historiography*, and for more detailed information see F. Rosenthal, *Muslim Historiography* (Leiden, 1968).

Seventh-Century Authors

Chronicle of Khuzistan: a short anonymous Christian Syriac chronicle from southwest Iran conveying "some episodes from the *Ecclesiastica*, that is, church histories, and from the *Cosmotica*, that is, secular histories, from the death of Hormizd son of Khusrau to the end of the Persian kingdom" (so 590–652).

Fredegar: a Latin chronicle in ninety chapters, which extends from the twenty-fourth year of Guntram, king of Burgundy (584), to the death of Flaochad, mayor of the palace in Burgundy (642), though with occasional references to later events. It has been known as the Chronicle of Fredegar ever since the sixteenth century, when a French scholar ascribed it to one "Fredegarium archidiaconum" for reasons never ascertained.

History of the Caucasian Albanians: an anonymous universal history concentrated on the author's homeland, though written in Armenian. It was put together in the early tenth century with the aim of documenting the career of the royal house of Albania and the development of the Church of Albania. Book two focuses heavily on the seventh century and modern experts are unanimous that it is based on contemporary and near-contemporary documents that were not subsequently revised.

John of Fenek: a native of Fenek in northwest Mesopotamia and a resident of the monastery of John Kamul. He wrote a "chronicle of the world" in Syriac in honor of the abbot of this convent. Though extending from Creation to "the severe chastisement of today," the work seeks only to treat "the salient points" of history and to do so "in a brief fashion." In the fifteenth and last chapter he devotes considerable attention to early Arab rule, concluding with a vivid account of the outbreak of the second Arab civil war and the famine and plague of AH 67/686–87, which he says is going on as he is writing.

John of Nikiu: a bishop of Nikiu, a town a few miles to the northwest of Fustat, and author of a chronicle relating in brief events from the Creation to the end of the Arab conquest of Egypt (ca. 643), with greater attention given to the latter event. The original work was most likely written in Coptic and translated into Arabic at an unknown date. Both these versions are lost, and there only survives an Ethiopic translation, which was rendered from the Arabic in 1602.

Maronite Chronicle: an anonymous Syriac chronicle, based on that of Eusebius, which covers events from Alexander the Great to at least the 660s. The chronicle is often defective and the part treating the late fourth century to the mid-seventh is entirely missing. The text halts abruptly at this point, in 665, and it is likely that it originally continued further. How much further is difficult to say, but it does contain some very accurately dated notices for the seventh century and the manuscript is of the eighth or ninth century.

Sebeos: Armenian author of a history that begins with a revolt in Armenia in the 480s, but then passes over much of the sixth century until a second revolt in 572, after which it recounts in detail those events concerning Armenia and its role in superpower politics up until the mid-650s, later adding stop-press news on the conclusion of the Arab civil war in 661. The attribution to the "lord Sebeos, bishop of the House of the Bagratunis" who attended the Council of Dvin in 645 is probably wrong, but since the text is now so well known as Sebeos's *History* I have continued to use this name in this book as shorthand for the history and its author.

Theophylact Simocatta: celebrated as the last of the classicizing historians. He was born most likely in Egypt around the year 580 and spent much of his life in the imperial bureaucracy. His history, written in Atticizing Greek and from a secular perspective, dealt with the reign of Maurice (582–602). Although he halts his work in the year 602, he alludes to the wars of the emperor Heraclius against the Persians, but not those against the Arabs, and so it is assumed that he wrote after 610, but died before 634.

Eighth-Century Authors

Chronicle of ca. 720: the common Greek source of Theophanes and Nikephoros (see later) for the period 669 to 720. It has been attributed to a certain Trajan, who held the rank of patrician and was a contemporary of Justinian II (685–95, 705–11) and who was said to have written "a most remarkable short chronicle." It certainly devotes a lot of attention to the reign of Justinian II, of whom it is highly critical, blaming him for provoking an unnecessary and costly war with the Arabs in 693. Otherwise, it gives a lot of information on the origins and raids of the Bulgars and on Arab campaigns against Byzantium, especially the siege of Constantinople in 716–18.

Chronicle of 741: an anonymous Latin chronicle covering events from 602 to 724, though since it reports that Leo III (717–41) ruled for twenty-four years it is assumed that the author wrote in 741 or shortly thereafter. Though probably produced in Spain, only a tenth of the work deals with Spanish affairs; mostly it treats Arab and Byzantine matters (62% and 28% respectively). It is well informed about the Umayyad caliphs and omits mention of 'Ali, so it is assumed to rely on a Syrian source written either in Syriac or Greek.

Chronicle of Zuqnin: an anonymous Syriac chronicle that begins with Creation and concludes with "the present year" 1086 of Alexander and 158 of the Muslims (AD 775). Scholars have named it the *Chronicle of Zuqnin* because the author makes clear that he is a resident of the monastery of that name in north Mesopotamia. From 717 onward the text constitutes a rich and detailed repository of information, occupying 240 pages in the printed edition, about the history of eighth-century Mesopotamia, much of which is not found in any other chronicle and is to a large extent based on first-hand experience.

Lewond: a priest who wrote a history covering events from Muhammad's death in 632 until the depredation of the Armenian church by an Arab governor in 789. The work focuses on politics and warfare and the country of Armenia, though with an eye to major events in Byzantium and the Caliphate. Lewond is patently hostile to Arab rule, but he is still able to present us with a reasonably clear account of early Arab rule in the Caucasus. It is uncertain when he wrote; the late eighth century is the favorite, just because that is where the history ends, but a date in the mid-ninth century has also been proposed.

Nikephoros: a native of Constantinople and its patriarch during the years 806–15. He chiefly authored theological works, but he is also credited with a "Short History" (*Historia syntomos*), which narrates in brief the course of the

Byzantine Empire from the accession of Phocas in 602 to the marriage of Leo IV to Eirene in 769. He presumably intended to continue it, but as it stands, it halts at a time when he could only have been about eleven years old. It is usually assumed to be an *oeuvre de jeunesse*, making the late eighth century the most plausible time of composition.

Theophilus of Edessa: an astrologer at the court of the early Abbasid caliphs until his death in 785. He wrote a chronicle that does not survive but which was used extensively for the period 630–750 by three later chroniclers: Theophanes the Confessor (d. 818), Dionysius of Telmahre (d. 845), and Agapius of Manbij (wr. 940s). The latter two explicitly name Theophilus as a source, and a comparison of the narratives of all three authors makes clear that they have a substantial amount of material in common.

Ninth-Century Authors

Baladhuri (Ahmad ibn Yahya, d. ca. 892): frequented the court of the caliph Mutawakkil (847–61) and wrote two major historical works. One is titled *Futuh al-buldan* ("The Conquests of the Countries"), which proceeds by region, beginning with Muhammad's campaigns in Arabia, recounting how each was captured and administered up until his own day. His second work, the *Ansab al-ashraf* ("The Genealogies of the Nobles"), is an enormous history (twenty volumes in the principal edition) that is arranged both by genealogy and by generations. It gives biographies of varying length of key figures, beginning with Muhammad and moving on to his kinsmen, and then on to various eminent personalities. It also retains some characteristics of a straightforward history, narrating major events and charting revolts.

Dinawari (Ahmad ibn Dawud, d. ca. 895): wrote a concise history that covers the period from Adam until the death of the caliph Mu'tasim in AD 842, "abbreviated from the biographies of men and curtailed for the sake of economy." Its focus is on kings and their wars, not prophets and their messages (even Muhammad gets no more than a page), with a clear Persian focus. Thus the account of the Sasanian emperors from the accession of Ardashir to the death of Yazdgird takes up more than a quarter of the work.

Ibn 'Abd al-Hakam ('Abd al-Rahman, d. 871): a native of Fustat from a scholarly family that traced its ancestry back to a freedman of the caliph 'Uthman. Although his history bears the title "The Conquest of Egypt" (*Futuh Misr*), it also deals with the Arab subjugation of the rest of North Africa and Spain, pre-Islamic Egyptian sacred history, Arab settlement and administration, and the history of the judges of Egypt and sayings of the Prophet transmitted by Egyptian scholars.

Khalifa ibn Khayyat (d. 854): also from a scholarly family as both his father and his grandfather were known for their expertise in the sayings of Muhammad. He grew up in Basra where his family had a business selling fabric dyes. He is the author of the earliest extant Arabic chronicle, which runs, after a brief note on the birth of Muhammad, from AH I to 232 (AD 622–846), arranging events annalistically. The work deals mainly with fighting between Arab groups, external conquests, and administrative matters. Events are for the most part narrated quite briefly and the work was presumably intended as a useful guide to Islamic history and a complement to his biographical dictionary of scholars, which also survives.

Tabari (Muhammad ibn Jarir, d. 923): lived into the tenth century and only completed his monumental *History of the Prophets and Kings* in 915. However, he is too important a source to leave out of this list. He was born in Amul in the Caspian region in 838 but spent most of his life in Baghdad. He worked for some time as a private tutor, but since he had a good income from his father he was not obliged to work and was able to devote much of his time to writing and study. In his universal history he strives to give the sources for all his narratives, which imparts an aura of accuracy and veracity to his history; modern historians have therefore given it greater credence than other less scrupulously validated histories (such as that of Dinawari and Ya'qubi), even though he relied on much the same sources as everyone else.

Theophanes the Confessor (d. 817): born of noble and rich parents, initially entered imperial service, but subsequently renounced his property and spent the rest of his life as a monk in northwest Anatolia. Late in his life, his friend George Syncellus, who was near to death, entrusted him with the materials necessary to complete a world chronicle that had been George's life work.

In the preface to the finished work Theophanes tells us how he "expended an uncommon amount of labor" on this task and, "after seeking out to the best of my ability and examining many books, wrote down accurately, as best I could, this chronicle from Diocletian down to the reign of Michael (811–13) and his son Theophylact."

Ya'qubi (Ahmad ibn Abi Ya'qub, d. ca. 897): author of a world history and a gazetteer of the Islamic world. We know nothing about him except that, to judge from his writings, he belonged to the bureaucratic circles of Baghdad. He also tells us in his gazetteer, written in 889, that in his youth he traveled much "and this kept me a long time in foreign climes." The first part of his world history, divided into two parts, deals with the world from Adam until the time of Muhammad, reviewing the kingdoms of a large variety of peoples. By contrast the second part, beginning with Muhammad, focuses solely on the Arab Empire and is organized according to the reigns of caliphs up until the Abbasid Mu'tamid, halting in 873.

TIMELINE

G⋆

105	Romans annex the kingdom of the Nabataeans, creating Roman Arabia
224	Sasanian dynasty comes to power
241	Persians annex the kingdom of the Hatrans, creating Persian Arabia
312	Conversion of Constantine to Christianity
582	Ghassanids dismissed from Byzantine service
594	Conversion of the Lakhmids to Christianity
ca. 610	Victory of Lakhmid army against the Persians at Dhu Qar
614–28	Persian occupation of Syria and Palestine
622	Muhammad founds his Muslim polity at Medina
628	Muhammad gains control of Mecca
630	Muhammad forms alliance with the town of Ta'if and the tribe of Thaqif
630	Heraclius restores the fragment of the Holy Cross to Jerusalem
632	Death of Muhammad
634	First documented encounter between West Arabian armies and the Byzantines
636	Battle of Yarmuk
638	Battle of Qadisiyya; capture of Jerusalem
640	Capture of Seleucia-Ctesiphon; raid against the Armenian capital of Dvin; Mu'awiya becomes governor of Syria
641	Capture of Caesarea
640–42	Arab conquest of Egypt
642	Arabs engage the Persian army at the Battle of Nihawand
643	Arabs launch an unsuccessful campaign into Armenia and the Caucasus
646	Byzantines briefly recapture Alexandria

649–50	Arabs raid Cyprus and Arwad
ca. 650	Failed Arab expedition into Nubia
650–53	Truce between the Arabs and Byzantines
651–52	Death of Yazdgird III
652–53	Armenia becomes a vassal of the Arabs
654	Media and Badhghis throw off allegiance to the Arabs
654–55	First major Arab expedition against Constantinople; Battle of the Masts
656–61	First Arab civil war
661	Mu'awiya becomes caliph
664	Juansher, prince of Albania, pledges allegiance to Mu'awiya
668–70	Arab offensive against Constantinople
670	Founding of Qayrawan and establishment of Arab army in Merv
670s	Guerrilla movement of the *mardaites* launched in the Lebanese mountains
673	Arab naval raid on Lycia; truce agreed between Mu'awiya and Contantine IV
674	Arab raiding party crosses the river Oxus for the first time
683–92	Second Arab civil war; Byzantine raids on Ashkelon and Caesarea
680s	Revolt of Kusayla in North Africa
685	Khazars raid Armenia, Georgia, and Albania
692	End of peace treaty between Byzantium and the Arabs; Battle of Sebastopolis
ca. 697	The death of the Berber leader known as "the prophetess" (*al-kahina*)
697	Failed Arab expedition in Zabulistan
698	Arab capture of Carthage
703	Arab garrison defeated by an Armenian army at Vardanakert
706	Arab capture of Paykand; slaughter of Armenian nobles
708	Arab capture of Tangiers
709	Arab capture of Bukhara
710	Arab expedition in Sind
711–14	Invasion of al-Andalus
712	Capture of Samarkand
717–18	Failed Arab siege of Constantinople
718	Byzantine forces raid Lattakia
726	Khazars kill the Arab governor of Armenia
728–30	Major uprising against the Arabs in Transoxania
730	Khazars capture Ardabil
731	Battle of the Defile in Transoxania
732	Battle of Poitiers/Tours
737	Arabs establish buffer against Khazars in north Caucasus
740	Arab army defeated in Anatolia by the Byzantines
740–42	Berber rebellion in North Africa
744	Baghawata Berber dynasty established on Atlantic coast

750	Abbasid dynasty takes power after overthrowing Umayyads; a branch of the Umayyad family establishes itself in Spain
751	Battle of Talas
757	Midrarid dynasty (from Miknasa Berbers) established in Sijilmasa
776	Rustamid dynasty (of Persian origin, supported by Berber Ibadis) established in Algeria
788	'Alid Idrisid dynasty established in Fez with support of Awraba Berbers
821	Tahirid dynasty (of Persian origin) established in east Iran
861	Saffarid dynasty (of Persian origin) established in Zaranj
875	Samanid dynasty (of Persian origin) established in Bukhara

Dramatis Personae

☪

'Abdallah ibn 'Amir, Quraysh, a conqueror of Iran and governor of Basra (649–56, 661–64).

'Abdallah ibn Sa'd, Quraysh, a conqueror of Libya and governor of Egypt (644–56)

'Abdallah ibn al-Zubayr, Quraysh, rival caliph to 'Abd al-Malik (683–92)

'Abd al-Malik, Quraysh, caliph (685–705)

'Abd al-Rahman ibn (Muhammad ibn) al-Ash'ath, Kinda, general (d. 704)

Abraha, Ethiopian ruler of Yemen (ca. 535–65)

Abu l-A'war, Quraysh/Sulaym, general and naval commander (d. ca. 670s)

Abu Bakr, Quraysh, caliph (632–34)

Abu Musa al-Ash'ari, Ash'ar (of Yemen), general and founder of Basra (d. ca. 660s)

Abu 'Ubayda ibn al-Jarrah, Quraysh, governor of Syria (634–39)

'Ali ibn Abi Talib, Quraysh, caliph (656–60)

'Amr ibn al-'As, Quraysh, a conqueror of Palestine and Egypt (d. 662)

Busr ibn Abi Artat, Quraysh, army general and naval commander (d. 689)

Constans II, Byzantine emperor (642–68)

Constantine IV, Byzantine emperor (668–85)

Cyrus, Chalcedonian patriarch of Alexandria (630–42)

Dewashtich, lord of Panjikent, rebel leader (d. 722)

Gao Xianzhi, Tang general of Korean origin (d. 756)

Gaozu, emperor of China (618–26), founder of Tang dynasty

Gaozong, emperor of China (650–83)

Ghurak, lord of Samarkand and king of Sogdia (710–37)

Gregory, governor of the Byzantine province of Africa (d. 647)

Habib ibn Maslama, Quraysh, conqueror of Armenia (d. 662)

Hajjaj ibn Yusuf, Thaqif, viceroy of the East (693–714)

Harith ibn Jabala, Ghassan, chief and ally of Byzantium (d. 569)

Hassan ibn Nu'man, Ghassan, a conqueror of Africa (d. 698)

Heraclius, Byzantine emperor (610–41)

Hormizdan, senior Persian general, defended Shush and Shushtar (d. 640s)

'Iyad ibn Ghanm, Quraysh, conqueror of Jazira (d. 640s)

Jayalbhata IV, king of Gurjara in northwest India (fl. 730s)

Juansher, king of Caucasian Albania (ca. 635–70)

Justinian II, Byzantine emperor (685–95, 705–11)

Kahina, "queen of the Berbers," rebel leader (d. late 690s)

Khalid ibn al-Walid, Quraysh, a conqueror of southern Iraq and Syria (d. 642)

Khatun, wife of the ruler of Bukhara and regent for her son (d. 690s)

Khurrazad, "prince of the Medes," commander of northwest Persia (d. ca. 650s)

Khusrau II, Persian emperor (591–628)

Kusayla, Berber chief, rebel leader (d. ca. 690)

Leo III, Byzantine emperor (717–41)

Martik, son of the Khazar khagan (fl. 720s)

Maslama, son of 'Abd al-Malik, Quraysh, general, besieged Constantinople (717–18)

Mu'awiya I, governor of Syria (640–60) and caliph (661–80)

Mu'awiya ibn Hudayj, Kinda, a conqueror of Africa (d. 670s)

Muhammad, Quraysh, prophet (d. 632)

Muhammad ibn Marwan, Quraysh, general and governor of Jazira and Armenia (d. 720)

Mukhtar ibn Abi 'Ubayd, Thaqif, rebel leader (d. 687)

Mundhir ibn Nu'man, Lakhm, chief and ally of Persian Empire (504–54)

Musa ibn Nusayr, son of a freedman, a conqueror of Mauritania and Spain (d. 716)

Peroz III, son of Yazdgird III, strove to restore Persian Empire (d. ca. 680)

Qutayba ibn Muslim, conqueror of Transoxania, governor of Khurasan (705–15)

Rustam, "prince of the Medes," commander of northwest Persia (d. 638)

Rutbil, title held by a number of rulers of Zabulistan in modern central Afghanistan

Sa'd ibn Abi Waqqas, Quraysh, a conqueror of Iraq and founder of Kufa (d. 675)

Shahrbaraz, Persian general and briefly Persian emperor (April–June 630).

Smbat Bagratuni, chief prince of Armenia (693–726)

Sophronius, patriarch of Jerusalem (ca. 634–38)

Suluk, Chabish-chor, leader of the Turgesh branch of the western Turks (715–38)

Tariq ibn Ziyad, Berber, a conqueror of Spain (fl. 711)

Theodore, Byzantine commander-in-chief of the Egyptian army (ca. 639–42)

Theodore Rshtuni, chief prince of Armenia (d. 655)

'Umar I, Quraysh, caliph (634–44)

'Umar II, Quraysh, caliph (717–20)

'Uthman, Quraysh, caliph (644–56)

'Uqba ibn Nafi', Quraysh, a conqueror of Africa (d. 683)

Vahan, senior Byzantine general (d. 636)

Valentine, senior Byzantine general (d. 643)

Wu, empress of China, de facto ruler due to sickness of her husband (655–705)

Yazdgird III, last emperor of Persia (632–52)

Yazid ibn al-Muhallab, Azd, governor of Khurasan (702–4, 715–17) and Iraq (716–17)

Ziyad ibn Abi Sufyan, adopted brother of Mu'awiya I and viceroy of the East (670–73)

For information on historians and chroniclers see the Appendix.

GENEALOGICAL TABLES OF QURAYSH AND THE UMAYYADS

☪

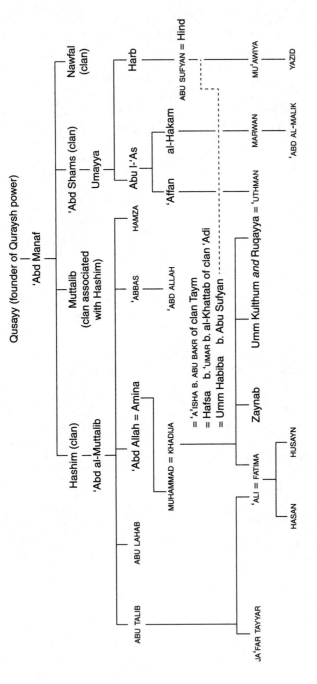

Note: Names of those who played an important role in Muhammad's lifetime or afterwards are in capitals.

Genealogical tree of the tribe of Quraysh

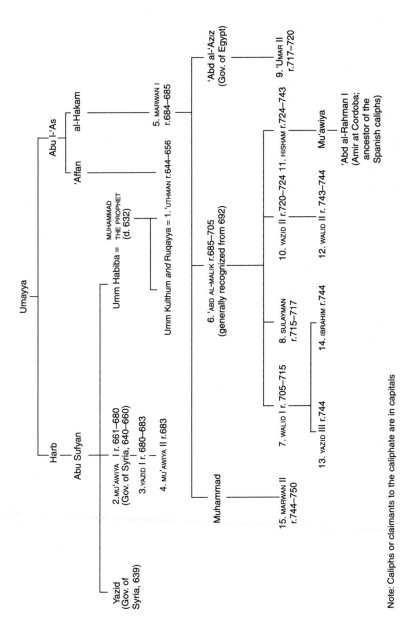

Note: Caliphs or claimants to the caliphate are in capitals

Genealogical tree of the clan of Umayya

NOTES

C⋆

Introduction

1. This is the Legend of the Seven Sleepers of Ephesus, which circulates in written form already in the fifth century AD and makes its way into the Qur'an in the seventh century.

2. D. W. Brown, *A New Introduction to Islam* (Chichester, 2009), 108 ("staggering"); Howard-Johnston, *Witnesses*, 448, 464 ("tsunami"); cf. F. M. Donner, "The Islamic Conquests" in Y. M. Choueiri, *A Companion to the History of the Middle East* (Oxford, 2005): "astonishing rapidity." Wickham, *Framing the Early Middle Ages*, 130 ("636–42").

3. Hoyland, *Seeing Islam*, 467; cf. D. Sourdel, "Un pamphlet musulman anonyme," *Revue des Etudes Islamiques* 34 (1966), 26.

4. Donner, *Muhammad and the Believers*, xii: "It is my conviction that Islam began as a religious movement—not as a social, economic or 'national' one." Yet even a cursory study of religious movements practicing violence, whether Christian (e.g., the Lord's Resistance Army in Uganda) or Muslim (al-Qa'ida, etc.) or Buddhist (Burma's 969 group), makes it clear that one cannot separate religion from socioeconomic issues and identity in such movements. If there were nothing material at stake, one would not need to fight.

5. The equivalent of our term "Arab" was "Saracen" in the Byzantine Empire and "Tayyaya" in the Persian Empire; both were originally names of particular tribes on the borders of the Byzantine and Persian Empires, respectively, but they were subsequently applied by imperial citizens to all the tribes of Arabia and the Syrian desert. Seventh-century Byzantines and Persians used the same term (i.e., Saracen or

Tayayya) for the Arab conquerors as they had used for the pre-Islamic Arabs, and so presumably they saw continuity between the two.

6. Procopius, *History of the Wars*, ed. and trans. H. B. Dewing (Loeb, 1916), 3.5.24–25.

Chapter 1

1. Theophylact, *History*, trans. M. and M. Whitby (Oxford, 1986), 4.11.2 (two eyes), 3.17.7 (Saracens).

2. Many scholars attacked Pirenne's *Mohammed et Charlemagne* (Brussels, 1937), in particular R. Hodges and D. Whitehouse (*Mohammed, Charlemagne and the Origins of Europe*, Ithaca, 1983), but it has recently been defended by E. Scott (*Mohammed and Charlemagne Revisited*, Nashville, 2012).

3. For convenience I will use the term "Persian" in this book to refer to the inhabitants of the area ruled by the Persian Sasanian dynasty (Iraq and Greater Iran, i.e., modern Iran, Turkmenistan, and Afghanistan) even though their rule ended in 652 and even though many of these inhabitants would have had other, more local identities. Medieval Muslim authors also use the term Persian (*furs*), or sometimes '*ajam*, which meant non-Arab generally but often served as a label for the Persians in particular. Some modern scholars prefer the term "Iranian," in the sense of speakers of an Iranian language, but the term is rarely used in our sources, has strong modern associations, and drags into its net various peoples of Transoxania/Central Asia who, even if they spoke an Iranian language, had distinctive cultures and identities of their own.

4. Letter of the head of the Georgian church to his Armenian counterpart, quoted in T. Greenwood, "Sasanian Reflections in Armenian Sources," *e-Sasanika* 5 (2008), 18.

5. Nikephoros, §17; *Chronicle of Khuzistan*, 29–30.

6. Kartir inscription: www.avesta.org/mp/kz.html, §4. For a full study of the inscription, see P. Gignoux, *Les quatre inscriptions du mage Kirdīr* (Leuven, 1991).

7. Philostorgius, *Historia Ecclesiastica*, ed. J. Bidez (Berlin, 1972), 3.4.

8. Cyril of Scythopolis, *Life of Euthymius*, ed. E. Schwartz (Leipzig, 1939), 24. Cf. Theodoret of Cyrrhus's comment about a monk called Abbas: "He grew from the Ishmaelite root, but was not expelled from the inheritance of Abraham" (cited by F. Millar, "The Theodosian Empire (408–50) and the Arabs," in E. S. Gruen ed., Cultural Borrowings and Ethnic Appropriations in Antiquity (Stuttgart, 2005), 307).

9. Cyril of Scythopolis, *Life of Euthymius*, 24.

10. For Sharahil and the point made here, see R. Hoyland, "Late Roman Provincia Arabia, Monophysite Monks and Arab Tribes," *Semitica et Classica* 2 (2009), and more generally Trimingham, *Christianity among the Arabs in Pre Islamic Times*.

11. J. Marcillet-Jaubert, *Les Inscriptions d'Altava* (Aix-en-Provence, 1968), 124–25 (no. 194).

12. Trans. D. Sinor in *id*. ed., *Cambridge History of Early Inner Asia* (Cambridge, 1990), 297.

13. Theophylact, *History*, 7.7.8. "Turk" is a term for numerous groups speaking Turkic languages; this specific group are referred to by scholars as Gok/Kok Turks (often translated as "Blue Turks").

14. Retsö, *The Arabs in Antiquity*.

15. Josephus, *Antiquities* (Loeb, 1930), I.220–21 (Nabataeans). Note that Emperor Justinian I in his Novella 102 referred to Arabia as *provincia araborum*. In 241 the Persians annexed the kingdom of the Hatrans, centered on the city of that name in modern northwest Iraq, and this was also called the province of the Arabs (*Bet Arabaye*); the situation was presumably comparable to Roman/Byzantine Arabia, but unfortunately we have almost no information about it.

16. P. J. Parr et al., "Preliminary Survey in N.W. Arabia," *Bulletin of the Institute of Archaeology* 10 (1971), 54–58 (Rawwafa Inscription).

17. References in R. Hoyland, "Arab Kings, Arab Tribes and the Beginnings of Arab Historical Memory," in H. Cotton et al., eds., *From Hellenism to Islam* (Cambridge, 2009), 379 (*araps*), 392 (*apo khoron tou Arabon ethnous*). For the monks' epitaphs, see K. M. Koikylides, *Ta kata ten lauran ton cheimarron Chouziva* (Jerusalem, 1901), 74–75 (Arab is written once as *Arabos* and once as *Araps*). In the fourth century there was an administrative reorganization of the division of territory between Palestine and Arabia in favor of the former, but the extent of the province of Arabia remained the same in the popular mindset.

18. Ahudemmeh, "Histoire," ed. and trans. F. Nau, *Patrologia Orientalis* 3 (1905), 21, 26–28. Missionaries told the Arabs that they were the descendants of Abraham via his son Ishmael, an idea that goes back to the Jewish historian Josephus (F. Millar, "Hagar, Ishmael, Josephus and the Origins of Islam," *Journal of Jewish Studies* 44, 1993).

19. See M.C.A. Macdonald, "Nomads and the Hauran," *Syria* 70 (1993), 374–76 (*parembole nomadon*). The document is the "Register of Dignitaries" (*Notitia dignitatum*), an official register of all the non-municipal offices and garrisons in the Roman Empire compiled by the "chief of the notaries" (recent edition by R. Ireland, Saur, 2002). The army, like Christianity, had an acculturating effect, as we can sometimes see in naming patterns; for example, the soldier Valens, who appears in a marriage contract of AD 537, has a father called al-Ubayy al-Ghubb, so probably he had changed his name from Arabic "Salih" to the Latin "Valens" (both mean "faring well") in order to fit in with army life (R. Katzoff and N. Lewis, "Understanding P. Ness. 18," *Zeitschrift für Papyrologie und Epigraphik* 84, 1990).

20. Procopius, *History of the Wars*, ed. and trans. H. B. Dewing (Loeb, 1916), I.19.7–11. For more on Abikarib, see F. Millar, "A Syriac Codex from near Palmyra and the Ghassanid Abikarib," *Hugoye* 16 (2013), 15–35.

21. Procopius, *History*, I.17.40 and I.17.48 (Mundhir and Harith); John of Ephesus, *Ecclesiastical History*, trans. R. Payne Smith (Oxford, 1860), 3.42 (Harith's son's rampage).

22. Cited and discussed in T. Khalidi, "Poetry and Identity in the Umayyad Age," *al-Abhath* 50–I (2002–3), 81. The term for nomads here is *a'rab*, which is used also in the Qur'an and is evidently closely related to the term *'arab*. It has been pointed out that Imru' al-Qays might have been saying that he was king of a geographical area known as *al-'arab*, but the two terms are inextricably linked: the inhabitants of *al-'arab* (*provincia Arabia*) would be known as Arabs (*'Arabaye*); see further J. B. Segal, "Arabs in Syriac Literature," *Jerusalem Studies in Arabic and Islam* 4 (1984), 99–I01.

23. It is often stated that the term *'arab* in the Qur'an characterizes only a language and not a people, but language is always a key facet of human identity and binds us to a wider group, so its usage in the Qur'an is highly significant and presupposes a community who spoke that language.

24. Cf. Halsall, *Barbarian Migrations*, 34: "The 'barbarian migrations' were, therefore, the product of the 'end of the Roman Empire', and not vice versa."

25. For these last two quotations, see Palmer, *Seventh Century*, xiv.

26. K.W. Butzer, "The Rise and Fall of Axum, Ethiopia," *American Antiquity* 46 (1981); D. Kennet, "On the Eve of Islam: Archaeological Evidence from East Arabia," *Antiquity* 79 (2005); J. Schiettecatte on "Shabwa, Marib et San'a" and R. Eichmann on "Tayma" in C. Robin and J. Schiettecatte, eds., *L'Arabie à la veille de l'Islam* (Paris, 2008); C. Foss, "Syria in Transition AD 550–750," *Dumbarton Oaks Papers* 51 (1997).

27. These two quotations are from Procopius and Agathias, respectively, and are quoted in Palmer, *Seventh Century*, xvii–xviii. A. Korotaev et al., "Origins of Islam," *Acta Orientalia* (Hungary) 52 (1999), argues for socioecological factors behind the rise of Islam; A. Walmsley, "Economic Developments and the Nature of Settlement," *Dumbarton Oaks Papers* 6I (2007), prefers to stress continuity across the sixth to eighth century.

Chapter 2

I. *History of the Caucasian Albanians*, 2.I4–16. Compare the remark of a Chinese observer: "Never had the western barbarians (i.e., Turks) been so powerful": Chavannes, 24–26. Albania is the Greek and Latin form of the local name, which is rendered in Persian and Arabic as Ran/Arran.

2. For this inscription, Kinda, Himyar, and Judaism, see C. Robin, "Les rois de Kinda" in A. al-Helabi et al., eds., *Arabia, Greece and Byzantium* (Riyadh, 2012), and his "Himyar et Israël," *Compte rendu de l'Académie des Inscriptions et Belles-Lettres* 148 (2004).

3. For example, the eighteen dynasties of Himyar mentioned in contemporary inscriptions are condensed into just one in Muslim histories of pre-Islamic Yemen. It may also be that the Judeo-Christian biblical worldview eroded local traditions, for other peoples too, like the Egyptians, had no real recollection of their pagan history by the seventh century except for what the Bible said about it.

4. *Chronicle of Siirt*, 469 (ch. 6I).

5. Such as Musaylima, Tulayha, Aswad, Sajah, Laqit, and Ibn Sayyad. See A. Makin, *Reconstructing the Enemy: Musaylima in Muslim Literature* (Frankfurt-am-Main, 2010); C. Robin, "Les signes de la prophétie en Arabie," in S. Georgoudi et al. eds., *La Raison des Signes* (Leiden, 2012).

6. For recent discussion of this view, see S. J. Shoemaker, *Death of a Prophet* (Philadelphia, PA, 2012), ch. 4.

7. Sebeos, 102. Since Sebeos then talks about launching sea raids against Iran, he presumably means east Arabia here. Ishmael/Ishmaelite is often used by Christian authors to refer to the Arab conquerors by virtue of the fact that the Arabs were regarded as the progeny of Ishmael, son of Abraham by the maidservant Hagar.

8. The earliest Muslim account is by Baladhuri, 59–61, who speaks of the tribes of 'Amila, Lakhm and Judham.

9. Theophilus of Edessa, 63–64 (raid of 610); Antiochus of Mar Saba, "Epistola ad Eustathium," *Patrologia Graeca* 89, col.1424; "Vita S. Georgii Chozebitae," ed. and trans. C. Houze, *Analecta Bollandiana* 1888, 134; Theophanes, 335–36 (dogs).

10. That does not mean these characterizations derive from the earliest period, but they do come across very strongly. On storytellers, see L. R. Armstrong, *The Qussas of Early Islam* (PhD; Chicago, 2013), and for problems in the Islamic tradition about the conquests, see the appendix chapter in this book.

11. Hoyland, *Seeing Islam*, 120; Baladhuri, 109.

12. Theophilus, 93–94.

13. Sebeos, 96–97 (Theodore brother of Heraclius); Theophilus, 91 (Theodore *vicarius*). On Areopolis, see S. Thomas Parker, *The Roman Frontier in Central Jordan I* (Washington, DC, 2006), 16–17.

14. Hoyland, *Seeing Islam*, 67–73 (Sophronius).

15. *Chronicle of 741*, §15 (Damascus); Theophanes, 337 (multitude). For this account of the Battle of Yarmuk, I draw on Theophilus, 100-3, and Sebeos, 97.

16. Hoyland, *Seeing Islam*, 219 (Fredegar—many men "died where they slept," perhaps afflicted by the plague), 615 n. 24 (the *Chronicle of 754*, §9, speaks of "the prophecy of the rats" and "the lumps in their throats swelling"); Theophilus, 106–8, where the references for Heraclius's order not to engage the Arabs are collected.

17. *Chronicle of 741*, §16 (Arabs capture Damascus); Tabari, 1.2390-1 (disputes); Theophilus, 98 (covenant). Edessa had submitted to the Persians for the same reasons: "the multitude of the Persian troops, their victory in battles, and since they [the Edessans] had not expectation of salvation from anywhere" (Sebeos, 63).

18. Theophanes, 339 (siege of two years); Sebeos, 98 (cross and oath); Hoyland, *Seeing Islam*, 221 (the pilgrim Arculf and the abbot Adomnan).

19. Theophilus, 114–17, where the Muslim sources are also given.

20. Theophilus, 123–24. J. Patrich, *Studies in the Archaeology and History of Caesarea Maritima* (Leiden, 2011), 114, contrasts Caesarea with Jerusalem and Scythopolis.

21. *Chronicle of Siirt*, 539 (ch. 87; Arabs disperse); Dinawari, 116–17 (Boran), and cf. Tabari, I.2189. For Dhu Qar and the next raid I mention at 'Ayn al-Tamr, see Tabari, I.1016, I.2062–4. For more on dating, see Pourshariati, *Decline and Fall*, 166–72.

22. The identity of the author is uncertain, but for convenience I use Sebeos, to whom the chronicle was first attributed. All quotations in the rest of this section are from Sebeos, 98–99, and *History of the Caucasian Albanians*, 2.18, unless otherwise indicated.

23. Ferdowsi, *Shahname*, ed. D. Khaleghi-Motlagh (New York, 1987–2008), 8.418 (Rostam); *Chronicle of Siirt*, 580 (ch. 94: taxes).

24. *Chronicle of Zuqnin*, 215.

25. Theophilus, 118–21, who is the source for this account about 'Iyad.

26. Theophilus, 185 n. 492 (citing Dionysius of Telmahre, d. 845).

27. Theophilus, 109. For examples of participants in the Arab conquests who said they had converted to Islam but knew little about it, see Tannous, *Syria between Byzantium and Islam*, 407–29. One can say, then, that the Arab conquests would have happened without Muhammad/Islam, but, as I go on to show in this book, they are less likely to have resulted in a new civilization; conversely, Islam would probably not have spread so far, and certainly not as fast, without the Arab conquests, the success of which dramatically backed up the Arabs' claims to be favored by God.

28. Modern scholars usually call this foundation agreement the "Constitution of Medina." For a recent translation of it, see S.A. Arjomand, "The Constitution of Medina," *International Journal of Middle East Studies* 41 (2009), who renders *mu'minun* as "faithful covenanters." However, F. Donner, "From Believers to Muslims," *al-Abhath* 50–1 (2002–3), feels that it is a wholly religious term.

29. One might compare them to those who fought in the Abbasid revolution in 750, who did not define themselves by ethnicity or religion, but by their role in the revolution and its ongoing implementation, using the label *ahl al-dawla*/"people of the revolution."

30. For the reference and discussion, see Sizgorich, *Violence and Belief*, 231–71.

31. Tabari, I.2190, 2192. For discussion and many other examples, see W. al-Qadi, "Non-Muslims in the Muslim Conquest Army," in A. Borrut et al., eds., *Christians and Others in the Umayyad State* (Chicago, 2014). Some Arab tribes—or sections within them—remained Christian at least until the ninth century, especially in northern Syria and Jazira.

32. J. Paul, "The State and the Military—a Nomad Perspective," *Orientwissenschaftliche Hefte* 12 (2003), n. 91 ("agriculture begins to suffer as more than a rather limited percentage of men is drafted—this percentage differs but does not exceed one in ten—whereas in nomadic societies the ratio can rise up to one in four or even more"); Bashear, *Arabs and Others*, ch. 1 (a'rab).

33. Tabari, I.2497, 2562–3 (asawira); Theophilus, 185-86 (Slavs).

34. Isfahani, *Kitab al-aghani* (Cairo, 1927–74), 3.257 (Tamim); A. Mingana, *Sources syriaques* (Leipzig, 1908), 147 and 175 (John of Fenek); Tabari, 1.2341 (Daylam). The question of who converted and when is complicated by the ambiguity of the verb *aslama*, which can mean to surrender to a human agent or to surrender to God and His messenger (i.e., become a Muslim). Medieval historians, along with quite a few modern ones, tend to assume that the religious sense was the only one, but probably the secular sense applied in many cases, especially in the early period.

35. For the point about the Persian cavalry, see Crone, *Slaves on Horses*, 237–38 n. 362. Note that collaboration/conversion was a two-way street; e.g., Sebeos reports that at the onset of the Arab civil war in 656 a large body of troops in Egypt, "some 15,000 men, believed in Christ and were baptized"—very likely these were Christian Arabs and/or Byzantines who had gone over to the Arab side after the conquest of Egypt, but who now, anticipating that the civil war spelled the end of the Arab regime, "united with the emperor of the Byzantines, made a treaty and [re-]joined him" (Sebeos, 154; Ibn 'Abd al-Hakam, 129, speaks of "the sons of Yanna, Azraq and Rubel" enrolled in 'Amr ibn al-'As' army, who may have been Byzantines).

36. Cited in Khalidi, "Poetry and Identity in the Umayyad Age," *al-Abhath* 50–1 (2002–3), 72–73, who notes that the term "Arab" becomes increasingly common in poetry in the course of the Umayyad period (661–750). Some Umayyad inscriptions (e.g., the Hammat Gader bath restoration text of 662) and documents (e.g., tax demands from the 670s found at Nessana in south Palestine) are dated to the years "according to the Arabs" (*kata arabas*), and Anastasius of Sinai (d. ca. 701) uses the terms Arab and Saracen interchangeably (A. Binggeli, *Anastase le Sinaïte*, PhD thesis, Paris IV, 2001, I.4, II.2, II.13).

37. Conversely, if the conquests had not led to a unfied empire, but either been repulsed or resulted in many separate polities, we would have spoken of the individual Arabian tribal groupings, like Ma'add and Kinda, in the same way as we speak of the individual Germanic groups, like the Goths and Vandals, in early Medieval Europe.

38. Bowersock, *Empires in Collision*, ch. 3 (Heraclius's gift). On ecological explanations, see notes 26–27 in Chapter I, this volume, and J. Haldon, "The Resources of Late Antiquity," in Robinson ed., *New Cambridge History of Islam 1*, 22–25.

39. Howard-Johnston, *Witnesses*, 464. It has periodically been cited as a major factor in the Arab conquests (e.g., Spuler, *Iran*, 6, and Pirenne, *Mohammed and Charlemagne*, 150–51), but has recently become the dominant explanation.

40. Donner, *Muhammad and the Believers*, xii; Donner, F., "Visions of the Early Islamic Expansion" in N. M. El Cheikh and S. O'Sullivan, *Byzantium in Early Islamic Syria* (Beirut, 2011), 28. Those who advocate the "non-violent conquest model" point to the lack of archaeological evidence for widespread destruction (citing P. Pentz, *The Invisible Conquest*, Copenhagen 1992), but the main fighting had consisted of field battles, rather than sieges, and this leaves corpses but no lasting physical trail. And

this is true of many conquests; for example, "it has been pointed out that from archaeological evidence we would have no idea at all that the Vandals had invaded North Africa" (Halsall, *Barbarian Migrations*, 327).

41. Sizgorich, *Violence and Belief*, ch. 3 (Ambrose); J. Howard-Johnston, "The Official History of Heraclius' Persian Campaigns," in E. Dabrowa, ed., *The Roman and Byzantine Army in the East* (Krakow, 1994), 85.

42. Tabari, I.2289.

Chapter 3

1. John of Nikiu, 116.2–9, 119.18–24, 120.1–6, and 39–69, gives a contemporary perspective on the struggles following Heraclius's death; see also Sebeos, 104, 106.

2. Pourshariati, *Decline and Fall*, 249–54.

3. Sebeos, 101 and 102.

4. Hoyland, *Seeing Islam*, 525, 585 (governor of Numidia); Nikephoros, §23 (John of Barqa). An inscription from Alexandria is dated to year 414 of the martyrs (AD 698) and the fifty-fifth year of "the Saracen nation having taken control of the country," which dates the start of the Arab conquests to 633 (S. Timm, *Das christlich-koptische Ägypten in arabischer Zeit 5*, Wiesbaden 1991, 2146).

5. The following narrative and quotations are taken from John of Nikiu, 111–21, unless otherwise indicated. I give a quite full account, as this is one of the few detailed contemporary conquest accounts that we possess.

6. Only two officials, not, as Charles translates, "the people," unwittingly giving fuel to the argument that the anti-Chalcedonian Christians of Egypt welcomed the Arabs. For this and other important revisions, see P. Booth, "The Muslim Conquest of Egypt Reconsidered," *Travaux et Mémoires* 17 (2013).

7. Namely, Philoxenus, duke of Arcadia, and Shenute, prefect of Antinoe: see John of Nikiu, 120.29–30, and F. Morelli, *L'archivio di Senouthios* (Berlin, 2010), who also cites papyri of Philoxenus.

8. This idea was put out by the anti-Chalcedonian Egyptians, once it became clear that Arab rule was likely to endure, in order to curry favor with the Arabs and to discredit their Chalcedonian rivals . See E. Coghill, "Minority Representation in the *Futuh Misr* of Ibn 'Abd al-Hakam" in R. Hoyland, ed., *The Late Antique World of Early Islam* (Princeton, 2014).

9. Nikephoros, §23.

10. Theophilus of Edessa, 111 (seemingly misplacing the notice); Baladhuri, 221; Ibn 'Abd al-Hakam, 191; Ya'qubi, 189; Nu'aym b. Hammad, *Kitab al-Fitan*, ed. S. A. al-Zuhayri (Cairo, 1991), 445–46 (no. 1286).

11. Baladhuri, 237. The wording of the truce between the Arabs and the Nubians is given by Ibn 'Abd al-Hakam, *Futuh Misr*, 189, on the authority of an old man who read it

in the chancellery of Fustat; it accords well with the allusions to the original in the papyrus of AD 758 (see next note).

12. *History of the Patriarchs*, ed. and trans. B. Evetts, *Patrologia Orientalis* 5 (1910), 144–45 (great king and patriarch); J. Plumley, "An Eighth-Century Arabic Letter to the King of Nubia," *Journal of Egyptian Archaeology* 61 (1975).

13. Pseudo-Methodius, "Apocalypse," in Palmer, *Seventh Century*, 237–38 (assuming that the Ethiopians are acting on behalf of the Byzantines).

14. Ibn 'Abd al-Hakam, 171, citing 'Uthman ibn Salih (d. 835).

15. Corippus, *Johannide*, 2.85, cited by Modéran, *Les Maures*, 45 and 49 (Luwata); Ibn 'Abd al-Hakam, 170, and Baladhuri, 224 (selling children); Augustine, *Epistolae*, ed. J. Divjak (Vienna, 1981), letter 10.

16. *Etymologies*, trans. S. A. Barney et al. (Cambridge, 2010), 14.5.7.

17. The account of 'Abdallah in Africa and his defeat of Gregory is taken from *Chronicle of 741*, §24; *Chronicle of 754*, §28; and Ibn 'Abd al-Hakam, 183. See also Khalifa, 159 (AH 27); Ya'qubi, 191 (who says that Gregory retreats back to Subeitla); Theophilus, 130 (who says that Gregory escaped to Constantinople). If, as scholars assume, this is the Gregory whose grandfather had been second-in-command to Heraclius's father, who was governor of Africa, and whose aunt, Gregoras, had married Heraclius's elder son, he might well have felt entitled to claim the imperial throne for himself.

18. Ibn 'Abd al-Hakam, 183.

19. *Chronicle of Khuzistan*, 36. This is also the source for the following account of the Arab conquest of Khuzistan; see also Dinawari, 136–40, who says that Hormizdan was the uncle of Shiroi, son of Khusrau II.

20. Sebeos, 104–5 (Nihawand), 102 (naval raids); Baladhuri, 386–91 (Fars).

21. Chavannes, 172 (Yazdgird spurned). Muslim sources say that Yazdgird acted arrogantly toward the nobles/governors of Kirman and Sistan, and that is why they refused to help him; e.g., Baladhuri, 315. Death of Yazdgird in 651–52: Sebeos, 135; Theophilus, 136–37; Baladhuri, 315–16; Dinawari, 148–49.

22. Chavannes, 172; *Cambridge History of China 3.1* (ed. D. Twitchett), 280; Daryaee, *Sasanian Persia*, 37–38.

23. Theophilus, 140, and Sebeos, 109–11, which are the sources I use for the rest of this section.

24. Theophilus, 131–34. What follows is a compressed and paraphrased version of the original narrative, the detail of which suggests that it derives ultimately from a well-informed contemporary source. Sebeos, 111–12, mentions Mu'awiya's sally toward Constantinople.

25. Soloi: *Dix campagnes de fouilles (1964–1974). Volume premier* (Sainte-Foy, 1985), 115–25.

26. Chavannes, 52, 171. For a maximal view on the destructive effects of the plague, see W. Rosen, *Justinian's Flea* (London, 2008).

27. Gabrieli, *Muhammad and the Conquests of Islam*, 103.

28. Pseudo-Zachariah, *Chronicle*, trans. G. Greatrex (Liverpool, 2011), 9.2. Early Arab poets boast a lot about the military prowess of their tribesmen and give the impression that they possessed all the standard military hardware of the day (F.W. Schwarzlose, *Die Waffen der alten Araber aus ihren Dichtern dargestellt*, Leipzig, 1886).

29. Ibn 'Abd al-Hakam, 116 (Bali); Theophilus, 101–2, citing Michael the Syrian, who is a late author but draws on much earlier material. Azdi (d. ca. 820), *Futuh al-Sham*, ed. A-M. Amir (Cairo, 1970), 97, 150, speaks of "the provincials" (*ahl al-balad*) helping the Muslims against the Byzantine soldiers (*al-rum*); he also divides the Bedouin into supporters of the Byzantines, supporters of the Muslims, and waverers.

30. Abu 'Ubayd (d. 837), *Kitab al-amwal*, ed. K. M. Harras (Beirut, 1978), 345 (*fi diyari-him*); Azdi, 218 (Iraq). Note that some demand notes on papyrus from southern Palestine, dated to the 670s, are made out in favor of clans from the Christian (possibly now Muslim) Arab tribes of Lakhm and Judham (C. J. Kraemer, *Excavations at Nessana 3*, Princeton, 1958, nos. 60–64: Sa'd ibn Malik and Sa'd ibn Zirr).

31. Sebeos, 98 (Heraclius); Baladhuri, 350 (census).

32. One might compare it to what we now call a jihadi ideology; as a Saudi jihadi in Syria told a Western reporter: "they (the jihadis) come from every country you could imagine" to fight the Asad regime and "create a caliphate" (*The Guardian Newspaper*, 9.9.13, 1 and 26).

33. Cited by P. J. Burton, *Friendship and Empire: Roman Diplomacy and Imperialism in the Middle East* (Cambridge 2011), 118. The Arabic terms *aman* and *dhimma* equate to the Latin *fides*, and Muslim lawyers also employed the Roman/Byzantine categories of voluntary surrender and forced surrender. The point here is not that the Arabs borrowed these concepts from the Romans/Byzantines, but rather that the Arabs belonged to the same world and so shared many of its presuppositions. For further discussion of surrender treaties see M. Levy-Rubin, *Non-Muslims in the Early Islamic Empire* (Cambridge, 2011), ch. 1.

34. Sebeos, 63, who notes that Edessa had resisted, but after facing an initial onslaught of Persian troops they decided to sue for peace "and requested an oath that they [the Persians] would not destroy the city."

35. Baladhuri, 158–61; Tabari, 1.2664. For a study of conquest agreements and the ancient background thereto, see Levy-Rubin, *Non-Muslims*, 8–57.

36. 'Abd al-Jabbar, *Tathbit dala'il al-nubuwwa*, ed. A-K. 'Uthman (Beirut, 1966), 328–29. Conversely, Mu'awiya was censured as "an emir who accumulates money like a merchant" (Khalifa, 230, AH 60).

37. Hoyland, *Seeing Islam*, 79–81 (Syrian author); Mingana, *Sources syriaques*, 156 and 184 (John of Fenek).

38. For what we can learn of early Arab rule from the papyri of Egypt, see Sijpesteijn, *Shaping a Muslim State*. She ponders why the Arabs adopted a "non-interventionist approach" (ibid., 64), but it is common for invaders to leave in place many of the

bureaucratic practices of the previous regime and its bureacurats, eliminating only the higher echelons, since they often do not themselves have the local knowledge to supervise the lower levels of government and do not embark on their venture with the aim of becoming administrators.

39. Tabari, I.962–3; Z. Rubin, "Reforms of Khusro Anushirwan" in Cameron, ed., *The Byzantine and Early Islamic Near East III*, 240–43. It is not impossible that the Persians introduced the poll tax during their occupation of Egypt and the Levant in the early seventh century; there is as yet no clearly dated reference to the poll tax from before the Arab conquests, but there are plenty of undated ones, and it is an unproven assumption that they belong to the Islamic period. For the papyri evidence, see Sijpesteijn, *Shaping a Muslim State*, 52, 72–74.

40. H. Kennedy, "Military Pay and the Economy of the Early Islamic State," *Historical Research* 75 (2002).

41. P. Crone, "The First-Century Concept of Hiğra," *Arabica* 41 (1994); K. Athamina, "A'rab and Muhajirun in the Environment of the Amsar," *Studia Islamica* 66 (1987); J. Gascou, "Sur la letter arabe de Qurra b. Šarīk P. Sorb inv. 2344," *Annales Islamologiques* 45 (2011). Note that in Sabaic and Ethiopic *hajar* means town or city; and in Sabaic we find the same contrast as in Arabic between *muhajirun* and *a'rab* (e.g., the inscription Ry508 speaks of the tribesmen of a region, "their town-dwellers and their Bedouin"/*hgrhmw w-'rbhmw*).

Chapter 4

1. Khalifa, 230 (AH 60).
2. Sebeos, 154. On the interests behind the internal Arab squabbles see M. Hinds, "Kufan Political Alignments" and "The Murder of the Caliph 'Uthman," *International Journal of Middle East Studies* 2 (1971) and 3 (1972).
3. *Chronicle of 741*, §31.
4. The following narrative and quotations are from Sebeos, 143–46. The Battle of Phoenix is also narrated by Theophilus, 141–44, *Chronicle of 741*, §24 ("Constans, gathering together a thousand and more ships, contended unsuccessfully against Mu'awiya and with scarcely any [of them] escaped in flight"), and Ibn 'Abd al-Hakam, 189–91, who is the first to call it the Battle of the Masts (though it is a confused account). Tabari, I.2867–71, gives a long account, whereas Khalifa, 167 (AH 32), and Ya'qubi, 195, just note that Mu'awiya led a campaign to "the straits of Constantinople." For naval matters in contemporary papyri, see C. Foss, "Egypt under Mu'awiya," *Bulletin of the School of Oriental and African Studies* 72 (2009), 18–19.
5. Theophilus, 153–61 and 166–68. The second part of the story, dealing with the assault on Constantinople, is also found in Nikephoros, §34, who is using the *Chronicle of ca 720*.

6. *Acta conciliorum oecumenicorum II.2*, ed. R. Riedinger (Berlin, 1984), 612–14 (Council of 680–81). See M. Jankowiak, "The First Arab Siege of Constantinople," *Travaux et Mémoires* 17 (2013).

7. *Chronicle of 741*, §27 (hunger and pestilence); Cosmas of Jerusalem, cited by C. Zuckermann, "A Gothia in the Hellespont in the Early Eighth Century," *Byzantine and Modern Greek Studies* 19 (1995); Theophilus, 166–68 (Greek fire).

8. *Chronicle of ca 720* (in Nikephoros, §34, and Theophanes, 354–55); Theophilus, 167–68.

9. My source for this section is primarily Sebeos, 136–43, supplemented by *History of the Caucasian Albanians*, 2.20–22, 27–28; Lewond, *History*, 53–54; Theophilus, 181.

10. Tabari, I.2898. The letter opens by invoking the God "who transfers kingship to whomever he pleases." Here there is no hint that the nobleman converted, though there are a number of cases where Iranian nobles are said to have disdained the idea of paying poll tax (Baladhuri, 314: *anifu min al-jizya*), and so converted to Islam; the elite were exempted from poll tax in the late Sasanian period, and so paying it would have been disagreeable to them, as it would have signified that they belonged to the lower ranks of society. However, in the first century or so of Arab rule many cities/regions paid their dues to the Arabs collectively rather than individually.

11. Baladhuri, 326 (dancing), 329 (Ardabil garrison), 338 (breaking of treaties), 335–37 (Masqala and Yazid); Chavannes, 173–74; Khalifa, 223 (AH 54: Masqala).

12. Xuanzang, *Travels in India*, ed. T. Watters (London, 1904), 102; *Life*, ed. S. Beal (London, 1914), 42. On the silk route trade and the role of Sogdians in managing it, see E. de la Vaissière, *Sogdian Traders* (Leiden, 2005).

13. For the following account, see Baladhuri, 404–11; Chavannes, 172 (Peroz); Khalifa, 211, 222, 224 (AH 50, 54, 56); Narshakhi, *History of Bukhara*, trans. R. Frye (Cambridge, MA, 1954), 9–10 (Khatun).

14. Khalifa, 167, 210 (AH 33, 50); Baladhuri, 393–38. The title is most often written as "Rutbil," but the diacritical marks are sometimes unclear or missing, which has led to the suggestion that it should be read as Zunbil because of an assumed connection with the local god Zun.

15. Modéran, *Les Maures*, 388 (Masuna), 401–14 (Masties), 420 (Cululis). The rest of the section is drawn from Theophilus, 164; Khalifa, 210 (AH 50); Ibn 'Abd al-Hakam, 193–97.

16. Baladhuri, 319 (Rayy); Sebeos, 147–48 (rebellion of the Medes).

17. Mardaites: Theophilus, 169 and 180–82; Baladhuri, 160–62; Nikephoros, §38 (using *Chronicle of ca 720*). For Byzantine coastal raids, see A. Elad, "The Coastal Cities of Palestine," *Jerusalem Cathedra* 2 (1982), who also notes the Arab policy of settling in these coastal cities groups, especially Persians, who would not be pro-Byzantine.

18. East Arabian tribesmen had close relations with Persia, but they were mostly not given senior positions in the Umayyad regime, which in part explains why so many anti-Umayyad rebels (Kharijites) came from their ranks.

19. *Maronite Chronicle*, 32 (move to Damascus), 31 (movements in Jerusalem); M. Mochiri, "A Sasanian-Style Coin of Yazid b. Mu'awiya," *Journal of the Royal Asiatic Society* (1982).

20. H. Gaube, *Arabosasanidische Numismatik* (Braunschweig, 1973), 22–25.

21. H. Lammens, *Etudes sur le règne du calife omaiyade Mo'awia I* (Paris, 1908), esp. 3–13 ('Abdarrahman ibn Khalid et les chrétiens de Homs), 419–41 (Yazid et la société des Chrétiens). Some indication of Christian Arab input comes from administrative terminology; for example, *chorion/kura* as a word for "district" occurs in early Islamic papyri in Egypt, where it had previously only meant "vineyard," but it did refer to a "district" in the province of Arabia before Islam (R. Hoyland, "Late Roman Provincia Arabia, Monophysite Monks and Arab Tribes," *Semitica et Classica* 2 (2009), 130: *kura*).

22. *Maronite Chronicle*, 32 (coinage); Baladhuri, 125 (church). Khalifa, 218 (AH 51), states, without explanation, that "the king of the holy land is Mu'awiya and his son too."

23. P. Sijpesteijn, "Army Economics," in R. E. Margariti et al., eds., *Histories of the Middle East: Studies. . . in Honor of A. L. Udovitch* (Leiden 2011), on stipends paid to dependents; H. Kennedy, "Military Pay and the Economy of the Early Islamic State," *Historical Research* 75 (2002), 159–60 (he cites another account from 892 that yields a figure of 89 percent for military expenditure). Ya'qubi, 258 (crown lands); a similar story about the crown lands is also attributed to 'Uthman, so Mu'awiya possibly did not devise the solution, but he certainly made more systematic use of it than anyone before him.

24. Baladhuri, 356–72, lists many land grants in southern Iraq apparently drawing on documentary evidence; Hoyland, *Seeing Islam*, 98–100 (Clysma and Dead Sea), 331 (prediction); Mingana, *Sources syriaques*, 153 and 181 (prosperity). John of Nikiu, 120.31, tells how the Arabs compelled the Egyptians to dredge the Trajan canal that ran between Babylon and the Red Sea. Note that Mu'awiya also owned estates in west Arabia according to literary texts (M. Kister, "The Battle of the Harra," *Studies in Memory of Gaston Wiet*, Jerusalem, 1977, 38–40), supported by epigraphic evidence (S. al-Rashid, *Dirasat fi l-athar al-islamiyya al-mubakkira*, Riyad, 2000, 46–60).

25. Foss, "Egypt under Mu'awiya" (Papas); Hoyland, *Seeing Islam*, 98 (enslavement).

26. Ya'qubi, 276. In general on Mu'awiya, see R. S. Humphreys, *Mu'awiya ibn Abi Sufyan* (Oxford, 2006).

27. He had for a long time excluded 'Ali as a legitimate caliph; cf. Ibn Abi Ya'la, *Tabaqat al-Hanabila* (Cairo, 1952), I.243, I.393 (When questioned by his colleagues about his change of heart, he replied that since the caliph 'Umar I "was satisfied with the idea of 'Ali as caliph of the Muslims. . . and since 'Ali called himself commander of the faithful, who am I to say that he was not?").

266 G NOTES

28. *Maronite Chronicle*, 32, says that "Mu'awiya did not wear a crown like other kings in the world," hinting that he was not as autocratic as later Muslim sources make him out to be. Similarly *Chronicle of 741*, §27, says of Yazid I that "he never, as is the wont of men, sought glory for himself because of his royal rank, but lived as a citizen along with all the common people," which might reflect the pro-Umayyad view.

29. Y. Ragib, "Une ère inconnue d'Egypte musulmane," *Annales islamologiques* 41 (2007), re two papyri, of 662 and 676, that are dated according to *qada' al-mu'minin*.

30. K-H. Ohlig and G. R. Puin, eds., *The Hidden Origins of Islam* (New York, 2010), esp. 40–41, 52, 144–45 (Christian); F. Donner, "From Believers to Muslims," *al-Abhath* 50–1 (2002–3), 26 ("non-confessional"); Y. Nevo, "Towards a Prehistory of Islam," *Jerusalem Studies in Arabic and Islam* 17 (1994), 110 ("indeterminate"); Donner, *Muhammad and the Believers*, 74 and *passim* (ecumenical). All include the Medinan period alongside the reign of Mu'awiya, but we have no public proclamations from the Medinan caliphs.

31. Sebeos, 144 (possibly originating with 'Uthman). The importance of Abraham to Muslims is noted in the mid-seventh-century *Chronicle of Khuzistan*, 38, and is empha-sized in the Qur'an. Late Antique Christians also thought that their faith "took its beginning from Abraham, the first of the fathers" (A. H. Becker, *Sources for the History of the School of Nisibis*, Liverpool 2008, 25, citing the sixth-century bishop Simeon of Bet Arsham). They also held to the idea of there being only one true religion, all else being heresy and error, and so the question of skeptical scholars as to why seventh-century Christian authors did not mention that the Arabs had a new religion reflects a very modern worldview.

32. Sebeos, 29–30 (decree); *Chronicle of Siirt*, 500 (head of Christians); Theophylact, 5.1.7, 5.13.5, 5.14.1 (Sergius); *Chronicle of Khuzistan*, 25 (cross). Also, both had Christian wives and many Christians at court and acted as arbiters in intra-Christian disputes (*Chronicle of Khuzistan*, 23, and Hoyland, *Seeing Islam*, 223).

33. P. Crone and M. Hinds, *God's Caliph* (Cambridge, 1986), 120 (succession letters), who provide good discussion about the nature of the early caliphate; Mingana, *Sources syriaques*, 146–47 and 175 (death penalty). A. Marsham, "Public Execution in the Umayyad Period," *Journal of Arabic and Islamic Studies* 11 (2011), 113, picks up on the word "brazenly" and suggests that John is talking about public violation/violence, which also merited the death penalty in Roman law. It is also possible that John is referring to Kharijites who were numerous in north Mesopotamia and who took a harsh line on infringement of God's law.

34. Ibn Sa'd (d. 845), *Tabaqat*, ed. E. Sachau (Leiden, 1904–40), 4.1.106, citing al-Sha'bi ('Abdallah); Fasawi (d. 890), *Kitab al-Ma'rifa wa-l-ta'rikh*, ed. A.D. al-'Umari (Beirut, 1981), 2.15 (Jabir ibn Zayd). From about the same time we get glimpses of this tussle between scholars and government; e.g. the mid-eighth-century Persian author Musa ibn 'Isa al-Kisrawi wrote a treatise on "the inconsistencies of those who assert

that judges do not have to follow the dictates of caliphs in their official duties" (Ibn al-Nadim, *Fihrist*, ed. G. Flügel, Leipzig, 1872, 128).

Chapter 5

1. Mingana, *Sources syriaques*, 155 and 183 ("zeal for the house of God"); Hoyland, *Seeing Islam*, 550–52 (coinage); *Chronicle of 741*, §31.

2. The Kharijite who captures central and eastern Arabia is Najda ibn 'Amir, and the one who minted coins in Iran is Qatari ibn Fuja'a. For these two characters, 'Abdallah ibn al-Zubayr, and the many other actors in the second Arab civil war, see A. A. Dixon, *The Umayyad Caliphate 65–86/684–705* (London, 1971), and G. Rotter, *Die Umayyaden und der zweite Burgerkrieg* (Wiesbaden, 1982).

3. Slavs and Sebastopolis: Nikephoros, §38, and Theophanes, 366 (both using the *Chronicle of ca. 720*); the Greek is *periousios laos*, a phrase used in the Greek translation of Exodus 19:5. On these two rulers and their times see C. Robinson, *'Abd al-Malik* (Oxford, 2005), and C. Head, *Justinian II of Byzantium* (Milwaukee, 1972).

4. *The Book of Pontiffs*, trans. R. Davis (Liverpool, 1989), 78 (also mentioning a ten-year peace signed by Justinian and the Arabs in 685); Khalifa, 251 (Kusayla; AH 63); Ibn 'Abd al-Hakam, 198–200 (Kusayla); Ibn al-Athir, *al-Kamil*, ed. 'U. al-Tadmuri (Beirut, 1997), 3.207–9 (AH 62); Theophanes, 370, and Nikephoros, §41 (Carthage: relying on the *Chronicle of ca 720*).

5. Khalifa, 268, 270 (AH 72, 74); Elias of Nisibis, *Opus Chronologicum*, ed. E. W. Brooks (Paris, 1910), 154 (AH 78); Baladhuri, 229; Ibn 'Abd al-Hakam, 200–201.

6. Ibn 'Abd al-Hakam, 201 (Hassan builds mosque, etc., *butr/baranis*); Corippus, 6.49 (Luwata "banished"), cited by Modéran, *Les Maures*, 644, who discusses the *baranis/butr* issue on pages 761–810. Arabs of pre-Islamic west Arabia may already have been using the term barbar for peoples on the east African coast (following Greco-Roman practice) and then simply applied it to the other peoples whom they encountered in Africa during the conquests (except the Egyptians/Copts, whom they also already knew about before Islam); see R. Rouighi, "The Berbers of the Arabs," *Studia Islamica* 1 (2011).

7. Ibn 'Abd al-Hakam, 201, 203–4 (Musa); *Chronicle of 754*, §51; Baladhuri, 230; Khalifa, 277–79 (AH 78–79).

8. This idea began with I. Olagüe's *La revolución islámica en Occidente* of 1966 (translated into French as *Les arabes n'ont pas envahi l'Espagne*) and has enjoyed more attention of late (e.g., K. De Villa, "Myth or Reality: The 'Invasion' and Spread of Islam in Spain," *The Fountain Magazine* 85, 2012). One argument used is that the Arab-Berber force was so small that the people of Spain could have easily defeated them if they had all risen up, just as they ejected Napoleon in 1807. However, before the era of nation-states people were divided into smaller ethnic, regional, sectarian, or social groups, and large-scale "national" resistance did not generally occur. For an interesting reassessment of how

England became Saxon, see A. Woolf, "Apartheid and Economics in Anglo-Saxon England," in N. Higham ed., *Britons in Anglo-Saxon England* (Woodbridge, 2007).

9. This section on Spain relies on *Chronicle of 754*, §§52, 54–57, 87; Ibn ʿAbd al-Hakam, 204–10; Baladhuri, 230–31; Khalifa, 304–5 (AH 92–93); E. M. Moreno, "The Iberian Peninsula and North Africa," in C. Robinson, ed., *New Cambridge History of Islam 1*, 385–89 (Theodemir and Hadrian); James, *Early Islamic Spain*, 50–51 (Ibn al-Qutiya). For historiographical issues, see Clarke, *Muslim Conquest of Iberia*.

10. H-S. Yang et al., *The Hye-Ch'o Diary* (Berkeley, CA, 1984), 48–56. The word for Arab in Chinese is *ta-shih*, which is a transcription of Persian *tazik/tajik*, which ultimately comes via Aramaic *tayayya* from Arabic *tayyiʾ*, the name of a pre-Islamic tribe that lived on the western borders of the Sasanian Persian Empire.

11. For Qutayba's campaigns, see Gibb, *The Arab Conquests in Central Asia*, 29–58. Tabari, 2.1218–27 (Nizak), 2.1244 (Ghurak).

12. The following account and quotations can be found in C. E. Bosworth, *Sistan under the Arabs* (Rome, 1968), 52–55 (ʿUbaydallah), 55–63 (Ibn al-Ashʿath).

13. Baladhuri, 401 (Rutbil); Chavannes, 161, 205–6 (embassies to China); K. van Bladel, "The Bactrian Background of the Barmakids," in A. Akasoy et al., eds., *Islam and Tibet* (Farnham, 2011), 54 (stupa); N. Sims-Williams, "The Arab-Sasanian and Arab-Hepthalite Coinage," *Cahiers de Studia Iranica* 39 (2008), 123–25 (coins).

14. This section relies primarily on Lewond, 59–61, 64–67; Theophilus, 195; Baladhuri, 205–6.

15. The close link between being Arab and being Muslim in the early period is clear from a number of cases where the word Arab is used to indicate Muslim; e.g., Papyrus London IV (ed. H. I. Bell, London 1910) 1375 (dated AD 711) speaks of "Arabs (*araboi*) and Christians" in the governor's retinue at Fustat, evidently meaning "Muslims and Christians"; the financial governor of Khurasan in the 720s wrote to the governor about the mass conversions to Islam, saying: "Who will you take the tax from now that all the people have become Arabs" (Tabari, 2.1508); *Chronicle of Zuqnin*, 155, notes that Yazid II (720–24) ordered that "the testimony of a Syrian [i.e., a Syriac-speaking Christian] against an Arab not be accepted."

16. Sometimes it is specified that the slaves given in tribute should be "free of defect and including neither boys nor old men" (Tabari, 2.1245), which would mean they were worth more, could do more work, and would not be available to fight for their homeland. Some served military purposes; for example, ʿAmr ibn Wabara "had slaves whom he used to hire out (for fighting) for thirty dirhams per day, but whom he would only pay ten dirhams each" (Tabari, 2.799–800).

17. Tabari, 1.2289 (the conquered as Arab booty); Mingana, *Sources syriaques*, 147 and 175 (John of Fenek).

18. Qurʾan 2:127–28 has Abraham and Ishmael ask God to make "from our descendants a people submissive to you (*umma muslima laka*)." There is a hint of a geneaological

qualifier to being a Muslim here, but it is too remote and vague to have become an enforceable requirement for conversion.

19. Arabic: *mawla*, plural *mawali*. This term shifted in meaning somewhat: initially the *mawla* was a retainer, and the key distinction among them concerned their free or unfree origins, not their ethnicity or religion (there were Arab Christian *mawali*, though probably the majority were non-Arab Muslims). Later it came to be used specifically to designate a non-Arab Muslim and it was postulated that the basis of the relationship between patron and freedman was not like that between master and servant (assuming dependency) but between two kinsmen (assuming reciprocity). See P. Crone, *Roman, Provincial and Islamic Law* (Cambridge, 1987), ch. 3. Non-Arab Muslims could also act as patrons, but initially most patrons would have been Arab Muslims.

20. Papyrus London IV (ed. H. I. Bell, British Museum 1910), 1447; C. E. Bosworth, "Raja' ibn Haywa al-Kindi and the Umayyad Caliphs," *Islamic Quarterly* 16 (1972).

21. John of Nikiu, 114.1, 121.10; Hoyland, *Seeing Islam*, 265 (without compulsion), 161–63 (Jacob).

22. Khatib al-Baghdadi, *Sharaf ashab al-hadith*, ed. M. S. Khatib Ughli (Ankara, 1971), no. 320 (al-A'mash). For the ways in which Iranian converts molded Islamic culture to make it more their own, see Savant, *New Muslims*. Note that Persians worked their mythical heroes into Islamic history by making them relatives of Shem, son of Noah (e.g., Dinawari, 4, who says that the grandfather of the legendary King Jamshid is Arphaxad son of Shem).

23. Cited by G. H. A. Juynboll, "The Role of Non-Arabs, *Mawali*, in the Early Development of *Hadith*," *Le Muséon* 118 (2005), 358, who gives more information on the non-Arab Muslim scholars I listed above as well as further examples. H. Motzki, "The Role of non-Arab Converts in the Development of Early Islamic Law," *Islamic Law and Society* 6 (1999), argues against this, but does not appreciate that the definition of Arab was changing and still speaks of "true Arabs."

24. Some tribes like Taghlib and Tanukh were probably native to Syro-Mesopotamia, but Muslim historians said that they originated in Arabia and had migrated north after the collapse of the Marib dam in the distant past.

25. Baladhuri, *Ansab al-ashraf* (Wiesbaden, 1978), 3.95 (al-Nakha'i); Baladhuri, 324 (al-'Ijl); Ibn 'Asakir, *Ta'rikh madinat Dimashq*, ed. A. Shibri (Beirut, 1995–98), 24.224–25 (Arab). On the Arab worry of being swamped by foreigners, see P. Crone, "Imperial Trauma," *Common Knowledge* 12 (2006).

26. Baladhuri, *Ansab al-ashraf* (Jerusalem, 1936–71), 4a.247 (Yazid's aunt); W. al-Qadi, "The Names of Estates in State Registers," in A. Borrut and P. Cobb, eds., *Umayyad Legacies* (Leiden, 2010), 263, which gives much detail on Qahdham's life.

27. Baladhuri, *Ansab al-ashraf* (Jerusalem, 1936–71), 5.300 ('Abd al-Malik), 4b.50 (Mundhir ibn al-Zubayr; *anbat al-Sham*; cf. Tabari, 2.1092: *jaramiqa min ahl al-sham*);

Jahiz (d. 869), *al-Bayan wa-l-tabyin*, ed. H. al-Sandubi (Cairo, 1926–27), 1.196 (Yazid ibn al-Muhallab); *Chronicle of Zuqnin*, 206 (Abbasid armies in the Jazira).

28. Herald: Tabari, 2.1024; Persian nobles with freedmen/slaves: Baladhuri, *Ansab al-ashraf*, ed. S. Zakkar and R. al-Zirkali (Beirut, 1996), 7.413 (Fayruz Husayn), and Baladhuri, 366 ('Abdallah al-Isfahani); P. Crone, *Slaves on Horses* (Cambridge, 1980), 37–38. On *chakars*, see E. de la Vaissière, "Chakârs d'Asie Centrale," *Studia Iranica* 34 (2005), who cites the passage above from Xuanzang.

29. Mingana, *Sources syriaques*, 158 and 185–86 (John of Fenek on events in Nisibis).

30. On Musa, see Tabari, 2.1145–64, and Baladhuri, 415–19.

Chapter 6

1. Theophanes, 411; *Chronicle of Zuqnin*, 162.

2. Or at least this is the motive for its construction given by al-Muqaddasi in his work *The Best Divisions for Knowledge of the Regions* (trans. B. A. Collins, Reading, 1994, 146). F. B. Flood, *The Great Mosque of Damascus* (Leiden, 2001), offers an insightful study of this magnificent building.

3. Theophilus, 272, 224. On Umayyad building, see D. Genequand, "Formation et devenir du paysage architectural Omeyyade," in A. Borrut, ed., *Umayyad Legacies* (Leiden, 2010), and A. Walmsley and K. Damgaard, "The Umayyad Congregational Mosque of Jarash," *Antiquity* 79 (2005).

4. There are many sources on this siege, some of which derive from contemporary Byzantine and Arab accounts. The following account relies on Theophilus, 209–15, supplemented by *Chronicle of Zuqnin*, 150–52; *Chronicle of ca 720* (in Theophanes, 396–99, and Nikephoros, §§54–56); Lewond, 109–13.

5. This is reported with very similar wording in both Theophilus, 215 (from Dionysius of Telmahre, d. 845), and Khalifa (d. 854), 320 (AH 99), who seem to share a Syrian source.

6. The following account and quotations are from *Chronicle of 754*, §§69, 74, 79–82, 84. The quotation of Bede is taken from his *Historia Ecclesiastica* (ed. C. Plummer, Oxford, 1896), 5.23.

7. For these quotations and further discussion, see D. L. Lewis, *God's Crucible: Islam and the Making of Europe* (London, 2008), 170–73.

8. This expression is found in both *Chronicle of 754*, §84 (*nudi prependiculis precincti*) and Ibn 'Abd al-Hakam, 219 ('*urāt mutajarradīn laysa 'alayhim illā al-sarāwīlāt*), suggesting a common source. My account of the Berber uprising is from *Chronicle of 754*, §84; Theophilus, 235; Khalifa, 352–56 (AH 122–24); Ibn 'Abd al-Hakam, 217–23.

9. J. Iskandar, "Devout Heretics: The Barghwata in Maghribi Historiography," *Journal of North African Studies* 12 (2007).

10. Chavannes, 203–5.

11. F. Grenet and E. de la Vaissière, "The Last Days of Panjikent," *Silk Road Art and Archaeology* 8 (2002).
12. Tabari, 2.1717–1718.
13. The Chinese version of the battle is found in the biography of General Gao preserved in Tang annals (Chavannes, 142–44 and notes thereto), but the Arab version is oddly not recounted by any historian before Ibn al-Athir (d. 1233) and al-Dhahabi (d. 1348). Western scholars also like to credit the battle with the introduction of paper to the Middle East, but paper had been available in Soghdia since the fourth century AD, and so its movement westward was probably just a result of the opening up of borders that accompanied the Arab conquests and that saw a number of products move from east to west and west to east (interestingly discussed, even if over-exaggerated, in A. M. Watson, *Agricultural Innovation in the Early Islamic World*, Cambridge, 1983).
14. L. Carrington Goodrich, *A Short History of the Chinese People* (Newton Abbot, 1969), 123; W. Barthold, *Turkestan Down to the Mongol Invasion* (London, 1968), 196; De la Vaissière, *Sogdian Traders* (Leiden, 2005), 218 (*History of An Lushan*).
15. This section principally relies on Khalifa, 328, 338, 340–44, 349, 351–52 (AH 103, 108, 110–13, 119, 121); Lewond, 69–70, 107–8; and *Chronicle of Zuqnin*, 159–60.
16. Baladhuri, 432, 434, 435–36 (Ruby Island), 436–40 (Muhammad ibn Qasim); Khalifa, 304 (AH 92–93).
17. The earliest Muslim source and the one I use here is Baladhuri (see previous note). On the *Chachnama*, see M. Ahmed, *The Many Histories of Muhammad b. Qasim* (PhD; Chicago, 2008) who also translates the Chalukya inscription I cite (ibid., 82).
18. The inscriptions are discussed by B. Chattopadhyaya, *Representing the Other: Sanskrit Sources and the Muslims* (Manohar, 1998), 28–35, and the Kollam plates in C. G. Cereti, "The Pahlavi Signatures on the Quilon Copper Plates," in *Festschrift for Nicholas Sims-Williams* (Wiesbaden, 2009).
19. Overtly dualist groups tended to fare badly though, because dualism clashed with Islam's stress on monotheism and because it was tainted by its connection to the former Persian regime. Labeled *zindiqs* (reinterpreters, heretics), such groups faced periodic persecution, especially the Manichaeans, though the label could be applied to anyone whom the government wanted to get rid of. See S. Arjomand, "Ibn al-Muqaffa'" *Iranian Studies* 27 (1994), 20–24.
20. Theophilus, 215–17, and *Chronicle of Zuqnin*, 155 (testimony of a Christian against a Muslim not accepted; blood-money of a Christian less than a Muslim). For more on this topic, see M. Levy-Rubin, *Non-Muslims in the Early Islamic Empire* (Cambridge, 2011), ch. 3.
21. The words for this in classical Islamic law are *jizya* and *kharaj* respectively, but this is an early Abbasid innovation; before this *kharaj* (Aramaic: *kharga*) was only used in the Persian realm and never features in the Egyptian papyri of the Umayyad period,

which use the term *jizya*, a generic term for tax or tribute (*jizyat al-ra's*/"head tax" or *jizyat al-ard*/"land tax" are used when clarification is required). Failure to recognize that the same word could refer to different things at different times and a desire to project the classical system back into the early decades of Arab rule has hindered our understanding of how the Islamic tax system developed.

22. Tabari, 2.1122 (Hajjaj); P. Crone, "The Pay of Client Soldiers," *Der Islam* 80 (2009).

23. H. A. R. Gibb, "The Fiscal Rescript of 'Umar II," *Arabica* 2 (1955), 3.

24. Sijpesteijn, *Shaping a Muslim State*, 314–15. I have massively simplified what was a very complex situation; for recent illustrations of this complexity, see Sijpesteijn's book and M. Campopiano, "Land Tax 'ala l-misaha and muqasama: Legal Theory and the Balance of Social Forces in Early Medieval Iraq," *Journal of the Economic and Social History of the Orient* 54 (2011).

25. Duri, *Early Islamic Institutions*, 114 (burning registers). In the Persian realm these local notables are often generically called *dihqans* by the Muslim sources; for their counterparts in Egypt and north Iraq, see Sijpesteijn, *Shaping a Muslim State*, 154–60, and Robinson, *Empires and Elites*, 90–97, respectively.

26. Abu l-'Arab al-Qayrawani, *Tabaqat 'ulama' Ifriqiya wa-Tunis*, ed. 'A. al-Shabbi and N. H. al-Yafi (Tunis, 1968), 84–87 ('Umar II); Tabari, 2.1507–9 (Ashras); Narshakhi, *History of Bukhara*, trans. R. Frye (Cambridge, MA, 1954), 48–49 (neophytes). It is an interesting question to what degree and/or at what point the Arab Muslim regime felt that it had a civilizing mission, that is, to bring enlightenment to others and not just feel superior that they had it and others did not; P. Crone, "Imperial Trauma," *Common Knowledge* 12 (2006), 109, calls the Arabs "missionary monotheists," but it is hard to discern a consistent policy and it often seems directed at areas where there were security concerns.

27. C. Wurtzel, "The Coinage of the Revolutionaries in the Late Umayyad Period," *American Numismatic Society Museum Notes* 23 (1978). See also M. Mochiri, *Arab-Sasanian Civil War Coinage* (Leiden, 1987).

28. Quoted in W. F. Tucker, *Mahdis and Millenarians* (Cambridge, 2011), 62, who also discusses the Janahiyya that I mention later and notes the links with Gnostic creation myths.

29. Tabari, 2.1566–86 (Harith ibn Surayj), 2.1575 (Murji'ite), 2.1918–19 (Muqatil and Jahm); *Akhbar al-dawla al-'abbasiyya*, ed. A. A. Duri and A. J. Muttalib (Beirut, 1971), 283 (Abu Muslim).

Chapter 7

1. Theophanes, 430 (Rawandis: "Persian wearers-of-black who were of the Magian religion"); Crone, *The Nativist Prophets*, 88—this work offers a rich and insightful study of Zoroastrian uprisings in Iran.

2. The duration of an empire is a contentious question: its members like to emphasize its longevity and continuity whereas modern historians like to periodize. For
example, the transfer of the capital of the Roman Empire from Rome to Byzantion/
Constantinople in AD 312 prompts us to rename it the Byzantine Empire, though
its citizens kept calling themselves Romans until 1453. We call the Achaemenid
(550–330 BC) and Sasanian (AD 224–652) states the first and second Persian Empire
respectively, because of the provenance of the dynasty (Fars/Persis), and distinguish
them from the intervening Seleucid and Arsacid/Parthian states, even though there
was arguably more similarity between the Parthians and Sasanians than between
the Achaemenids and Sasanians. Note that already in the fourteenth century Ibn
Khaldun had noted the short duration of Muslim dynasties and explained it with
reference to the prevalence of pastoral nomads in Muslim-ruled lands (see E. Gellner,
Muslim Society, Cambridge, 1981, ch. 1).

3. Thus the Turk and Mongol dominance of the Middle East in this period; see R.
Bulliet, *Cotton, Climate and Camels in Early Islamic Iran* (New York, 2011).

4. *Chronicle of Zuqnin*, 181–83, 190–91 (John son of Daddi, Kushan the Armenian, and
Gregory the Urartian).

5. Grabar, *Formation*, ch. 3; Fowden, *Qusayr ʿAmra*, ch. 8. Yazid III's mother was allegedly
the daughter of Peroz III. These two examples fit with the report about Yazid I's
striking of coins dated to the years of his reign (see Chapter 4 n. 19, this volume).

6. Madrasas changed the Muslim religious scene substantially, for they sponsored
an Islamic curriculum and supported salaried staff to teach it. Before this, rulers
employed judges and big city mosques employed preachers, but otherwise, religious
specialists (imams, mullahs, ʿulamaʾ, etc.) were unofficial and unsalaried; they gained
standing by dint of becoming recognized for their religious learning and/or pious
behavior and could only earn money in this capacity unofficially, by giving advice on
religio-legal and other matters.

7. On Ibn al-Muqaffaʿ's manual, see S. Goitein, *Studies in Islamic History and Institutions*
(Leiden, 1966), ch. 8 ("a turning point"), and S. Arjomand, "Ibn al-Muqaffaʿ," *Iranian
Studies* 27 (1994), 31–33. For further thoughts on Islam's antipathy to empire, see
Crone, *Slaves on Horses*, 61–91, and on the Arab Empire's demise, see H. Kennedy, "The
Decline and Fall of the First Muslim Empire," *Der Islam* 81 (2004).

8. J. Paul, "The State and the Military—a Nomadic Perspective," *Orientwissenschaftliche
Hefte* 12 (2003), esp. 35: "redistribution as a basic feature of royal behaviour is (in
the nomad perspective) contrasted to accumulation, which is seen as the principle on
which settled administration is founded." With this goes a sense of social equality
and mobility; see L. Marlow, *Hierarchy and Egalitarianism in Islamic Thought* (Cambridge,
2002), and cf. M. Hodgson, *Rethinking World History* (Cambridge, 1993), 114, who
argues that it was impossible to maintain an empire "under the conditions of high
social mobility which the Arab conquests had brought about" and which favored

"cosmopolitan mercantile elements" at the expense of "an effective agrarian bureau-cratic order."

9. The last reference to African Latin comes from the traveler Muhammad al-Idrisi (d. 1165), who says that it is spoken by most of the inhabitants of Gafsa in modern Tunisia. Coptic is rarely used for documents or literature after the eleventh century, surviving only as a liturgical language.

10. Narshakhi, *History of Bukhara*, trans. R. Frye (Cambridge, MA, 1954), 3.

11. Thus in the *Life of Muhammad* by Ibn Ishaq (d. 767), as transmitted to us by Ibn Hisham (d. 833), the pre-Islamic section focuses exclusively on Arabia, considers all its inhab-itants to be Arabs (even the South Arabians, whose inscriptions distinguish between themselves and Arabs), has Ishmael marry into an Arab tribe and designates all his offspring Arabs, and it locates the origins of all Arabophone tribes in Arabia (even those like Taghlib and Tanukh who were very likely native to Syro-Mesopotamia).

12. For recent discussion, see P. Crone, "Post-Colonialism in Tenth-Century Islam," *Der Islam* 83 (2006).

13. This did not mean that there was no persecution of non-Muslims by Muslim authori-ties, but it was always illegal and so tended to be small scale and of short duration. Works on the topic of the non-Muslim contribution to Islamic civilization often have an apologetic tone (consider the subtitle of the popular book of M. R. Menocal, *Ornament of the World*, New York, 2002: "How Muslims, Jews and Christians Created a Culture of Tolerance in Medieval Spain"). Yet it is true that nowhere else in medieval Europe was as open to scholars of all three religions as Spain. For Baghdad, see S. H. Griffith, *In the Shadow of the Mosque* (Princeton, 2007), ch. 5.

14. There are no survey works for this topic and one has to read about each subject area in turn. It is also nowadays somewhat contentious, since it is often thought to be somehow demeaning to Islam to imply that it contains foreign elements (though of course all religions and civilizations do). Some scholars play up the inventiveness of Islamic civilization (the message that the Arabs/Muslims gave science to Europe is very popular, for example), whereas others emphasize its derivative nature (e.g., S. Gouguenheim, *Aristote au Mont Saint-Michel*, Paris, 2008, argues that the Europeans preserved Greek science themselves and that it was Christians who preserved it in the Middle East, not Muslims).

15. E.g., Ibn Samura, governor of Sistan for Mu'awiya, took with him to Basra captives from Kabul and they built a mosque for his villa "in the Kabul style of building" (Baladhuri, 397).

16. Mingana, *Sources syriaques*, 151 and 179 ("no distinction"), 147 and 175 (captives).

17. K. van Bladel, "The Bactrian Background of the Barmakids," in A. Akasoy et al., eds., *Islam and Tibet* (Farnham, 2011); D. Sourdel, *Le vizirat 'abbaside* (Damascus, 1959–60), 134–81 (Yahya al-Barmaki, vizier of Harun al-Rashid, and his sons), 195–217 (Fadl ibn Sahl, vizier and viceroy of the east for the caliph Ma'mun, and his brother Hasan).

18. Jahiz, *Dhamm al-kuttab*, cited in C. Pellat, *Life and Works of al-Jahiz* (London, 1969), 274–75. On the translation of Greek scholarship, see D. Gutas, *Greek Thought Arabic Culture* (London, 1998). On Sasanian Persian literature/culture in Islam and Persianization (referred to as Iranization by some scholars), see M. Zakeri, *Persian Wisdom in Arabic Garb* (Leiden, 2007); H. Kennedy, "Survival of Iranianness," in V. Curtis and S. Stewart, eds., *The Rise of Islam* (London, 2009); A. Peacock, "Early Persian Historians and the Heritage of Pre-Islamic Iran," in E. Herzig and S. Stewart, eds., *Early Islamic Iran* (London, 2011).

19. Imam just means the person at the front (someone to follow, a model); in Sunni Islam it primarily designates a prayer leader, but in Shi'ism it refers to the leaders of the community, who are generally always descendants of the prophet's son-in-law 'Ali.

20. For the quotations and further discussion, see Crone, *Nativist Prophets*, ch. 19. I am not saying that Shi'ism and Sufism are specifically Persian phenomena but that they were open to Persian religious ideas; both also flourished outside of Persia, and Sufism in particular spread and developed localized forms in places as diverse as Senegal and Pakistan, especially before the rise of modern fundamentalist Islam.

21. The four sources are present in the Mishna and Talmud (J. Wegner, "Islamic and Talmudic Jurisprudence: The Four Roots of Islamic Law and Their Talmudic Counterparts," *American Journal of Legal History* 26, 1982). On the Roman side compare the statement of Emperor Justinian (*Digest*, 1.3.32) that the order of primacy for deriving laws is *scripti leges* ("written laws"/scripture; Arabic *kitab*), *mores et consuetudinis* (customary practice; Ar *sunna*), *proximum et consequens* ("near and following logically," that is, analogy: Ar *qiyas*), *iudicium populi . . . consensus omnium* ("the judgement of the people . . . the consensus of all"; cf. Ar *ijma'*). For more on the links between Roman and Islamic law, see B. Jokisch, *Islamic Imperial Law* (Berlin, 2007) and for the idea that Umayyad governors used the late Roman rescript system, whereby major litigations were referred in the first instance to the governor's office, see M. Tillier, "Dispensing Justice in a Minority Context," in R. Hoyland, ed., *The Late Antique History of Early Islam* (Princeton, 2014).

22. E.g., H. Motzki, *The Origins of Islamic Jurisprudence* (Leiden, 2002), who locates the origins in Mecca. For the unwillingness of Islamicists to engage with the idea of the non-Arabian origins of Islamic law, see P. Crone, *Roman, Provincial and Islamic Law* (Cambridge, 1987), 1–17. But, as I. Goldziher notes, Islam has an "ability to absorb and assimilate foreign elements so thoroughly that their foreign character can be detected only by the exact analysis of critical research" (*Introduction to Islamic Theology and Law*, Princeton, 1981, 4–5).

23. P. Crone and A. Silverstein, "The Ancient Near and Islam: The Case of Lot-casting," *Journal of Semitic Studies* 55 (2010).

24. A. Marsham, "Public Execution in the Umayyad Period," *Journal of Arabic and Islamic Studies* 11 (2011), 116–23; G. Hawting and D. Eisenberg, "'Earnest Money' and

the Sources of Islamic Law," in B. Sadehgi et al., eds., *Islamic Cultures Islamic Contexts* (Leiden, 2014).

25. M. J. Kister, "Do Not Assimilate Yourselves. . .," *Jerusalem Studies in Arabic and Islam* 12 (1989).

26. For some discussion of this topic, see F. Donner, *Narratives of Islamic Origins* (Princeton, 1998), and S. C. Lucas, *Constructive Critics: Hadith Literature and the Articulation of Sunni Islam* (Leiden, 2004).

27. One is reminded of a speech of 'Amr ibn al-'As to a Byzantine commander about how the sharing out of land had been unfavorable to the Arabs and that they were now seeking to exchange half of their thorns and stones for half of the cultivable lands (Ibn 'Asakir, *Ta'rikh Madinat Dimashq 1*, ed. S. al-Munajjid, Damascus, 1951, 461–62).

28. W. M. Sloane, *Greater France in Africa* (New York, 1924), 91–92. More generally, see G. Jenkins, "For Love of Country? Britain, France and the Multiethnic Imperial Army 1815–1919," http://ida.academia.edu/GrahamJenkins, accessed September 30, 2013. A similar policy was followed by the Arabs in settling Persians, Indians, and Jews in the Mediterranean coastal cities, reasoning that they would not aid any Byzantine attempts to recapture these cities (see Chapter 4 n. 17, this volume).

29. This does not mean their conversion was insincere or solely for material gain; one might compare it to immigrants seeking to become American citizens—they hope thereby to find a better life and are usually sincere in their belief about the virtues of American democracy and freedom.

30. Most lawyers accepted the legality of Muslim men marrying non-Muslim women, and in any case there was no other option for men on campaign in foreign lands: "We married women of the people of the book (i.e., Jews, Christians, and usually Zoroastrians too) as we did not find enough Muslim women" (Tabari, 1.2375).

31. Nu'aym ibn Hammad, *Kitab al-Fitan*, ed. M. al-Shuri (Beirut, 1997), no. 655 (nine out of ten). I should emphasize what I said in Chapter 5, namely, that in the first century or so after the Arab conquests one needed a Muslim patron to convert to Islam; in the case of a prisoner-of-war this was readily available in the form of one's Arab captor; he did not have to free his captives when they converted, but it was common, especially in return for payment or service.

32. Most recently, see C. Wickham, *Inheritance of Rome* (Penguin, 2010). An exception is M. Hodgson, *Rethinking World History* (Cambridge, 1993), 113–14: "the history of the first century of the Muslim empire was the history of its gradual reconstitution as an Irano-Semitic agrarian empire such as the Sasanian had been." Medieval Persians, by contrast, were well aware of the Arabs' debt to them: "Our ancestors gave you your kingdom, but you showed no gratitude for our generosity" (poem by Ibn Mamshadh of Isfahan, cited by M. Stern in C. E. Bosworth, ed., *Iran and Islam*, Edinburgh 1971, 541–42).

33. This may at first seem unlikely, but Islam in the Qur'an is quite close to its Judaeo-Christian roots, and it is what has happened since the early Islamic period, to both Christianity and Islam (as well as their long history of mutual antagonism), that has led the two to diverge. Islam might have maintained the same relationship to Christianity as is held today by Mormonism, which like Islam has its own prophet and scripture and certain distinctive practices.

Appendix

1. The author of a late eighth-century treatise on taxation records a government attempt to amend the tax rate for the people of Edessa by making a claim about what was in their original conquest treaty, to which the Edessans replied: "You are now ignorant, as we are ignorant, of how things were at the beginning; so how can you see fit to impose on us something for which you can provide no established precedent" (Robinson, *Empires and Elites*, 2–4, citing Abu Yusuf). For examples of legal and pious material inserted into conquest accounts, see the articles of Brunschwig and Noth in Donner, *Expansion of the Early Islamic State*.

2. In general, see Crone, *Slaves*, 3–17, and the works listed in the Historiography section of the Select Bibliography.

3. Thus J. Koren and Y. D. Nevo, "Methodological Approaches to Islamic Studies," *Der Islam* 68 (1991), though within these broad groupings there is a fair diversity of opinion. See also C. Robinson, "The Ideological Uses of Early Islam," *Past and Present* 203 (2009), 216–17, who uses the labels "mistrusting minimalists" and "trusting maximalists."

4. An example of the former is Donner's *Muhammad and the Believers* (see P. Crone's review in *Tablet Magazine*, August 10, 2010: "Donner's book has already been hailed in a manner showing that its thesis appeals deeply to American liberals: Here they find the nice, tolerant, and open Islam that they hanker for"). See also C. F. Foss on "trendy political correctness" in a review of Walmsley's *Early Islamic Syria* for *Journal of Roman Archaeology* 21 (2008), 739–40. For the opposing trend, see the publications on http://www.inarah.de/cms/ and their English volume *The Hidden Origins of Islam* (ed. Ohlig and Puin), and Günter Lüling, *A Challenge to Islam for Reformation* (Delhi, 2003), which is a serious book, but, as the title suggests, has polemical overtones.

5. P. Crone, *Roman, Provincial and Islamic Law* (Cambridge, 1987), 6: after the Second World War, "Islamicists increasingly preferred to study Islam as an autonomous system developing internally in response to its own needs and by the use of its own resources."

6. To take just one example, the substantial correspondence of three north Syrian Christian figures (Jacob of Edessa, John of Litarb, and George, bishop of the Arabs) from the late seventh/early eighth centuries has still not been published, let alone studied, even though one Islamicist pointed out long ago its usefulness for

understanding the rise of predestinationist thinking in Islam (M. Cook, *Early Muslim Dogma*, Cambridge, 1981, 145–52). It is hard to imagine European medievalists being so neglectful if a similar corpus were available to them.

7. *Chronicle of 741*, §28; Baladhuri (A), 9.291, and Tabari, 3.2173–75.
8. P. Brown, *The Rise of Western Christendom* (Oxford, 2003), 301.

SELECT BIBLIOGRAPHY

☪

Late Antiquity and Early Islam have of late spawned a vast literature, and so, in order to keep this list manageable and useful, I have given only the most important and most recent works. My choice reflects those works that have helped form my views on the subjects covered in this book and/or those that I think will be useful for readers wanting to explore in greater depth an issue that I raise. For general reference, see the *Encyclopaedia of Islam, Encyclopaedia Iranica,* and *Dictionary of Byzantium.*

General Studies on the Conquests and Military Affairs

Donner, F. *The Early Islamic Conquests* (Princeton, 1980).

Donner, F., ed. *The Expansion of the Early Islamic State* (Farnham, 2008).

Gabrieli, F. *Muhammad and the Conquests of Islam* (Eng. Trans.; New York, 1968).

Kaegi, W. *Byzantium and the Early Islamic Conquests* (Cambridge, 1992).

Kennedy, H. *Armies of the Caliphs* (London, 2001).

Kennedy, H. *The Great Arab Conquests* (Cambridge, MA, 2007).

Lee, A. D. *War in Late Antiquity* (Oxford, 2007).

Nicolle, D. *The Great Islamic Conquests* (Oxford, 2009).

Southen, P., and Dixon, K. R. *The Late Roman Army* (London, 1996).

The Late Antique Setting

Banaji, J. *Agrarian Change in Late Antiquity* (Oxford, 2001).

Bowersock, G. W. *Empires in Collision in Late Antiquity* (Waltham, MA, 2012).

Bowersock, G. W. et al., eds. *Late Antiquity: A Guide to the Postclassical World* (Cambridge, 1999).

Brown, P. *The World of Late Antiquity* (London, 1971).

Cameron, Av. et al., eds. *The Byzantine and Early Islamic Near East 1–6* (Princeton, 1992–).

Cameron, Av. et al., eds. *The Cambridge Ancient History XIV: Late Antiquity* (Cambridge, 2000).

Cameron, Av. *The Mediterranean World in Late Antiquity: AD 395–700* (London, 2011).

Daryaee, T. *Sasanian Persia* (London, 2009).

Dignas, B., and Winter, E. *Rome and Persia in Late Antiquity* (Cambridge, 2007).

Fowden, E. *The Barbarian Plain: Saint Sergius between Rome and Iran* (Berkeley, 1999).

Fowden, G. *Empire to Commonwealth: Consequences of Monotheism in Late Antiquity* (Princeton, 1994).

Fowden, G. *Before and After Muhammad: The First Millennium Refocused* (Princeton, 2014).

Greatrex, G., and Lieu, S. *The Roman Eastern Frontier and the Persian Wars* (London, 2007).

Halsall, G. *Barbarian Migrations and the Roman West 376–568* (Cambridge, 2007).

Howard-Johnston, J. *East Rome, Sasanian Persia and the End of Antiquity* (Variorum; Aldershot, 2006).

Johnson, S., ed. *Oxford Handbook of Late Antiquity* (Oxford, 2012).

Lieu, S. N. C. *Manichaeism in the Later Roman Empire and Medieval China* (2nd revised edition; Tübingen, 1992).

McCormick, M. *Origins of the European Economy AD 300–900* (Cambridge, MA, 2001).

Pirenne, Henri. *Mohammed and Charlemagne* (English trans.; London, 1939).

Pourshariati, P. *Decline and Fall of the Sasanian Empire* (London, 2008).

Sarris, P. *Empires of Faith: The Fall of Rome to the Rise of Islam* (Oxford, 2011).

Sizgorich, T. *Violence and Belief in Late Antiquity* (Philadelphia, PA, 2009).

Wickham, C. *Framing the Early Middle Ages* (Oxford, 2006).

Wood, P., ed. *History and Identity in Late Antiquity* (Oxford, 2013).

Continuity/Decline and the Environment

Bray, R. S. *Armies of Pestilence: The Effects of Pandemics on History* (Cambridge, 1996).

Christensen, P. *The Decline of Iranshahr: Irrigation and Environments in the History of the Middle East* (Copenhagen, 1993).

Gunn, J. *The Years without Summer: Tracing A.D. 536 and Its Aftermath* (Oxford, 2000).

Kennedy, H. "From Polis to Madina," *Past and Present* 106 (1985).

Liebeschuetz, J. H. W. G. *The Decline and Fall of the Roman City* (Oxford, 2001).

Little, L. K., ed. *Plague and the End of Antiquity: The Pandemic of 541–750* (New York, 2007).

Walmsley, A. "Economic Developments and the Nature of Settlement," *Dumbarton Oaks Papers* 61 (2007).

Ward-Perkins, B. *The Fall of Rome and the End of Civilisation* (Oxford, 2006).

Historiography and the Beginnings of Islam

Berg, H., ed. *Method and Theory in the Study of Islamic Origins* (Leiden, 2003).

Cook, M. *Studies in the Origins of Early Islamic Culture and Tradition* (Variorum; Aldershot, 2004).

Crone, P. *Meccan Trade and the Rise of Islam* (Princeton, 1987).

Crone, P., and Cook, M. *Hagarism: The Making of the Islamic World* (Cambridge, 1977).

El-Hibri, T. *Parable and Politics in Early Islamic History: The Rashidun Caliphs* (New York, 2010).

Hawting, G. *The Idea of Idolatry and the Emergence of Islam* (Cambridge, 1999).

Howard-Johnston, J. *Witnesses to a World Crisis* (Oxford, 2010).

Hoyland, R. G. *Seeing Islam as Others Saw It* (Princeton, 1997).

Humphreys, S. *Islamic History: A Framework for Enquiry* (Princeton, 1991).

Nevo, Y., and Koren, J. *Crossroads to Islam* (New York, 2004)

Noth, A. (with L. I. Conrad). *The Early Arabic Historical Tradition* (Princeton, 1994).

De Prémare, A-L. *Les Fondations de l'Islam* (Paris, 2002).

Robinson, Chase. *Islamic Historiography* (Cambridge, 2003).

Shoshan, B. *Poetics of Islamic Historiography* (Leiden, 2004).

Wansbrough, J. *The Sectarian Milieu* (Oxford, 1978).

The Making of Islamic Civilization

Al-Azmeh, A. *Muslim Kingship* (London, 1997).

Berkey, J.P. *The Formation of Islam: 600–1800* (Cambridge, 2002).

Calder, N. *Studies in Early Muslim Jurisprudence* (Oxford, 1993).

Cook, M. *Early Muslim Dogma* (Cambridge, 1981).

Crone, P. *Slaves on Horses* (Cambridge, 1980).

Crone, P. *Medieval Islamic Political Thought* (Edinburgh, 2005).

Crone, P. *From Arabian Tribes to Islamic Empire* (Variorum; Aldershot, 2008).

Dabashi, H. *Authority in Islam* (New Brunswick, NJ, 1989).

Décobert, C. *Le Mendiant et le Combattant: l'institution de l'Islam* (Paris, 1991).

De Prémare, A. *Les Fondations de l'Islam: entre écriture et histoire* (Paris, 2002).

Donner, F. *Muhammad and the Believers* (Cambridge, MA, 2010).

Donner, F., ed. *The Articulation of Early Islamic State Structures* (Farnham, 2012).

Duri, A. A. *Early Islamic Institutions* (London, 2011).

Friedmann, Y. *Tolerance and Coercion in Islam* (Cambridge, 2003).

Grabar, O. *The Formation of Islamic Art: Revised and Enlarged Edition* (New Haven, 1987).

Hawting, G. *The First Dynasty of Islam: The Umayyad Caliphate* (London, 2002).

Holu, K. G., and Lapin, H., eds. *Shaping the Middle East: Jews, Christians and Muslims in an Age of Transition* (Bethesda, 2011).

Judd, S. C. *The Third Fitna: Orthodoxy, Heresy and Coercion in Late Umayyad History* (PhD; Michigan, 1997).

Kennedy, H. *The Prophet and the Age of the Caliphates* (2nd edition; London, 2004).

Kennedy, H. *The Byzantine and Early Islamic Near East* (Variorum; Aldershot, 2006).

Marsham, A. *Rituals of Islamic Monarchy* (Edinburgh, 2009).

Milwright, M. *An Introduction to Islamic Archaeology* (Edinburgh, 2010).

Robinson, C., ed. *The New Cambridge History of Islam I* (Cambridge, 2011).

Van Bladel, K. *The Arabic Hermes* (Oxford, 2009).

Van Ess, J. *The Flowering of Muslim Theology* (Cambridge, MA, 2006).

Walzer, R. *Greek into Arabic* (Oxford, 1963).

Key Primary Sources

Baladhuri, *Futuh al-buldan*, ed. M. J. de Goeje (Leiden, 1866).

Chavannes, E. *Documents sur les Tou-Kiue (Turcs) Occidentaux* (Paris, 1903): assembles in French translation the major Chinese sources on the "western peoples."

Chronicle of 741 trans. in Hoyland, *Seeing Islam*, Excursus B.

Chronicle of 754 trans. in K. B. Wolf, *Conquerors and Chroniclers of Early Medieval Spain* (Liverpool, 1999), 91–128.

Chronicle of Khuzistan, ed. I. Guidi (Paris, 1903).

Chronicle of Siirt, ed. and trans. A. Scher, *Patrologia Orientalis* 13 (1918).

Chronicle of Zuqnin, trans. Amir Harrak (Toronto, 1999).

Dinawari, *al-Akhbar al-tiwal*, ed. V. Guirgass (Leiden, 1888).

History of the Caucasian Albanians by Movses Dasxuranci, trans. C. J. F. Dowsett (Oxford, 1961).

Ibn 'Abd al-Hakam, *Futuh Misr*, ed. C. Torrey (New Haven, 1922).

John of Nikiu, *Chronicle*, trans. R. H. Charles (London, 1916).

Khalifa (ibn Khayyat), *Ta'rikh*, ed. A. D. al-'Umari (Riyad, 1975).

Lewond, *History*, trans. Z. Arzoumanian (Wynnewood, PA, 1982).

Maronite Chronicle, trans. in Palmer, *Seventh Century*, 29–35.

Mingana, A., ed. and trans. *Sources syriaques* (Leipzig, 1908): includes the chronicle of John of Fenek.

Nikephoros, *Short History*, ed. and trans. C. Mango (Washington, DC, 1990).

Palmer, A., et al. *The Seventh Century in West Syrian Chronicles* (Liverpool, 1993): presents translations of the main Syriac historical texts for the period 582–717.

Sebeos, *The Armenian History*, trans. R. Thomson (Liverpool, 1999).

Tabari, *Ta'rikh al-rusul wa-l-muluk*, ed. M. J. de Goeje et al. (Leiden, 1879–1901).

Theophanes, *Chronographia*, trans. C. Mango and R. Scott (Oxford, 1997).

Theophilus of Edessa, *Chronicle*, trans. R. G. Hoyland (Liverpool, 2011).

Ya'qubi, *Ta'rikh 2*, ed. M. T. Houtsma (Leiden 1883).

Regional Studies
Africa and Spain

Bowersock, G. *The Throne of Adulis: Red Sea Wars on the Eve of Islam* (Oxford, 2013).

Clarke, N. *The Muslim Conquest of Iberia* (Abingdon, 2012).

Conant, J. *Staying Roman: Conquest and Identity in Africa and the Mediterranean 439–700* (Cambridge, 2012).

Fenwick, C. "From Africa to Ifriqiya: Settlement and Society in Early Medieval North Africa (650–800)," *al-Masaq* 25 (2013).

Hatke, G. *Aksum and Nubia: Warfare, Commerce, and Political Fictions in Ancient Northeast Africa* (New York, 2013).

James, D. *Early Islamic Spain: The History of Ibn al-Qutiya* (Abingdon, 2009).

Kaegi, W. *Muslim Expansion and the Byzantine Collapse in North Africa* (Cambridge, 2010).

Manzano Moreno, E. *Conquistadores, emires y califas: Los omeyas y la formación de al Andalus* (Barcelona, 2006).

Merrills, A., ed. *Vandals, Romans and Berbers: New Perspectives on Late Antique North Africa* (Aldershot, 2004).

Modéran, Y. *Les Maures et l'Afrique Romaine* (Rome, 2003).

Munro-Hay, S. *Axum: An African Civilisation of Late Antiquity* (Edinburgh, 1991).

Takla, H., and Gabra, G., eds. *Christianity and Monasticism in Aswan and Nubia* (Cairo, 2013).

Welsby, D. *Medieval Kingdoms of Nubia: Pagans, Christians and Muslims in the Middle Nile* (London, 2002).

Arabia and the Arabs

Bashear, S. *Arabs and Others in Early Islam* (Princeton, 1997).

Beaucamp, J. et al., eds. *Le massacre de Najran II: Juifs et Chrétiens en Arabie* (Paris, 2010).

Fisher, G. *Between the Empires: Arabs, Romans and Sasanians* (Oxford, 2011).

Gajda, I. *Le royaume de Himyar à l'époque monothéiste* (Paris, 2009).

Hoyland, R.G. *Arabia and the Arabs* (London, 2001).

Peters, F.E. *The Arabs and Arabia on the Eve of Islam* (Variorum; Aldershot, 1999).

Retsö, J. *The Arabs in Antiquity* (London, 2003).

Shahid, I. *Byzantium and the Arabs* (Washington, DC, 1984–).

Trimingham, J. S. *Christianity among the Arabs in Pre Islamic Times* (London, 1979).

Byzantium

Brubaker, L., and Haldon, J. *Byzantium in the Iconoclast Era* (Cambridge, 2011).

Cameron, Av. *The Byzantines* (Chichester, 2010).

Haldon, J. *Byzantium in the Seventh Century* (2nd revised edition: Cambridge, 1997).

Herrin, J. *Byzantium: The Surprising Life of a Medieval Empire* (London, 2007).

Jeffreys, E. et al., eds. *The Oxford Handbook of Byzantine Studies* (Oxford, 2008).

Pohl, W. *Die Awaren: ein Steppenvolk in Mitteleuropa* (Munich, 1988).

Whittow, M. *The Making of Orthodox Byzantium 600–1025* (Berkeley, 1996).

Caucasia

Bais, M. *Albania Caucasica: ethnos, storia, territorio attraverso le fonti greche, latine, armene* (Milan, 2001).

Gippert, J. *The Caucasian Albanian Palimpsests of Mt. Sinai* (Brepols, 2008).

Golden, P. et al., eds. *The World of the Khazars* (HdO; Leiden, 2007).

Greenwood, T., ed. *Languages and Cultures of Eastern Christianity: Armenian* (Farnham, 2013).

Rapp, S. H., ed. *Languages and Cultures of Eastern Christianity: Georgian* (Farnham, 2012).

Egypt

Bagnall, *Egypt in the Byzantine World 300–700* (Cambridge, 2010).

Butler, A. *The Arab Conquest of Egypt* (revised edition; Oxford, 1978).

Chagnon, L. *La conquête musulmane de l'Egypte* (Paris, 2008).

Legendre, M. *La Moyenne Egypte du VIIe au IXe siècle* (PhD; Leiden, 2013).

Power, T. *The Red Sea from Byzantium to the Caliphate* (Cairo, 2012).

Sijpesteijn, P. *Shaping a Muslim State* (Oxford, 2013).

Levant and Jazira

Avni, G. *The Byzantine-Islamic Transition in Palestine: An Archaeological Approach* (Oxford, 2014).

Cook, D. *The Beginnings of Islam in Syria during the Umayyad Period* (PhD; Chicago, 2002).

Elad, A. *Medieval Jerusalem and Islamic Worship* (Leiden, 1995).

Flood, B. *The Great Mosque of Damascus: Studies on the Making of Umayyad Visual Culture* (Leiden, 2001).

Fowden, G. *Qusayr 'Amra and the Umayyad Elite in Late Antique Syria* (Berkeley, 2004).

Haldon, J. *Money, Power and Politics in Early Islamic Syria* (Farnham, 2010).

Johns, J., and Raby, J., eds. *Bayt al-Maqdis: 1. 'Abd al-Malik's Jerusalem; 2. Jerusalem and Early Islam* (Oxford, 1992 and 1999).

Khalek, N. *Damascus after the Muslim Conquest* (Oxford, 2011).

Robinson, C. *Empires and Elites after the Muslim Conquest* (Cambridge, 2006).

Sivan, H. *Palestine in Late Antiquity* (Oxford, 2008).

Tannous, J. *Syria between Byzantium and Islam* (PhD; Princeton, 2010).

Walmsley, A. *Early Islamic Syria: An Archaeological Appraisal* (London, 2007).

Wood, P. *We Have no King but Christ: Christian Political Thought in Greater Syria on the Eve of the Arab Conquest* (Oxford, 2010).

Persia: Iraq and Greater Iran

Agha, S.S. *The Revolution Which Toppled the Umayyads: Neither Arab nor Abbasid* (Leiden, 2003).

Choksy, J. K. *Conflict and Cooperation: Zoroastrian Subalterns and Muslim Elites in Medieval Iranian Society* (New York, 1997).

Crone, P. *The Nativist Prophets of Early Islamic Iran* (Cambridge, 2012).

Curtis, V., and Stewart, S., eds. *The Rise of Islam: The Idea of Iran IV* (London, 2009).

Frye, R. *Islamic Iran and Central Asia* (Variorum; London, 1979).

Luce, M. D. *Frontier as Process: Umayyad Khurasan* (PhD; Chicago, 2009).

Madelung, W. *Religious Trends in Early Islamic Iran* (Albany, NY, 1988).

Morony, M. *Iraq after the Muslim Conquest* (Princeton, 1984).

Oxford Handbook of Iranian History, ed. T. Daryaee (Oxford, 2012).

Payne, R. *Christianity and Iranian Society in Late Antiquity* (PhD; Princeton, 2010).

Savant, S. *The New Muslims of Post-Conquest Iran* (Cambridge, 2013).

Shaked, S. *From Zoroastrian Iran to Islam* (Variorum; Aldershot, 1995).

Spuler, B. *Early Islamic Iran* (English trans.; Leiden, 2014).

Toral-Niehoff, I. *Al-Hira: eine arabische Kulturmetropole im spätantiken Kontext* (Leiden, 2013).

Transoxania/Central Asia

Beckwith, C. *Empires of the Silk Road* (Princeton, 2009).

De la Vaissière, E. *Samarcande et Samarra: élites d'Asie Centrale* (Paris, 2007).

Foltz, R. *Religions of the Silk Road* (New York, 1999).

Frye, R.N. *The Heritage of Central Asia* (Princeton, 1996).

Gibb, H. A. R. *The Arab Conquests in Central Asia* (London, 1923).

Haug, R. J. *The Gate of Iron: The Making of the Eastern Frontier* (PhD; Michigan, 2010).

Heirmann, A., and Bumbacher, S. P., eds. *The Spread of Buddhism* (HdO; Leiden, 2007).

Litvinsky, B. et al., eds. *History of Civilisations of Central Asia 3: 250–750* (Paris, 1996).

Soucek, S. A History of Inner Asia (Cambridge, 2000).

INDEX